AFRICAN
FOREIGN POLICIES

SAIS African Studies Library

I. William Zartman, General Editor

AFRICAN FOREIGN POLICIES

Power and Process

edited by
Gilbert M. Khadiagala & Terrence Lyons

LYNNE
RIENNER
PUBLISHERS

BOULDER
LONDON

Published in the United States of America in 2001 by
Lynne Rienner Publishers, Inc.
1800 30th Street, Boulder, Colorado 80301
www.rienner.com

and in the United Kingdom by
Lynne Rienner Publishers, Inc.
3 Henrietta Street, Covent Garden, London WC2E 8LU

Library of Congress Cataloging-in-Publication Data
African foreign policies : power and process / edited by Gilbert M. Khadiagala
and Terrence Lyons.
    p. cm. — (SAIS African studies library)
Includes bibliographical references and index.
ISBN 1-55587-990-X (hardcover : alk. paper)
ISBN 1-55587-966-7 (pbk. : alk. paper)
    1. Africa—Foreign relations—1960– 2. Geopolitics—Africa. 3. Africa—
Strategic aspects. I. Khadiagala, Gilbert M. II. Lyons, Terrence. III. SAIS
African studies library (Boulder, Colo.)
DT30.5.A35587   2001
327.6—dc21   2001019071

British Cataloguing in Publication Data
A Cataloguing in Publication record for this book
is available from the British Library.

Printed and bound in the United States of America

      The paper used in this publication meets the requirements
 ∞   of the American National Standard for Permanence of
      Paper for Printed Library Materials Z39.48-1984.

    5 4 3 2 1

Contents

Acknowledgments

This book grew out of a SAIS African Studies Conference, an annual event that brings together scholars and policymakers from Africa, Europe, and North America to debate significant African issues. As these conferences have become one of the key sources in the production and collation of knowledge about Africa, they have benefited immensely from the contributions and critiques of many people who take their time to attend every year. We wish to thank the participants and look forward to their continued support. We also want to thank our students at SAIS who generously make the effort to ensure the success of the conferences.

A number of scholars who participated in the conference on which this book is based are not included in the book. We particularly want to acknowledge the contributions of Korwa Adar, Ibrahim Gambari, Okechukwu Iheduru, Makumi Mwagiru, and Thandika Nkiwane. Julius Mutwol kindly agreed to work on the index. Finally, we are indebted to Theresa Simmons for her organizational skills that brought the conference and the book to fruition.

—*G. M. K.*
—*T. L.*

1

Foreign Policy Making in Africa: An Introduction

Gilbert M. Khadiagala & Terrence Lyons

Studies of African foreign policy seek to shed light on actors, contexts, and outcomes. Foreign policy makers attempt to reconcile domestic interests with external circumstances, taking account of the available means, resources, and institutions for doing so. Important to understanding foreign policy are specific domestic and external contexts and the interaction between these two environments. As major players in foreign policy, elites operate within institutions that continually constrain them, but oftentimes, these policymakers can work around such limits and manage the tensions between domestic and international society. Outcomes are interesting because they answer far-reaching questions about how elites achieve their foreign policy goals, specifically how they balance means and objectives. Despite the postcolonial conundrum of multiple motives and meager means, African elites have treated foreign policy as a way for nation-states to become effective participants and claimants in the international arena.

The focus on actors and contexts, on the sources and sites of policy formulation and implementation, reveals the institutional bases of actors and their links to each other and society as a whole. In studies of decisionmaking in Africa, most scholars have concentrated on the cultural and organizational contexts of conception and execution of policy in light of domestic and international resources. These studies have highlighted that decisions are outcomes of a wide array of variables ranging from the nature of leadership, ideology, modes of domestic mobilization, organizational resources, and the impediments and opportunities that emanate from the external environment.

African foreign policy has been essentially a matter of deliberate actions by elites. Limited by a dearth of resources and competing domestic concerns of nation and state building, African elites, for the most part, have chosen to participate in external realms. After independence, foreign policy makers sought to resolve the choice (and oftentimes trade-offs) between national and continental identity, sovereignty and supranationalism, and differentiation and integration. Continental identity, supranationalism, and integration in various forms proceeded from the desire to unite disparate geographic units, to pool resources in concerted action, and to increase the leverage of the continent as a whole in the global and regional affairs of new African states. In contrast, through sovereignty, national identity, and differentiation, African states sought to maximize individual political autonomy, strengthen territorial borders, and guarantee unilateral advantages from privileged relations with external actors. Thus the competing choices and practices of nationalism and Pan-Africanism have coexisted, though uneasily, in African foreign policy, a testimony to the success of elites in straddling these broad concerns.

In this book we explore contemporary trajectories in African foreign policy, building on new and old themes. We are interested in explaining the impact of the seismic changes of the 1990s on foreign policy actions in Africa's major regions. A diverse body of work has over the years analyzed the consequences of the post–Cold War global order on African domestic political and economic structures. Our authors broaden this research by focusing on some of the salient actors and issues that animate foreign policy. A focus on the intersection of African domestic and international politics provides insight into the challenges and uncertainties of the 1990s and beyond. We analyze decisionmakers, their capabilities and goals, in an effort to understand the continuities and transformations in foreign policy behavioral and structural contexts.

Our primary focus is on foreign policy making in regional contexts, since they are arenas for dense patterns of common and conflicting interests with wider implications for multiple actors. For a majority of weak African states, regions are sources of authoritative foreign policies, places where power is displayed and exerted. They are also the closest and generally most salient threat to regime survival, thereby warranting particular attention. Through regional prisms we are able to illuminate the persistence of policy preoccupations such as economic integration and the emergence of such new ones as intervention and peacebuilding.

■ PAST THEMES IN AFRICAN FOREIGN POLICY

The dominant approaches to analyzing African foreign policy proceed from recognition of the severe constraints on the freedom of actors. In the 1960s, analysts emphasized that African decisionmakers were constrained by the need to consolidate power and meet socioeconomic demands at home. In addition to the fact that African elites had only tenuous control over the postcolonial states, external actors, particularly the former colonial powers, retained considerable influence over most facets of African life. This influence was partly why anticolonialism and the opposition to external intrusion formed significant aspects of Africa's foreign policy behavior. As discussed by P. B. Harris, African foreign policy in the formative decade was a product of distinct fears of exploitation from both the West and East and the need to reduce the penetration of the Cold War into emergent Africa.[1] The goals of preempting intrusive outsiders and solidifying Africa's identity led to the construction of norms of diplomatic behavior and regional institutions.

In subsequent decades, African elites continued to labor under what Clapham aptly described as the constraints of "poverty, disunity, domestic expectations and external penetration."[2] Political economy analyses in the 1970s and 1980s proposed a structural perspective on African elite constraints that concentrated on the pervasive influence of global economic and military asymmetries. These analyses identified structures of dependence, penetration, and subordination that influenced African foreign policy making. As McGowan and Gottwald pointed out: "Within a context of powerlessness and dependence, character and ideas alone cannot overcome a passive-subordinate role in international affairs."[3]

Constraints defined national interests and how elites articulated them in the external world. Limited resources confined African foreign policy largely to regional and continental contexts, the spheres of the most intense diplomatic efforts and institution building. When elites articulated national interests beyond the continent, they did so to win prestige, establish a presence in the proliferating international institutions, and forge strategic alliances with other global underdogs in an effort to extract resources from dominant power blocs. International institutions, in turn, reinforced the norms of noninterference in the domestic affairs of African states and support for juridical sovereignty.[4] In addition, some African leaders, such as Haile Selassie and Kwame Nkrumah, tried to translate an international profile into political or economic resources that would serve domestic purposes.

To overcome their inherent weaknesses, African states also constructed their own continental and regional institutions. Building alliances is a well-tested strategy for weak states in search of security; hence African states banded together into blocs that would enhance their leverage in world affairs. These institutions also became vital in solving problems collectively and in the quest for economic integration. As the most important institution, the Organization of African Unity (OAU) was established to give meaning to Africa's collective action in matters of internal economic development and liberation from colonial regimes in southern Africa. Over time, as some states strove for preeminence in intra-African relations, the OAU emerged as a forum for leadership competition.

Contests for leadership at regional and continental levels were inextricably tied to variations in national capabilities and ideological resources. Despite Africa's weak global position, internal differences in resources engendered variations in the degree of independent foreign policy action. Nigeria's role in the creation of the Economic Community of West African States (ECOWAS) in 1975 demonstrated the links between economic capabilities and leadership, a trend that has remained constant despite dramatic shifts in Nigeria's political landscape. The collapse of the East African Community in the 1970s was in part due to unresolved competition for leadership among three more equally matched states—Kenya, Uganda, and Tanzania. Elites also tried to mobilize ideas and symbols to compensate for economic weaknesses. Kwame Nkrumah and Julius Nyerere are examples, particularly in their ability to usurp ideological resources for purposes of African integration and unity. Under Nkrumah, Ghana assumed the leadership in continental institution building in the 1960s. Nyerere demonstrated similar organizational skills by spearheading Tanzania's leadership of southern African liberation in the 1970s and 1980s. Unlike economic leadership, as in the case of Nigeria and its enduring role as a regional hegemon, ideological leadership adhered to specific personalities.

African foreign policy decisionmaking has always been the province of leading personalities. Foreign policy as the prerogative of presidents and prime ministers dovetailed with the postcolonial patterns of domestic power consolidation. In environments where the structures of participation and contestation, particularly political parties and legislatures, declined appreciably, the charismatic leader became the source, site, and embodiment of foreign policy. Weak and manipulatable bureaucratic structures compounded the lack of effective representative institutions, affording ample opportunities for individual leaders to dabble in their countries' external affairs. Power centralization coincided with the pervasive belief that controlling the complexities of the external arena entailed unanimity of purpose, which could be guaranteed only by strong executives. From this exalted vantage point, foreign policy making emerged as a tool for leaders to both disarm their domestic opponents and compensate for unpopular domestic policies.

The behavioral patterns in inter-African relations and organizations reinforced the predominance of presidents as foreign policy makers. Through summits and other high-level meetings, continental and regional organizations nurtured the perception of foreign policy as a conclave of the mighty. The tendency of leaders to dominate decisions on momentous issues such as economic cooperation and mediation of conflicts limited the roles of opposing institutions. As Zartman observed:

> Specific, even minute, decisions may be made by the president whose prestige in Africa and experience in dealing with other leaders gives him a special competence in inter-African relations. His anger and his ardor, his whims and his convictions, may become the mood of his country's policy, and his friendships and acquaintances mark its limits. . . . Within this pattern of relations and decisions, the role and influence of all other groups and institutions work through the president and must be seen as modifications of the rule of centralized personalized power.[5]

Throughout the formative decades of African independence, the relative security of states and measurable levels of economic prosperity formed the most tangible outcomes of foreign policy. Before the lost economic decade of the 1980s, for instance, there was a meaningful and reciprocal engagement between Africa and international economic institutions that jump-started development efforts. The benefits of economic prosperity justified Africa's participation in a wide array of regional and international institutions and blunted some of the edges of powerlessness. Furthermore, broad-based African diplomatic practices fostered the evolution of institutions for capacity building and identity formation in political and security areas.

■ NEW TRENDS IN AFRICAN FOREIGN POLICY

Africa underwent a far-reaching transformation in the 1990s. As Clapham stated, "The post-colonial era in Africa is now, and only now, coming to an end; and the problem confronting the continent, and those who seek to understand it, is to discern what is taking place."[6] The Cold War and apartheid ended, and with their departure two issues that shaped much of African foreign policy were removed. Domestically, continued economic crisis and the collapse of the neopatrimonial postcolonial state—and, in response, a surge in pressures for reform—shifted political calculations. These international and domestic transformations altered the topography of power and institutional arrangements across the continent and, hence, the context in which foreign policy decisions were made. In some cases, African leaders responded with strained and fragile efforts to reform their economies and political systems; in others, the pressures led to state collapse. Many states fall somewhere between these two extremes with the future still in the balance.

The Cold War never explained the sources of foreign policy on the continent, but the willingness of the two superpowers to provide assistance to states regarded as important to their global strategies allowed a number of African leaders to hold on to power. International financial institutions similarly bolstered the prospects of many neopatrimonial regimes on the continent. In some cases, client regimes fell soon after Cold War patronage stopped. It is notable, for example, that among the six top recipients of U.S. aid during the Cold War, five (Ethiopia, Liberia, Somalia, Sudan, and Zaire) suffered from severe conflict during the 1990s; the sixth (Kenya) faced increasing domestic pressures for political liberalization.[7] The loss of patronage and diplomatic support from the Soviet Union altered the prospects for governments in Ethiopia, Angola, and Mozambique and the strategies of liberation forces in Namibia and South Africa. At the same time the International Monetary Fund and the World Bank imposed structural adjustment policies on African states weakened by debt, economic decay, and corruption.

In part in response to the demonstrated inability of the state to respond to the economic crisis and in part the result of international pressures, a number of African states held elections in a bid to construct new domestic and international sources of legitimacy. In some cases (Kenya, Cameroon, Gabon, Togo) these elections were manipulated to keep incumbents in power, but in others (Benin, Mali, Namibia, Malawi, and most notably South Africa) leadership changed as a result of popular participation.[8] These experiments with democracy have created a new set of institutions such as political parties, legislatures, and increasingly independent press and advocacy groups that have the potential to alter the ways by which African foreign policies are made and implemented.

Whereas some states faced the new challenges resulting from reform or other processes, others collapsed when confronted with the stark choices forced upon them from both above and below.[9] The UN, the major powers, and African states have struggled to develop effective mechanisms to respond to change. The early promise of multilateral intervention that convinced the United States and the UN to send troops to Somalia faded in the face of local opposition. The international community disengaged from Rwanda once genocide began and left the difficult tasks of developing effective peace processes in places like Liberia, Sierra Leone, Sudan, Lesotho, the Democratic Republic of Congo, and Burundi to weak African regional organizations. More ominously for vulnerable African states, the norm of noninterference in a sovereign state's internal affairs— one of the signature elements of the African regional order—lost its credibility as neighbors in much of central and West Africa broke away from that norm.

African foreign policy at the beginning of the twenty-first century is still dominated by overarching constraints on the survival of weak states. The imperatives of state survival, Clapham notes, force elites to use foreign policy to garner political and economic resources from the external environment.[10] Whether made singly or collectively, foreign policy reflects the continual attempts by elites to manage threats to domestic security and insulate their decision-making from untoward external manipulation. Contemporary African elites, like their predecessors, are preoccupied with political stability, legitimacy, and economic security, issues whose importance seems to increase rather than diminish.

Continuities in structural weaknesses, however, compete in importance with marked changes in actors, issues, institutions, and strategies for African foreign policy. The bulk of the postcolonial independence leaders have exited the scene, and new actors have emerged, promising to handle old constraints differently, innovating where their predecessors stumbled, and learning to appreciate the limits of their capabilities. They are reshaping institutions and alliance patterns to meet new challenges in the face of remarkable changes in domestic and external contexts. In style and substance, new actors are trying to lend a different flavor to policymaking by mobilizing diverse constituencies and remaking rules.

The demise of apartheid, and the shift of South Africa from pariah to potential hegemon, has transformed regional relations in southern Africa, as detailed in Chapter 7 by Gilbert Khadiagala. In East and central Africa, leadership changes have occasioned what is billed as a "new generation of African leaders," particularly Yoweri Museveni of Uganda, Meles Zenawi of Ethiopia, Isaias Afewerki of Eritrea, and Paul Kagame of Rwanda. Seeking to inject a new pragmatism in decisionmaking, these leaders have had a major imprint on their domestic and regional environments. René Lemarchand shows in Chapter 5 that although the cohesion of the new leadership was always exaggerated, the core of this group is making considerable changes to international relations in the Great Lakes region. John Clark's chapter (4) points to the pattern of personal alliances in the foreign policy of central Africa, which thrives on generational and family links. Ruth Iyob points out in Chapter 6 that contemporary leaders in the Horn of Africa operate in a context where the past, particularly as it shapes myths and traditions of statehood, continues to shape foreign policy outlooks. The allure of new leaders may be on the wane in light of the resurgence of previous behavioral patterns and practices, most notably the Ethiopia-Eritrea conflict, raising questions about the institutional sturdiness of the African renaissance.

No less important than individual policymakers is the reinvigoration of decisionmaking institutions. The wave of transitions to democracy in the 1990s has expanded the policy roles played by parliaments, interest groups, civic organizations, and the mass media. Peter Schraeder's contribution (Chapter 3) details the multifaceted roles of these institutions in Francophone West Africa. Denis Venter, in Chapter 8, enumerates the many organizations coalescing about South Africa's foreign policy. His analysis demonstrates the enormity of building a coherent foreign policy in a newly democratic state amid conflicting interests and perspectives. In most of Africa, the leaderships face scrutiny from independent media, policy analysts, and advocacy groups in national and regional institutions. As it ceases to be the *domaine réserve* of the head of state, the domestic context of African foreign policy making takes on an increasingly complex character, increasingly determined by the interaction of a broad range of actors, institutions, and norms.

The interplay between economic functionalism and new sources of political disintegration at regional levels is a key issue in contemporary African foreign policy. Regional organizations in the 1990s increasingly assumed more assertive security roles to deal with the specter of civil conflicts. The decision to establish the OAU's Mechanism for Conflict Management, Prevention, and Resolution in 1993 spawned diverse efforts by various states to preempt more virulent forms of nation-building and state-making conflicts. Clement Adibe's Chapter 2 on Anglophone West Africa, Khadiagala and Venter on southern Africa, and Iyob on the Horn demonstrate the role of regional hegemons Nigeria, South Africa, and (potentially) Ethiopia in steering ECOWAS, the Southern African Development Community (SADC), and the Intergovernmental Authority on Development (IGAD) across the uncertain terrain of intervention, security coordination, and peacebuilding. These roles are new and largely untested, but they underscore an interesting trend of revising the practices of sovereign independence toward notions of collective responsibility.[11]

African regions also have retained their infrastructural bases for experiments with economic coordination. The renewed emphasis on regional economic integration is part of a worldwide trend to promote trade and investments in geographical zones. Although economic integration slowed considerably in the 1980s, African states now see it as one antidote to global economic marginalization. Yet these efforts remain tentative, stymied like before by fragile political foundations, the tensions between differentiation and integration, and the inability of states to cede meaningful responsibility to regional organizations.

As foreign policy elites try to restructure institutions for conflict prevention and economic development, there are other threats lurking in regional environments that thus far defy Africa's limited resources. Ethnic and communal conflicts are boiling across the ever-porous African borders, spreading dangers of refugees, arms, disease, and environmental degradation. Although not entirely new, these threats are partly outcomes of a broader political disintegration of authority and the deepening militarization of African societies. Adibe, Clark, and Lemarchand describe how the scourge of refugees and displaced peoples in West Africa and the Great Lakes regions fuels the proliferation of arms. More poignantly, the warlords and private armies that William Reno discusses in Chapter 9 reflect a larger trend of states unable to tame their peripheries entering into Faustian bargains to shore up their diminishing power. Reno shows that arms traders, smugglers, and private security forces have become major players in foreign policy, blurring the tenuous boundaries between state and nonstate actors, legal and illegal actions. To the extent that transnational nonstate actors such as militia groups, arms merchants, and diamond dealers forge alliances with African weak states and their challengers, they invariably nullify the growing influence of civil society actors on foreign policy making.

The international context has changed as well, creating new obstacles and opportunities for vulnerable African states. Foreign assistance has shifted from a largely bilateral engagement with a former metropole, particularly with regard to Francophone Africa, to increased multilateral interactions with a wider array of donors and international financial institutions, as detailed by Peter Schraeder in Chapter 3. The shift to multilateralism allows African states to appeal to a range of donors and to diversify their relationships. States now go beyond the traditional governmental and intergovernmental relationships to seek assistance from international nongovernmental and corporate groups. These groups control significant resources and can help or hinder the mobilization of public support for actions ranging from foreign investment to peacekeeping and military intervention.

But overall aid levels remain insufficient; moreover, the economic orthodoxy required to remain within the good graces of the international financial institutions severely constrains African states' organizational ability.[12] The legacy of the economic collapse of the 1980s persists, and with it the escalation of political conditionalities that African states are required to comply with before obtaining economic assistance. As demands for human rights, good governance, and elections have become standard in the international lending and aid community, the leverage of African actors has decreased. Under these constraints, some states have opted, as Reno discusses, to draw resources from sometimes-shadowy international actors that have a financial interest in protecting very weak states.

Africa's security relations in the international arena have also changed. Prior to the 1990s, many African states joined with either the great powers or with the former colonial power, most notably France, to strengthen security. Much of the motivation for these Cold War patterns ended in the late 1980s, and even France seemed to be reassessing its security guarantees. In the early 1990s, UN involvement in Namibia, Angola, Mozambique, Western Sahara, Somalia, and Rwanda seemed to suggest that new multilateral means for managing conflicts were being constructed. Following the debacles in Angola and Somalia and the tragic events in Rwanda and eastern Zaire, however, the international community distanced itself from the continent. The United States began to promote the African Crisis Response Initiative and to encourage Africans to manage their own crises. The international community seems unwilling to support large multilateral interventions involving external forces in response to state collapse or major humanitarian emergencies.

In addition to constraints and demands, the international system also offers potential resources and protection for regimes threatened by internal dissent and opposition. African leaders employ a variety of strategies to attract attention and rewards from the international community. Some, such as Ghana and Uganda, have played the role of test cases for economic reform, attracting the interest of donor governments and international financial institutions. Others have played critical roles in managing African conflicts or humanitarian crises in a way that permits external forces to keep their distance; examples are Mobutu's influence for a period in the Great Lakes region and the role Nigeria played in Liberia and Sierra Leone. Participation in the Francophone and Commonwealth summits and support for UN peacekeeping operations are other ways that African leaders have sought to attract the attention of the broader world and win resources that strengthen their regimes.

Foreign policy outcomes are difficult to assess with certainty in an Africa mired in violent conflict and socioeconomic disintegration. The era when foreign policy was linked to strengthening African nation-states has given way to a time of healthy skepticism. Building African institutions for conflict management and economic integration remains a critical foreign policy objective, but economic retrogression, the escalation of wars, and the decline of norms of interstate relationships continually cast a shadow of doubt on these efforts. Neither Nigeria's leadership of ECOMOG in Sierra Leone nor its quest for a seat on the UN Security Council has resonance with ordinary citizens preoccupied with basic survival.

The problem of outcomes is closely tied to the vital one of measuring substantive change. Although democratization has broadened the range of actors in the policy process, most have no meaningful impact on policies because the issues either are beyond their competence or are secondary in their priorities. How much input, for instance, does Uganda's parliamentary committee on foreign affairs have on Paris Club economic negotiations with the government or the military's execution of the war in the Congo? Do civil society groups serve as effective checks on foreign policy decisionmaking in Ghana or Benin?

The foreign ministry or presidency in present-day Bangui, Bamako, Lagos, or Lusaka confronts a multitude of interests and pressures converging to lay some claim to discrete matters conceived as foreign policy. Irrespective of their source, these interests have a tremendous impact on the processes and outcomes of African foreign policy. For most of the postindependence period, relatively benign domestic and external contexts afforded elites more latitude to maneuver in foreign policy arenas. Internal and external policy environments have become increasingly complex, testing the mettle of policymakers and limiting their authority to routinely manage these competing claims. Ultimately, foreign policy in Africa, as elsewhere, is about the opportunities and burdens of participating in transnational affairs.

■ NOTES

1. P. B. Harris, *Studies in African Politics* (London: Hutchinson University Library, 1970): 60–82.
2. Christopher Clapham, "Sub-Saharan Africa," in Clapham, ed., *Foreign Policy Making in Developing States: A Comparative Approach* (New York: Praeger, 1977): 79.
3. Patrick McGowan and Klaus-Peter Gottwald, "Small State Foreign Policy Policies: A Comparative Study of Participation, Conflict, and Political and Economic Dependency in Black Africa," *International Studies Quarterly* 19, no. 4 (1975): 469. For structural theories of African foreign policy see Timothy Shaw and Olajide Aluko, *The Political Economy of African Foreign Policy: A Comparative Analysis* (New York: St. Martin's Press, 1984); Timothy Shaw, "Foreign Policy, Political Economy and the Future: Reflections on Africa and the World System," *African Affairs* 79,

no. 315 (April 1980): 260–268; Eduard Bustin, "The Foreign Policy of the Republic of Zaire," *Annals* 489 (January 1987): 63–75; Martin Staniland, "Francophone Africa: The Enduring French Connection," *Annals* 489 (January 1987): 40–50; and Edmond Keller, "The Politics of State Survival: Continuity and Change in Ethiopian Foreign Policy," *Annals* 489 (January 1987): 76–87.

4. Robert H. Jackson, *Quasi-States: Sovereignty, International Relations and the Third World* (Cambridge: Cambridge University Press, 1990).

5. I. William Zartman, "Decision-Making Among African Governments in Inter-African Affairs," *Journal of Development Studies* 2, no. 2 (1966): 100.

6. Christopher Clapham, "Discerning the New Africa," *International Affairs* 74, no. 2 (1998): 263.

7. Michael Clough, *Free at Last: U.S. Policy Toward Africa and the End of the Cold War* (New York: Council on Foreign Relations, 1992): 77.

8. For a survey see Crawford Young, "The Third Wave of Democratization in Africa: Ambiguities and Contradictions," in Richard Joseph, ed., *State, Conflict, and Democracy in Africa* (Boulder: Lynne Rienner, 1999).

9. I. William Zartman, ed., *Collapsed States: The Disintegration and Restoration of Legitimate Authority* (Boulder: Lynne Rienner, 1995).

10. Christopher Clapham, *Africa and the International System: The Politics of State Survival* (Cambridge: Cambridge University Press, 1996): 4. See also Stephen Wright, ed., *African Foreign Policies* (Boulder: Westview Press, 1999); William Cyrus Reed, "Directions in African International Relations," in Mark W. DeLancey, ed., *Handbook of Political Science Research in Africa* (Westport, CT: Greenwood Press, 1992): 73–103; David Williams, "Africa and International Relations," *Africa* 68, no. 3 (1998): 425–449; and Stuart Croft, "International Relations and Africa," *African Affairs* 96, no. 385 (October 1998): 607–611.

11. For discussion of these evolving norms see Olusegun Obasanjo, "A Balance Sheet of the African Region and the Cold War," in Edmond J. Keller and Donald Rothchild, eds., *Africa in the New International Order: Rethinking State Sovereignty and Regional Security* (Boulder: Lynne Rienner, 1996). See also Francis M. Deng, "African Policy Agenda: A Framework for Global Partnership," and Terrence Lyons, "Can Neighbors Help? Regional Actors and African Conflict Management," in Francis M. Deng and Terrence Lyons, eds., *African Reckoning: A Quest for Good Governance* (Washington, DC: Brookings Institution, 1998).

12. Thomas M. Callaghy, "Africa and the World Political Economy: More Caught Between a Rock and a Hard Place," in John W. Harbeson and Donald Rothchild, eds., *Africa in World Politics: The African State System in Flux* (Boulder: Westview Press, 2000).

2

Foreign Policy Decisionmaking in Anglophone West Africa

Clement A. Adibe

At the dawn of the twentieth century, much of Africa was a colonial enclave under the domination of competing European states. As the dominant actor in international life in the aftermath of the Treaty of Westphalia, the state was conspicuously absent in Africa in the early periods of this century. Part of the obligations arising from Europe's dual mandate, therefore, was to transmute to Africa the system of states that had characterized inter-European relations for three centuries. According to Lord Lugard, the quintessential administrator and colonial thinker of the twentieth century, it was the rivalry of the "Great [European] Continental Powers which was the immediate cause of the modern 'partition of Africa,'" upon which the modern African states are based.[1] A century later, European states have closed ranks and have replaced their rivalry for the most part with an unprecedented level of cooperation under the aegis of the European Union; their African colonies have become a historical artifact; and the state system they erected with impunity appears to be shaky and in some places has indeed collapsed outright.[2] On the eve of the twenty-first century, according to some scholars and commentators, Africa was indeed "back to the future."[3] Dispirited, disorganized, and marginalized in the post–Cold War era, the African state, Ali Mazrui contends, has become "a political refugee" of the international system, much like its people.[4]

Nowhere is Mazrui's description of the fragility of the African state system more appropriate than in West Africa. In a much-publicized 1994 essay, Robert Kaplan depicted this region, particularly Sierra Leone and Liberia—two of the region's Anglophone states—as the epicenter of the onrush of a (Western) civilizational Armageddon:

> West Africa is becoming *the* symbol of worldwide demographic, environmental, and societal stress, in which criminal anarchy emerges as the real 'strategic' danger. Disease, overpopulation, unprovoked crime, scarcity of resources, refugee migrations, the increasing erosion of nation-states and international borders, and the empowerment of private armies, security firms, and international drug cartels are now most tellingly demonstrated through a West African prism.[5]

For students of foreign policy, this depiction of West Africa's sociopolitical environment as anarchic poses an interesting research problem: What is the *nature* of foreign policy decisionmaking in West Africa? That this question is inherently cynical is rather obvious. But it is also challenging because according to some theorists, foreign policy decisionmaking is essentially a process of *rational* choice, for which the West African political environment is hardly conducive.[6] Herein lies the puzzle: If the state is collapsing and the region is dissolving into utter chaos, what, then, is the purpose, objective, or essence of foreign policy, and who are the relevant actors? These questions underscore the central hypothesis of this chapter: The more weakened and unstable state structures and institutions become, the greater importance political actors attach to their external relations, and hence the primacy of foreign policy. I shall argue, therefore, that the challenging political environment of West Africa has led to the proliferation of actors and issues and that the resulting redefinition of interests and alliances is consistent with the globalizing tendencies of late-twentieth-century neoliberalism.[7]

This chapter is divided into four sections. Following this introductory section, I discuss the cultural roots of the nuances and practices of foreign policy in Anglophone West Africa. The third section addresses the main issues and actors that have dominated the foreign policy process of the region, and the final section draws some conclusions for the future of foreign policy in West Africa.

■   THE CULTURE OF FOREIGN POLICY
    DECISIONMAKING IN ANGLOPHONE WEST AFRICA

As the name suggests, Anglophone West Africa is both a linguistic
and a geographical expression. It refers to the societies or states on
the West Coast of Africa, which are distinguished by their common
use of the English language and common law for diplomatic and administrative purposes. The English language and English administrative practices form part of the core symbols of their collective imagination in relation to others.[8] There are five states that make up the
category called Anglophone West Africa—Gambia, Ghana, Liberia,
Sierra Leone, and Nigeria. As a matter of geopolitical definition,
these states are also the Anglophone members of the Economic
Community of West African States (ECOWAS). In this chapter, the
phrase Anglophone West Africa refers to the English-speaking members of ECOWAS that are distinguished by a sense of collective
identity that has been formed and nourished by a common historical,
ideological, and institutional experience.

The modern Anglophone states of West Africa are the products
of two important forces in the nineteenth century—British colonialism and the Garveyist impetus for reverse migration of the African
diaspora from the Caribbean and the Americas.[9] With respect to the
first, Colin Newbury has argued that the British strategic desire to
check French expansion in West Africa compelled Britain to seek
"agreements which extended British jurisdiction, often in advance of
administrative occupation, [and these] roughed out the main lines of
future advances from bases in the Gambia, Gold Coast, Sierra Leone
and Nigeria."[10] Thereafter, Britain systematically sought to "peg out
claims for futurity" through an extensive program of social, political, cultural, and administrative practices that fundamentally
changed the character and identity of its West African colonies.[11]
The second source of state creation in Anglophone West Africa, the
return of the African diaspora, found its unique expression in
Liberia. Here, African-American repatriates from the United States
settled in 1847 and established what Dunn and Tarr have described
as a "repatriate state" under their unchallenged hegemony.[12] According to Ungar, these two forces of state creation in West Africa, the
British colonialists and the repatriates, shared a contempt for the native population and utmost faith in their mission and status as "the

guardians, the protectors, and the teachers of [the native] tribes."[13] It is not surprising, therefore, that despite their different origins, Liberia and the British colonies of West Africa would be similarly affected by the unifying force of Pan-Africanism at the dawn of the twentieth century.

■ FOREIGN POLICY AND
   THE IDEOLOGY OF PAN-AFRICANISM

Given the differences in the origins of the state in Anglophone West Africa, it is hardly surprising that Pan-Africanism emerged as the principal ideological tool for ensuring some semblance of sociopolitical cohesion through its emphasis on common racial identity. In the half-century since decolonization, Pan-Africanism has been at the center of African foreign policy decisionmaking. By Pan-Africanism, I refer to the idea of uniting disparate African states under one continental nation-state or, failing that, under some common intergovernmental institutions.[14] This idea came with the diaspora states of Anglophone West Africa, especially in Sierra Leone, where racial consciousness was taking root. Faced with the threat of race war, Sierra Leone's political elites promoted the idea of common racial consciousness and pride among *all* blacks, natives and repatriates, as the basis of relations within and among West African societies. This message struck a particular chord in Liberia, where the liberal-minded repatriate educator and diplomat Edward Blyden provided an intellectual core to Pan-Africanism that departed markedly from the pretentious arrogance of his colleagues in Liberia's conservative True Whig Party.[15] In a speech he delivered in Freetown in 1891, Blyden underscored the racial basis of the Pan-Africanist ideology when he admonished his fellow repatriates with extraordinary candor:

> Your first duty is to be *yourselves*. You need to be told constantly that you are Africans, not Europeans—black men not white men . . . ; and that in your endeavors to make yourself something else, you are not only spoiling your nature and turning aside from your destiny, but you are robbing humanity of the part you ought to contribute to its complete development and welfare, and you become as salt which has lost its flavor—good for nothing—but to be cast out and trodden down by others.[16]

Although Blyden's political goal was a West African community with its nucleus in Liberia, the essence of his message was African unity, and this message rang even louder in the ears of a new generation of Pan-Africanists in the twentieth century. Faced with the contradictions of European colonial consolidations in Africa and the specter of war in Europe, the new generation of elites "oriented Pan-Africanism to mean self-determination for the African peoples"—a "right" that would later be reinforced with great eloquence by U.S. president Woodrow Wilson at the postwar peace conference in Versailles. During this period, a culture of consultations and reliance on personal acquaintances began to emerge among Anglophone West African elites. This culture resulted in early efforts to harmonize policies and demands, especially in their external relations. In the 1920s, these elites formed a common political party, the National Congress of British West Africa (NCBWA). In the words of one of its founders, Joseph Casely-Hayford of Ghana, the objective of the NCBWA was "[the] desire . . . , as the intelligentsia of British West Africa, to promote unity among our people. . . . Nigeria has joined hands with Gambia and Gambia with Sierra Leone and Sierra Leone with the Gold Coast, etc. and it is our hope, by this combination, to express our views in a way that can be effective."[17]

The flowering of institutional cooperation throughout Anglophone West Africa was also caused by British colonial policies that, on the eve of World War I, were geared toward conservation and optimal use of scarce resources in the colonies. These policies resulted in the creation of common institutions, such as a single commodity marketing board and a unified army in the form of the West African Frontier Force (WAFF). Such common institutions with their shared administrative and legal practices, rules, norms, and principles provided immense opportunities for intellectual and emotional bonding that made possible the successful imagination of a West African Anglophone community.[18]

After World War II, Kwame Nkrumah inherited the mantle of leadership in West Africa and later personified the emotional and political aspirations of Pan-Africanism in the mid-twentieth century. For British colonialism in West Africa, Nkrumah's successful demand for independence for his homeland, Ghana, in 1957 amounted to a coup de grâce. The consequent independence of the remaining British colonies in the early 1960s set the stage for a new era in foreign policy decisionmaking. The foreign policy process that emerged in the first decade of independence may be distinguished by three principal characteristics: a pragmatic redefinition of Pan-Africanism; the reduction of regional institutional linkages and a growing preference for a loose continental organization; and the enunciation of the national interest as an integral part of the nation-building process.

At the dawn of independence, Pan-Africanism was used instrumentally for the consolidation of state power in much of Anglophone West Africa. Nowhere was this strategy more manifest than in Ghana, where Nkrumah proceeded to establish himself and Ghana as the Black Star. For Nkrumah, the passion for an all-African federation was still there, but, not unlike Blyden, he envisioned himself and his new nation as the nucleus of such a modern federation.[19] It is indeed a remarkable tribute to Nkrumah's strategic vision that he theorized a causal relationship between the physical survival of the infant Ghanaian state and the autonomy or sovereignty of its neighbors from colonial rule. According to Kwesi Krafona, Nkrumah's strategic dilemma at independence was simply this: How secure would Ghana be if it continued to be "surrounded by colonial neighbors: Upper Volta (now Burkina Faso), Togo and Ivory Coast, on her northern, eastern and western flanks, respectively?"[20] Nkrumah's response to this dilemma was to predicate his foreign policy on the proposition that "the independence of Ghana is meaningless, unless it is linked up with the total liberation of Africa."[21] Accordingly, Nkrumah retooled Pan-Africanism to serve two urgent foreign policy objectives of the Ghanaian state: first, the unimpeded decolonization of Africa and second, the consolidation of freedom, once attained, through the establishment of an overarching continental institution endowed with supranational powers. For these reasons, according to Krafona, "Pan-Africanism [became] the core of Ghana's foreign policy in relation to Africa and . . . it was in consonance with Ghanaian and African interests."[22]

In my view, it is such conflation of national interest with continental interest that readily underscored the essentially realist character of West African diplomacy in the early postindependence era. Nkrumah spared no efforts to bring to fruition his scheme for African integration in the form of the Organization *for* African Unity, an institutional forerunner of the United States of Africa.[23] He stumped the major capitals and cajoled the leaders of the newly independent states of sub-Saharan Africa to support his plans. At the cost of neglecting domestic socioeconomic needs, Nkrumah often deployed his enormous foreign reserves to extract the consent of those African leaders who were not easily swayed by the power of his ideas and distinctive elocution.[24] Nkrumah also used his personal prestige and marital ties to President Gamal Nasser of Egypt to win the support of Africa's Arab states.[25] Indeed, he inaugurated the era of shuttle and personal diplomacy in West Africa as the preferred method of conducting foreign affairs, and this strategy continued for three decades after Nkrumah's political exit.

Despite his remarkable activism, Kwame Nkrumah did not hold a monopoly on Afrorealism and Pan-Africanism in the 1960s. In Liberia, for instance, President V. S. Tubman was suspicious of Nkrumah's "grand design" even as he supported the idea of closer unity among African states in principle. Not to be outdone by Nkrumah, however, Tubman proposed an alternative idea for African unity. He assembled what became known as the Monrovia bloc, which roundly criticized the Nkrumah plan for an OAU endowed with supranational authority as being too "radical" and unrealistic. Tubman particularly objected to the provision in Nkrumah's plan for an African high command—a standing African army—which he feared would be dominated by Ghana and used to undermine the sovereignty of those states that were aligned against Nkrumah. Tubman's alternative proposal to the Nkrumah plan was that of a loose intergovernmental organization that adhered strictly to the principle of noninterference in the domestic affairs of its members. Remarkably, the consensus to establish OAU in 1963 was centered on this "moderate" vision of "pan-Africanism as inter-governmentalism."[26] In Anglophone West Africa, the formation of the OAU was the culmination of efforts to find alternative diplomatic structures after Nkrumah withdrew Ghana from preindependent common institutions such as the West African Clearing House and the West African Marketing Board. It was also a victory for what would become the cardinal principle of African diplomacy: nonintervention in the affairs of a sister state. This principle would, in subsequent years, be jettisoned in West Africa with the eruption of violent conflict in Liberia in 1990.

Anglophone West Africa's foreign policy in the immediate postindependence era was also characterized by an early effort to articulate an independent national foreign policy based on individual assessments of the national interest. For many of these states, vocal anticolonialism was a preferred plank on which to base their national

foreign policy. Unlike their Francophone neighbors in the years following independence, Anglophone West African states sought to distance themselves from their former colonial power, with all the attendant loss of "privileges" and access to much-needed resources.
For these states, the annual summit meetings of the Commonwealth
were perceived to be little more than an opportunity to socialize with
Her Majesty and protest British support for white minority rule in
southern Africa.[27] The staunch anti-apartheid stance adopted by Anglophone West African states reflected (1) an innate, psychological
desire to embarrass Britain and (2) the growing public demand to
hasten the complete liberation of Africa by bringing to a quick end
the last bastions of colonial rule in southern Africa.[28] Nkrumah's
Ghana used every opportunity in domestic and international forums
to drum up support for a strong anti-apartheid policy. As the leading
sub-Saharan economy in the early 1960s, Ghana also played a leading role in financing and training fledgling armed liberation movements in southern Africa. Nigeria continued this policy when it
emerged as the region's leading state in the 1970s.

In sum, the immediate postcolonial period witnessed the begin-
nings of a foreign policy framework rooted firmly in the ideology of
Pan-Africanism. This idea largely contributed to the region's choice
of multilateralism over unilateralism in its external behavior. Pan-
Africanism was also the source of the region's commitment to the
anti-apartheid struggle in southern Africa and the complete eradica-
tion of European colonialism in Africa. In this framework, the principal actor was unquestionably the region's strongman, Nkrumah;
his example gave rise to the personality of rulers as the principal determinant of the regional pecking order. The problem, however, was
that foreign policy objectives were hardly met, mainly because of
excessive rhetoric and grandiosity. The goal of uniting and liberating
Africa is fuzzy as a foreign policy objective. Taken at face value, it
is doubtful that it can be realized. In terms, therefore, of evaluating
the relationship among actors, issues, and outcomes, this example
manifests the disjuncture between capability and foreign policy objectives as one problematic aspect of the Anglophone West African
foreign policy process in the immediate postindependence period.
Attempts to establish a balance between national capability and foreign policy objectives would receive their greatest impetus from the
shrinking strategic and economic importance of West Africa following the end of the Cold War.

■ INSTABILITY, NEW ACTORS, AND FOREIGN POLICY
  ISSUES IN ANGLOPHONE WEST AFRICA

The instability that rocked West Africa in the late 1960s and became increasingly chronic throughout the 1980s had its roots in Anglophone West Africa, especially Nigeria and Ghana, where military intervention in politics destroyed constitutional rule and civil bureaucracy.[29] Although the impact of this political change on the region's economic fortunes was quite severe, it was no less drastic and traumatic for regional diplomacy.[30] The coup d'état that toppled Ghana's first republic in 1966 raised serious questions about Nkrumah's lopsided devotion to foreign policy at the expense of domestic needs. In the language of contemporary scholarship, Nkrumah neglected the domestic component of the independence "social contract" while devoting too much energy and resources to the side of the contract dealing with Ghana's relations with departing colonialists.[31] Nkrumah's successors in Ghana and elsewhere in the subregion did not learn from his mistake. The tragic consequences of this failure would be dramatized throughout the subregion by Nigeria's civil war between 1967 and 1970.[32]

The diplomacy of the Nigerian civil war sharpened existing differences between Anglophone West Africa and its Francophone neighbors. For the Anglophone states, the Nigerian conflict was an internal matter, a crisis that should be handled by the Anglophone community. Even after the initial mediation efforts by Ghana had failed, Nigeria's Anglophone neighbors struggled, albeit unsuccessfully, to limit regional interference in the conflict and, in the process, incurred the wrath of their Francophone neighbors, especially Côte d'Ivoire.[33] The key lesson of that experience was the need for an institutional mechanism that, for the first time, would bridge the gap between Anglophone and Francophone West Africa.

In 1975 the Economic Community of West African States (ECOWAS) was established with the expectation that it would become the principal institutional mechanism and focus of West African diplomacy.[34] ECOWAS was also designed as a collective response to the presumed negative externalities of globalization. For this reason, the founders of ECOWAS hoped that it would deal with problems of economic underdevelopment in West Africa by acting as the engine of free trade and investment. According to some scholars, this has yet to happen, largely because the economic pre-conditions for successful integration do not presently exist in West Africa.[35] But even more important, the operation of ECOWAS over the years has tended to reinforce rather than bridge the Anglophone-Francophone divide. This is especially true with respect to political and security issues that dominated the organization in the 1990s.

Quite in contrast to its relative dormancy in the economic issue area, ECOWAS has been remarkably proactive in political and security matters. In the unstable political environment of the late 1970s and 1980s, regime insecurity was the dominant issue confronting much of West Africa. This concern produced intense diplomatic activities within ECOWAS that resulted in a groundbreaking agreement on mutual assistance that became the basis for a collective security mechanism in the 1990s. Thus when the Liberian conflict broke out in 1990, the hitherto dormant Protocol on Mutual Assistance was readily invoked by Liberia's Anglophone "brothers" to justify their plans for a direct military intervention, despite serious reservations by the majority of their Francophone partners.[36] The regionalization of the Liberian conflict from 1990 onward clearly illustrates the seriousness with which the threat of insecurity is perceived in West Africa, especially among the more politically unstable Anglophone members of the subregion, primarily Sierra Leone, Gambia, Ghana, and Nigeria. Equally important, it also reveals the persistence of personal ties as a determinant of foreign policy processes and behavior in West Africa. As Stephen Ellis has shown, ECOWAS intervention in Liberia derived in part from a sense of obligation arising from arcane business relationships and complex familial bonds:

> The personal interests, which linked various West African heads of state, were both the sinews of political relationships and a reflection of national aspirations. . . . As Presidents Babangida and Doe cemented an alliance with their joint business ventures, so a rival potentate, President Houphouët-Boigny of Côte d'Ivoire, had a similar system of personal foreign relations. His goddaughter had married A. B. Tolbert, the son of Doe's predecessor. The Tolberts, father and son, both perished during the 1980 putsch which brought Doe to power, after which A. B. Tolbert's widow married Captain Blaise Compaore, later president of Burkina Faso. The Doe-Babangida axis during the late 1980s was therefore seen by Houphouët-Boigny not only as the perpetuation of the personal humiliation he had suffered when the upstart Doe had been responsible for the murder of his son-in-law, but also as the reversal of a previous diplomatic alliance linking Abidjan and Monrovia.[37]

Such personal relationships lead to two explanations for the doggedness of Ivorian opposition to the ECOMOG presence in Liberia: First, personal animosity was based on Houphouët-Boigny's familial links; second, it was in the Ivorian national interest to thwart Nigeria's regional hegemonic aspirations. This latter explanation, which is widely popular among scholars, has its origins outside the region in what Asteris Huliaras recently described as France's deep-seated fear of "the Anglo-Saxon conspiracy," of which Nigeria is an instrument in West Africa.[38]

In the course of the ECOWAS intervention in Liberia, it appeared also that the age-old political aspiration of West Africa's statesmen for a united political framework and collective action might have been realized. To say this is not to argue that ECOWAS was hugely successful in stopping the carnage in Liberia (for it contributed to it) or that it erased the problem of realpolitik from West African diplomacy. Quite to the contrary, the ECOWAS intervention in Liberia clearly demonstrated that realist thought and practices are very much alive in West Africa, where Nigeria's domination of ECOMOG is rightly considered to be a matter of serious concern to its neighbors as well as to its citizens.[39] The point, however, is that such exercise of regional hegemony is taking place within the multilateral framework of ECOWAS with all its attendant limitations.[40] The normative significance of this action lies in the choice of collective action over unilateralism in West African diplomacy. This choice represents a continuation from the past. Even more important, the ECOWAS intervention in Liberia conforms to the century-old Anglophone West Africa's political philosophy and Pan-Africanist ethos, namely that the "black man has the ability and the right to define and take charge of his destiny."[41] It is this particular consideration that may help explain the applause received by former Nigerian military rulers from African states for spearheading regional multilateral efforts to restore democracy in Liberia despite their own anti-democratic practices at home. Liberia, therefore, shattered the long-standing principle of nonintervention in internal affairs as the holy grail of regional diplomacy.

I have so far discussed the intervention in Liberia as an ECOWAS (Anglophone and Francophone) project. This perspective is largely correct because the Anglophone members provided the core of the operation and displayed greater staying power. The organization, operation, and decisionmaking structure of ECOMOG in Liberia is a case study in the complex politics of state power and group identity in West Africa. As Figure 2.1 shows, with the exception of the deputy force commander from Guinea, the command positions in General Joshua Dogonyaro's ECOMOG between 1990 and 1992 were held by Nigerian and Ghanaian officers.

We can explain the virtual exclusion of Francophone ECOWAS states from the command structure of ECOMOG in strategic terms, for example, in terms of the so-called struggle for regional hegemony

Figure 2.1 ECOMOG Command Structure Under General Dogonyaro

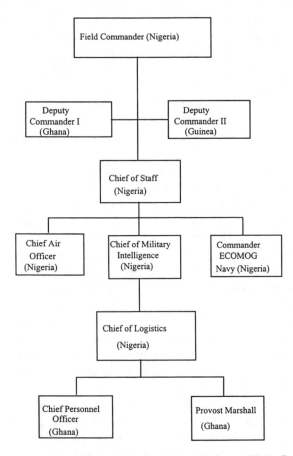

Source: Adapted from Nkem Agetua, *Operation Liberty: The Story of Major General Joshua Nimyel Dogonyaro* (Lagos: Hona Communications, 1992), pp. 83–85.

between Nigeria and Houphouët-Boigny's Côte d'Ivoire or, indeed, in terms of the sometimes visible, sometimes invisible hand of U.S. diplomacy (especially with regard to the Senegalese participation in ECOMOG). Indeed, according to Ofuatey-Kodjoe, the underlying strategy of West Africa's Anglophone powers, particularly Nigeria, was to keep out "the influence of [other] powers from . . . the region."[42] My position, however, is that we should look at the century-old efforts to build a *sense* of community in Anglophone West Africa in order to understand why Gambia and Sierra Leone joined Ghana and Nigeria in committing their extremely limited resources to such a complex and expensive operation as the ECOMOG involvement in Liberia turned out to be. The same is even truer for the continuing perseverance of Ghana and Nigeria in Sierra Leone since the beginning of the Revolutionary United Front (RUF) insurgency. Realpolitik alone cannot explain the current foreign policy behavior of Anglophone West African states. The nuances of Anglophone African foreign policy may be found in its cultural evolution through centuries of community building.

■   STATE COLLAPSE AND THE
     ASCENDANCE OF NONSTATE ACTORS

The foreign policy context of Anglophone West Africa in the past decade has assaulted the statecentric model of classical international politics. Since the 1990s, new actors have emerged to jostle for political relevance in the diplomatic arena that was dominated by the postcolonial state. Prominent among these nonstate actors are insurgent groups, local and international human rights advocacy and nongovernmental organizations, and transnational organizations.

❏   *Insurgency Movements*

The lack of responsible and legitimate government in Anglophone West Africa has generated a desire by a growing segment of the population who seek change to form insurgency movements with operational bases in neighboring states. Although guerrilla movements have been in existence in eastern and southern Africa (e.g., the Mau Mau movement in Kenya and the South West African People's Organization [SWAPO] in Namibia), where they resulted "from failures in decolonization," their appearance in Anglophone West Africa is a relatively recent phenomenon.[43] In a recent study, Christopher Clapham suggested that the emergence of insurgency movements in West Africa in the 1990s "can be ascribed to an experience of post-independence government *so bad* as to lead to a resistance born of desperation, and to the consequences of prolonged immiseration, exploitation and *state decay*."[44] Predictably, the appearance and spread of these insurgency movements in Liberia and Sierra Leone have had a convulsive effect on the international relations of the entire West African subregion. For this particular reason, insurgency movements may be characterized as the most significant new actor in West Africa's diplomacy since colonialism; they therefore warrant closer scholarly attention.

In December 1989, some 100 insurgents belonging to a little-known organization, the National Patriotic Front of Liberia (NPFL), attacked a border town in eastern Liberia from neighboring Côte d'Ivoire. This event was the start of a war that was to last for more than seven years and, in the process, secure a place for insurgency movements in West African diplomacy.[45] Led by Charles Taylor, a maverick and mercurial character par excellence, the NPFL established itself very early on in the campaign as an effective fighting force. Barely three months after they launched their campaign, NPFL forces were controlling about 90 percent of Liberia's mineral-rich countryside and had succeeded in effectively degrading the Armed Forces of Liberia (AFL), thereby leaving President Samuel Doe virtually imprisoned in his presidential mansion in Monrovia.

The success of the NPFL, however, triggered quick and fierce reaction from Nigeria and Ghana, Liberia's Anglophone sister states, for several reasons. First, Nigeria's president at the time, Ibrahim Babangida, and Ghana's president, Jerry Rawlings, were military dictators who were finessing plans for self-succession, just as Doe had done in Liberia a few years earlier. Self-interest and military camaraderie dictated that they support President Doe, if only to deter their civilian opponents in their respective countries from copying the NPFL. Second, information available to the leaders of Nigeria and Ghana confirmed that elements of the NPFL had been trained and armed by Libya, whose ideology and expansionist policies in sub-Saharan Africa had been viewed with suspicion and concern by the Nigerian and Ghanaian political elites.[46] Worse still, the NPFL was being actively supported by some Francophone neighboring states. In fact, in the first wave of the attack on Liberia, invading NPFL forces were "joined by regular Burkinabe soldiers on secondment from their own government."[47] For Nigeria and Ghana, the NPFL had become an instrument both of Libya's suspicious intentions and of the Francophone bloc in West Africa. Accordingly, repelling the NPFL attack and denying Charles Taylor and his organization control of Liberia's state apparatus became the paramount policy objective of the leadership of the two Anglophone powers, especially Nigeria's General Babangida, during the various phases of international intervention in the conflict.[48] Although the NPFL would later splinter into various factions as the civil war dragged on, it nevertheless retained its premier status and influence, which assured it a place at the negotiating table throughout the duration of the conflict. Its dominance during the period of war enabled it also to win the elections that followed the formal end of the conflict in 1997.

The influence of insurgency movements on West African diplomacy did not end with the NPFL. When the war in Liberia spilled into Sierra Leone in 1991, the RUF saw an opportunity to wrest power from the "corrupt and inept government in Freetown."[49] Like the NPFL, the invading RUF forces numbered only a few hundred armed men initially, and they too had ties to Libya. According to Ibrahim Abdullah and Patrick Muana, the leader of the RUF, Foday Sankoh, had "military and ideological training" in guerrilla warfare in Benghazi, Libya, between 1987 and 1988.[50] Sankoh's links with NPFL's leader, Charles Taylor, were rather obvious as well. According to one account, "Some RUF members [had] fought alongside National Patriotic Front of Liberia (NPFL) combatants in Liberia, so that by 1991, when the RUF entered Sierra Leone, they were supported by an NPFL group."[51] Such glaring associations quickly revealed the following pattern: The insurgency movements in Anglophone West Africa were closing ranks across national boundaries against their equally united and determined adversaries, the military dictators. Clearly, the line had been drawn.

The immediate impact of the RUF invasion was the destabilization of Sierra Leone. Between 1991 and 1996 the governments of President Joseph Momoh, Captain Valentine Strasser, Brigadier Maada Bio, and President Ahmed Tejan Kabbah collapsed in rapid succession because of the difficulties generated by the occupation of Sierra Leone's countryside by RUF militia and its virtual monopoly of the underground diamond economy in the areas under its control.[52]

When the RUF came to power in 1997 by taking advantage of existing cracks within the politico-military alliance that brought President
Kabbah to power, the organization became the central target of a
Nigerian-led counterinsurgency plan. Almost immediately, the RUF
government, led by Major Johnny Koromah, was forced into a series
of military confrontations with ECOMOG forces, which resulted in
their defeat in February 1998 and the subsequent reinstallation of the
Kabbah administration on March 10. Although the leadership of the
RUF was significantly degraded after the clash with ECOMOG—
Koromah disappeared into the Futa Jalon mountains, and Sankoh
was imprisoned in Nigeria—the RUF has retained its influence as
the principal threat to stability in Sierra Leone and hence is a significant player in any efforts toward conflict resolution in the country.

❑   *Rights Advocacy Groups*

Aside from insurgency movements, other nonstate actors with growing diplomatic influence in West Africa include opposition movements and human rights organizations. These organizations have
been produced mainly, but not exclusively, in Nigeria, where the
Third Republican democratic transition program was unceremoni-
ously terminated in 1993 by the military junta.[53] The opposition to
the military from elements in the civil society that followed the annulment of the June 12 elections was swift and widespread enough
to threaten the already fragile state. In response, the military further
curtailed civil liberties as it struggled to impose order. This particular move had the unintended consequence of uniting disparate civil
rights activists under the umbrella of the National Democratic Coalition (NADECO) and the Campaign for Democracy (CD). By calling
for the de-annulment of the 1993 presidential elections, these organizations became the champions of democracy and civil rights and in
no time became the symbol of mass resistance against military rule
in Nigeria.

In oil-rich southeastern Nigeria, the Ogoni nation mobilized
under the aegis of the Movement for the Survival of Ogoni People
(MOSOP) to agitate for greater autonomy, respect for minority rights,
improved access to national resources, and respect for the fragile
ecosystem in the Niger Delta. The prosecution of these protests, especially between 1993 and 1995, also exposed the legendary ethnic,
class, and religious fault lines of the Nigerian body politic.

If the voice of these organizations and their demands did not resonate abroad, they probably would have had very little impact on Nigerian external relations from 1993 onward. However, the leaders of these organizations had resources and contacts in the United States and Europe that gave them access to global institutions and the media. In the global economy of the late twentieth century, such access was an invaluable asset. According to Reno, "Concerns from abroad about Nigeria's political situation . . . interfered with Abacha's efforts to legitimate his coup to outsiders. The regime's U.S. representatives, the Washington, D.C., firm of Washington and Christian, were losing the public relations battle against, for example, the pro-Abiola Campaign for Democracy's Beko Ransome-Kuti . . . and criticism from Nobel Laureate Wole Soyinka."[54]

To these pressures we should add MOSOP and its venerable leader, Ken Saro-Wiwa, a renowned author and playwright who enjoyed significant goodwill outside Nigeria, especially among liberal-minded activist organizations in the West. Saro-Wiwa's message of Nigeria's genocidal actions toward its minority population in the oil-rich Niger Delta region found a ready and friendly audience in the Geneva-based Working Group on Indigenous People, as well as in the Unrepresented Nations and Peoples Organization, based in The Hague, Netherlands.[55] Saro-Wiwa also became an instantaneous hit, a cause célèbre, among environmental nongovernmental organizations such as the Sierra Club, Greenpeace, and the World Wildlife Federation when he pointed to the environmental atrocities perpetrated by irresponsible oil exploration activities undertaken in the Niger Delta by global oil giant Royal Dutch Shell.[56] His unyielding demand that "Shell must pay more than the four billion dollars which the Ogoni have demanded in reparation for the ecological damage to the people and the land"[57] made him a hero among his people, a threat to Shell's profitability, and a traitor in the eyes of Nigeria's military government, which desperately needed every dime of oil revenue to maintain its vast but ailing patronage network.[58] When the Abacha regime summarily executed Saro-Wiwa in November 1995, the Sierra Club, Amnesty International, and other rights NGOs joined MOSOP and NADECO in lobbying Western governments to adopt punitive measures against Nigeria. As a measure of their success, the Abacha administration reaped an unexpected windfall of hate, worldwide condemnation, and ostracism, including suspension from the much-prized Commonwealth of Nations. Nigeria's humbling pariah status, which lasted until Sani Abacha's sudden death in June 1998, greatly enhanced the image and standing of human rights groups in Nigeria and made them a serious player in the diplomatic game. Even more important, their existence and tactics made the cost of dictatorships much higher—a lesson that Abacha's military successors took to heart. The Abacha regime was forced to hire expensive public relations firms in Europe and the United States to launder its image; it took out advertisements in costly international newspapers, such as the *New York Times,* to sell itself to an increasingly skeptical foreign audience; and it even spent scarce foreign exchange in an effort to bribe relevant foreign policy constituencies in the West, particularly the United States.[59]

❑   *Transnational Organizations*

I use the more generic term "transnational organizations" to characterize both the traditional nongovernmental organizations (NGOs) that are not driven by profits and those other profit-oriented organizations, such as Executive Outcomes, whose increasing presence and activities in Africa do not fit standard descriptions of a multinational corporation. To many international NGOs, West Africa has become a useful arena for establishing their credentials as a dependable alternative to the state. A symptom of state collapse par excellence, these NGOs are involved in the provision and distribution of food and other social services that the state is no longer able to provide in much of Africa.[60] Indeed, during the worst years of the conflict in Liberia, food delivery to the desperately needy population was handled almost entirely by the World Food Program (WFP), Catholic Relief Services (CRS), the International Committee of the Red Cross and Red Crescent (ICRC), and Lutheran World Service. Health care delivery in war-torn Liberia was the domain of the Médecins sans Frontières (MSF), ICRC, and Save the Children Fund; UNICEF, the ICRC, and the World Health Organization handled water supply.[61] Neither the NPFL nor the government of Liberia cared about the welfare of the population. Indeed, their choice of these agencies as the target of their looting frenzy led to some of the worst cases of human rights violations during the war. In Liberia, the conventional NGOs not only performed traditional humanitarian tasks but also became reliable sources of information for foreign governments interested in determining the culpability of warring parties in particular atrocities. Some of these organizations, such as the Atlanta-based International Negotiation Network (INN), became key participants in peace negotiations between the disputing parties.[62] In the later phase of the peace process in Liberia, NGOs played a prominent role in the verification of the disarmament process and in election monitoring.

But the operational scope of NGOs is not limited to collapsed states. In the area of election monitoring and human rights, for instance, NGOs have had unofficial responsibilities for establishing the institutions of ombudsmen in Ghana, the Gambia, and Nigeria. In these countries, as in others, human rights NGOs have become the eyes and ears of Western governments. This role has often resulted in a love-hate relationship between these organizations and their host governments. Consequently, these organizations should be considered a component of any theoretical or analytical framework for understanding the dynamics of foreign policy decisionmaking in contemporary West Africa.

Aside from traditional NGOs, a new threshold was reached in Sierra Leone when Executive Outcomes (EO), a South African–based outfit, was hired by the Strasser regime in Freetown to flush out RUF forces operating in the hinterland. According to Herbert Howe, Executive Outcomes is a "private army" comprising some 2,000 combat veterans of the apartheid-era South African Defence Force.[63] For a handsome price, they are available for hire by a foreign government that is being threatened by an insurgency. Following EO's impressive debut in Angola in 1993, the Sierra Leonean government learned about it and contracted its services in May 1995. EO's task was to help the government dislodge RUF forces from the lucrative diamond- and bauxite-mining districts that they had controlled since the outbreak of the war. Within weeks of arriving in Sierra Leone, EO was able to "push RUF away from Freetown, protect the Kono diamond district, and open the roads to Freetown for food and fuel transport. By late January 1996, EO-backed forces had retaken the southern coastal rutile and bauxite mines."[64] If EO helped bring back commerce to Sierra Leone, its role in reanimating political life is equally significant. According to Reno, EO's "presence established enough security to hold elections in March 1996."[65] EO's success reverberated rather ominously throughout West Africa and beyond. As the British Parliamentary Human Rights Group put it, EO's experience in Sierra Leone "may lead to a situation where any government in a difficult position can hire mercenaries to stay in power."[66]

The significance of EO's involvement in Sierra Leone goes beyond the obvious normative considerations. My interests lie instead
in the implications of EO's involvement for West African diplomacy
and political economy. EO is an affiliate of the Branch Group of
Companies, which has extensive interests in mineral mining in
southern Africa as well as in Sierra Leone. According to Howe, the
synergy between EO and the Branch Group has been troubling for
even Western businesses and diplomats. Sources in the United States
note that it was hardly a coincidence that "as soon as EO cleared the
rebels out of the diamond fields, the government of Sierra Leone
awarded Branch Energy a huge diamond concession."[67] Even worse,
as Reno has noted, EO's involvement gravely distorted the structure
of political alliances in Sierra Leone, a fact that has implications for
long-term national reconciliation: "The election helped to consolidate a reconfigured political alliance rooted in Executive Outcomes'
presence—the firm's alliance with a new group of politicians and the
destruction of Sierra Leone's old bureaucracies, including much of
the military. All of this left the political alliance heavily dependent
on the presence of foreigners."[68]

Although such reconfigurations are inimical to stability, as was
soon reflected in the hasty removal of President Kabbah in the coup
of 1997, the fact remains that the presence of EO makes creditor
representatives, diplomats, and members of major NGOs happy because EO "prop[s] up rulers who can address mutual interests without forcing diplomats to acknowledge the true nature of political authority" in weak states.[69] Therein lies the danger of the latest
scramble for Africa, in which unaccountable nonstate actors have assumed unprecedented supremacy.

■ CONCLUSION

The foreign policy of Anglophone West Africa displays remarkable
instances of continuity and change. Despite the chronic instability in
the subregion, successive regimes have maintained a preference for
multilateralism over unilateralism in international affairs. The century-old tradition of Pan-Africanism may explain this preference for
multilateralism, but we should not underestimate the political and
economic constraints that limit the capacity of these states to opt for
a unilateral course in their external relations. Despite the obvious

irrelevance of the principle of nonintervention in internal affairs, it is unlikely that the region will experience a spate of interventions in the foreseeable future. The reasons are twofold: First, few states in the region possess the internal capacity required to engage in unilateral military deployment beyond their borders. Even those few states that could project military force beyond their borders for a limited period of time, such as Nigeria and Ghana, are likely to be constrained by the ever-watchful eyes of Western powers. After all, the Nigerian-led ECOMOG operation went ahead largely because the United States gave a nod of approval; it lasted as long as it did because the relevant Western powers saw no strategic or political reasons to risk their forces in the region. Second, and more important, ECOWAS emerged from the Liberian conflict a much stronger organization capable of containing the divisive tendencies of West Africa's linguistic divide. Faced with the prospects of greater marginalization in the global economy of the twenty-first century, West African states will be more likely to commit to greater integration under the aegis of ECOWAS.

In terms of the issues, the current prominence of security considerations in the foreign policy agenda of Anglophone West African states is likely to continue in the medium term given the major reversals of democracy's "third wave" in much of West Africa.[70] The absence of transparent and accountable governments in the subregion will continue to engender pressures for revolt and instability. For this reason, the unregulated operation of diverse NGOs and transnational organizations is worrisome in West African diplomacy and nation-building processes.

■ NOTES

1. See the authoritative account of British colonialism by Lord Lugard *The Dual Mandate in British Tropical Africa* (London: N.p., 1922; Hamden, CT: Archon Books, 1965).

2. I. William Zartman, ed., *Collapsed States: The Disintegration and Restoration of Legitimate Authority* (Boulder, Colo.: Lynne Rienner, 1995).

3. See, among others, Thomas Callaghy, "Africa: Back to the Future," *Journal of Democracy* 5, no. 4 (1994): 133–145; Robert Kaplan, "The Coming Anarchy," *Atlantic Monthly,* no. 273, February 1994: 44–65; William Pfaff, "A New Colonialism? Europe Must Go Back into Africa," *Foreign Affairs* 74 (January-February 1995); and Oliver Furley, ed., *Conflict in Africa* (London: Tauris Academic Studies, 1995).

4. Ali Mazrui, "The African State as a Political Refugee," in David R. Smock and Chester A. Crocker, eds., *African Conflict Resolution* (Washington, DC: U.S. Institute of Peace Press, 1995), chapter 2.

5. Kaplan, "The Coming Anarchy," p. 47 (emphasis in the original).

6. See Sidney Verba, "Assumptions of Rationality and Non-Rationality in Models of the International System," *World Politics* 14 (1961): 93–117; and James Rosenau, "Pre-Theories and Theories of Foreign Policy," in R. Barry Farrell, ed., *Approaches to Comparative and International Politics* (Evanston, IL: Northwestern University Press, 1966), pp. 27–93.

7. See Christopher Clapham, *Africa and the International System: The Politics of State Survival* (Cambridge: Cambridge University Press, 1996); and Ankie Hoogvelt, *Globalization and the Postcolonial World: The New Political Economy of Development* (Baltimore, MD: Johns Hopkins University Press, 1997).

8. See Benedict Anderson, *Imagined Communities,* rev. ed. (New York: Verso, 1991), p. 84; and E. J. Hobsbawm, *Nations and Nationalism Since 1780: Program, Myth, Reality* (Cambridge: Cambridge University Press, 1990), chapter 2.

9. For details, see J. D. Fage, *A History of West Africa: An Introductory Survey* (Cambridge: Cambridge University Press, 1969); and J. F. Ade Ajayi and Michael Crowder, eds., *History of West Africa* (New York: Columbia University Press, 1972).

10. Colin W. Newbury, ed., *British Policy Towards West Africa: Select Documents, Volume II* (Oxford: Oxford University Press, 1971), pp. 157–158.

11. Lugard, *The Dual Mandate* (London: 1922), p. 10.

12. D. Elmwood Dunn and Byron S. Tarr, *Liberia: A National Polity in Transition* (Methuen, NJ: Scarecrow Press, 1988), p. 50.

13. Sanford Ungar, *Africa: The People and Politics of an Emerging Continent,* rev. ed. (New York: Simon and Schuster, 1986), p. 92, footnote.

14. This is a rather minimalist definition of Pan-Africanism, for the ideal of Pan-Africanism was a common African homeland (preferably a United States of Africa) for all Africans in the diaspora. For details, see V. B. Thompson, *Africa and Unity: The Evolution of Pan-Africanism* (London: Longmans, Green, 1969); and Immanuel Geiss, *The Pan-African Movement* (London: Methuen, 1974).

15. Blyden also served as the first African ambassador to the court of St. James between 1877 and 1879.

16. Edward Blyden, quoted in Hollis R. Lynch, *Edward Wilmot Blyden: Pan-Negro Patriot* (London: Oxford University Press, 1967), p. 215 (emphasis in the original).

17. J. Casely-Hayford, quoted in Thompson, *Africa and Unity,* p. 28.

18. This policy was also pursued in British colonies in East Africa, and its remarkable success there laid the foundation for the establishment of the East African Community following the attainment of independence. For details, see Arthur Hazlewood, ed., *African Integration and Disintegration: Case Studies in Economic and Political Union* (London: Oxford University Press, 1967).

19. See Kwame Nkrumah, *Africa Must Unite* (London: Mercury Books, 1965).

20. Kwesi Krafona, *The Pan-African Movement: Ghana's Contribution* (London: Afroworld, 1986), p. 22.

21. Ibid., p. 9.

22. Ibid.

23. See Olatunde Ojo, D. K. Orwa, and C.M.B. Utete, *African International Relations* (London: Longman, 1985).

24. Such domestic economic sacrifices were considered by Nkrumah's military successors to be an unnecessary price to pay for Nkrumah's personal ambitions and Pan-Africanist ideals. For details, see the personal account of the military coup against Nkrumah by A. A. Afrifa, *The Ghana Coup* (London: Frank Cass, 1967).

25. Nkrumah was married to General Nasser's daughter, and this union became an invaluable source of political capital that he skillfully deployed in support of his continental aspirations. For details, see Ali Mazrui, *Africa's International Relations: The Diplomacy of Dependency and Change* (Boulder: Westview Press, 1979).

26. For details, see W. Thompson, *Ghana's Foreign Policy, 1957–66* (Princeton: Princeton University Press, 1969); and Olajide Aluko, *Ghana and Nigeria, 1957–1970: A Study in Inter-African Discord* (London: Rex Collings, 1976).

27. Understandably, Liberia is the only Anglophone country in West Africa that is not a member of the Commonwealth.

28. In 1960, Liberia joined Ethiopia in initiating a lawsuit against South Africa before the World Court. According to Ungar, *Africa: The People and Politics of an Emerging Continent* (p. 95), this action contributed to the eventual "revocation of Pretoria's old League of Nations mandate over Namibia."

29. For a detailed discussion, see Victor T. Levine, "The Fall and Rise of Constitutionalism in West Africa," *Journal of Modern African Studies* 35, no. 2 (1997): 181–206.

30. See, for instance, John Stremlau, *The International Politics of the Nigerian Civil War, 1967–1970* (Princeton: Princeton University Press, 1977); O. Oyediran, ed., *Nigerian Government and Politics Under Military Rule* (New York: St. Martin's Press, 1979); Joseph N. Garba, *Diplomatic Soldiering: The Conduct of Nigerian Foreign Policy, 1975–1979*, rev. 2nd ed. (Ibadan: Spectrum Books, 1991).

31. For a theoretically insightful discussion of African independence as a social contract, see I. William Zartman, "Governance as Conflict Management in West Africa," in Zartman, ed., *Governance as Conflict Management* (Washington, DC: Brookings Institution, 1997), pp. 18–24.

32. See Stremlau, *The International Politics of the Nigerian Civil War* and Aluko, *Ghana and Nigeria.*

33. See G. Aforka Nweke, *External Intervention in African Conflicts: France and French-Speaking West Africa in the Nigerian Civil War, 1967–1970* (Boston: African Studies Center, Boston University, 1976); and Daniel Bach, "The Politics of West African Economic Cooperation: CEAO and ECOWAS," *Journal of Modern African Studies* 21, no. 4 (1983): 605–623.

34. See Olatunde Ojo, "Nigeria and the Formation of ECOWAS," *International Organization* 34, no. 4 (1980): 571–604.

35. For further discussions, see Julius E. Okolo, "Obstacles to Increased Intra-ECOWAS Trade," *International Journal* 44, no. 1 (1989–1999): 171–214; and Clement Adibe, "ECOWAS in Comparative Perspective," in Timothy M. Shaw and Julius E. Okolo, eds., *The Political Economy of Foreign Policy in ECOWAS* (New York: St. Martin's Press, 1994), pp. 187–217.

36. See Clement Adibe, *Managing Arms in Peace Processes: Liberia* (Geneva: UN, 1996).

37. Stephen Ellis, "Liberia's Warlord Insurgency," in Christopher Clapham, ed., *African Guerrillas* (Oxford: James Currey, 1998), p. 166.

38. Asteris C. Huliaras, "The 'Anglo-Saxon Conspiracy': French Perceptions of the Great Lakes Crisis," *Journal of Modern African Studies* 36, no. 4 (1998): 593–609.

39. W. Ofuatey-Kodjoe, "Regional Organizations and the Resolution of Internal Conflict: The ECOWAS Intervention in Liberia," *International Peacekeeping* 1, no. 3 (1994): 261–302.

40. For an insightful account, see Robert A. Mortimer, "Senegal's Role in Ecomog: The Francophone Dimension in the Liberian Crisis," *Journal of Modern African Studies* 34, no. 2 (1996): 293–306.

41. This is the very essence of Nkrumah's political thought, the genealogy of which may be traced to James Africanus Horton, *West African Countries and Peoples* (Edinburgh: Edinburgh University Press, 1868, 1969). See also Davidson Nicol, *Black Nationalism in Africa* (New York: Africana, 1969).

42. Ofuatey-Kodjoe, "Regional Organizations and the Resolution of Internal Conflict," p. 273.

43. Christopher Clapham, "Introduction: Analyzing African Insurgencies," in *African Guerrillas*, p. 3.

44. Ibid. (emphasis added).

45. Ellis, "Liberia's Warlord Insurgency," p. 155.

46. I would like to thank Steve Weigert for drawing my attention to the significance of this variable in West Africa's contemporary diplomacy.

47. Ellis, "Liberia's Warlord Insurgency," p. 155.

48. For details, see Clement E. Adibe, "The Liberian Conflict and the ECOWAS-UN Partnership," *Third World Quarterly* 18, no. 3 (1997): 471–488.

49. Ibrahim Abdullah, "Bush Path to Destruction: The Origin and Character of the Revolutionary United Front/Sierra Leone," *Journal of Modern African Studies* 36, no. 2 (1998): 203.

50. Ibrahim Abdullah and Patrick Muana, "The Revolutionary United Front of Sierra Leone," in Clapham, *African Guerrillas*, p. 177.

51. Ibid., p. 117.

52. For insightful analysis of the warlord economy in Liberia and Sierra Leone, see William Reno, *Warlord Politics and African States* (Boulder: Lynne Rienner, 1998), chapters 3–4; and Herbert Howe, "Private Security Forces and African Stability: The Case of Executive Outcomes," *Journal of Modern African Studies* 36, no. 2 (1998): 307–331.

53. For details of the annulment of Nigeria's presidential election in mid-1993, see, among others, Julius Ihonvbere, "Where Is the Third Wave? A Critical Evaluation of Africa's Non-Transition to Democracy," *Africa Today* 43, no. 4 (1995): 343–368; Larry Diamond et al., eds., *Transition Without End* (Boulder: Lynne Rienner, 1997); Pita O. Agbese, "The Military as an Obstacle to the Democratization Enterprise: Towards an Agenda for Permanent Military Disengagement from Politics in Nigeria," *Journal of Asian and African Studies* 31 (1996): 82–98; and Richard Joseph, ed., *State, Conflict, and Democracy in Africa* (Boulder: Lynne Rienner, 1999).

54. Reno, *Warlord Politics and African States,* p. 199.

55. Ken Saro-Wiwa, *Genocide in Nigeria: The Ogoni Tragedy* (London: Saros International, 1992).

56. For details, see Saro-Wiwa's own chilling account of his activities and the fate that befell him in *A Month and a Day: A Detention Diary* (New York: Penguin Press, 1995).

57. Ibid., pp. 169–170.

58. See Reno, *Warlord Politics and African States,* chapter 6; and Joseph, *State, Conflict, and Democracy in Africa,* chapter 9.

59. In *Warlord Politics,* Reno writes that Randall Robinson, a critic of Nigeria's military dictatorship and head of the influential TransAfrica Coalition in the United States, "reported that he was offered $1 million" by agents of the Nigerian government to stop his opposition to the Abacha regime (p. 208).

60. See Michael Bratton, "Beyond the State: Civil Society and Associational Life in Africa," *World Politics* 41 (April 1989); Thomas G. Weiss and Leon Gordenker, eds., *NGOs, the UN, and Global Governance* (Boulder: Lynne Rienner, 1996); and Eboe Hutchful, "The Civil Society Debate in Africa," *International Journal* 51, no. 1 (1995–1996): 54–77.

61. Colin Scott, "Humanitarian Action and Security in Liberia, 1989–1994," occasional paper no. 20, Watson Institute for International Studies, Providence, R.I., 1995.

62. For details see Adibe, *Managing Arms in Peace Processes.*

63. Howe, "Private Security Forces," p. 307.

64. Ibid., p. 314.

65. Reno, *Warlord Politics and African States,* p. 133.

66. Quoted in Howe, "Private Security Forces," p. 323.

67. Ibid., p. 318.

68. Reno, *Warlord Politics and African States,* p. 134.

69. Ibid., p. 135.

70. See Ihonvbere, "Where Is the Third Wave?" pp. 343–368.

3

New Directions in Francophone West African Foreign Policies

Peter J. Schraeder

In 1995, Senegal hosted an international conference commemorating the 100-year anniversary of France's creation of Afrique Occidentale Française (AOF—French West Africa), a colonial unit that grouped together the present-day countries of Benin, Burkina Faso, Côte d'Ivoire, Guinea, Mali, Mauritania, Niger, and Senegal.[1] Although the primary purpose of France's colonial enterprise of bolstering its power and influence did not survive the contemporary independence era, French policymakers nonetheless left behind an important foreign policy legacy: a unique and distinct group of Francophone countries whose leaders identify with a greater French-speaking community (*la francophonie*). This foreign policy legacy is not simply limited to the cultural realm but also incorporates economic, political, and military dimensions.[2]

Understanding the foreign policy implications of this French colonial legacy in West Africa has been based on one of three sets of narrowly defined arguments: the overriding importance of the personal whims of authoritarian leaders—the so-called big-man theory of African foreign policy; the positions of the newly independent countries of Francophone West Africa within the larger geopolitical setting of the Cold War struggle between the United States and the former Soviet Union; or the continuation of dependency relationships between French policymakers and their West African counterparts. In essence, the formulation and implementation of Francophone West

African foreign policies was simplistically explained as primarily derivative of the personal interests of its leaders or the foreign policy interests of the French, U.S., and Soviet policymaking establishments. Such arguments were not limited to Francophone West Africa but instead captured the overall thrust of scholarship devoted to the African subfield of comparative foreign policy analysis.

Even if one were to accept the validity of these arguments during the Cold War era, three historical turning points suggest their declining utility in the post-1989 era. First, the third wave of democratic transition that spread to the African continent beginning in 1990 contributed to the democratization of Francophone West African foreign policy establishments by strengthening power centers outside of the presidential mansion that are capable of challenging the supremacy of African leaders.[3] For example, the democratically elected members of national assemblies should be able to exert their newfound influence in shaping foreign policy agendas and provide a potential avenue of influence for historically weak representatives of civil society, such as the media, human rights organizations, and religious groups.

The demise of the Cold War served as a second historical turning point, signaling the end of superpower rivalry in Francophone West Africa. An important outcome was the growing unwillingness of the northern industrialized democracies to accept French portrayals of Francophone Africa as constituting part of France's *chasse gardée* (exclusive hunting ground) to the exclusion of other major powers.[4] As noted by Jeffrey Garten, a "cold peace," in which the northern industrialized democracies compete for economic markets and influence in all regions of the world, including Francophone West Africa, has replaced the Cold War between the United States and the former Soviet Union.[5] The foreign policy implication of this trend is that Francophone West African leaders should be able to take advantage of intensifying international competition to reduce the ties of external dependency.

A third historical event with equally important implications for dependency explanations of foreign policy was Paul Kagame's assumption of power in 1994 under the banner of the Rwandan Patriotic Front (RPF), a guerrilla army supported by Uganda and perceived by French policymakers as hostile to France and "under Anglo-Saxon influence."[6] According to French policymakers, the RPF's military victory constituted the first time that a Francophone country had fallen to Anglo-Saxon influence. Some French policy-makers even characterized Kagame's military victory as the first of a series of falling dominoes that could successfully transform the foreign policy relationships of central Africa to the detriment of French foreign policy interests. This perception was reinforced in 1997 by the emergence of Laurent Désiré Kabila as the head of a new military regime in Congo-Kinshasa that was closely allied with Rwanda, Uganda, and the United States.[7] Kagame's victory was a poignant reminder that the process of regime change—regardless of whether carried out by the barrel of a gun or the ballot box—entails significant risks for France's carefully crafted Francophone network in Africa: the potential replacement of staunchly pro-French, undemocratic elites with Francophone leaders less aligned to France and more sympathetic to closer ties with other great powers.[8]

In this chapter I argue that traditional personal rule, Cold War, and dependency-oriented explanations constitute at best exaggerations and at worst mere caricatures of more complex and dynamic foreign policy processes. Other neglected factors, such as public opinion, religious beliefs, and regional interests, require attention to achieve a more nuanced and valid understanding of Francophone West African foreign policies. These factors are even more salient at the beginning of the new millennium as these leaders confront popular pressures for democratization and the intensification of international economic competition. This analysis draws upon the shared cultural experiences of nine Francophone West African states: the eight countries that historically composed France's AOF colonial administration (Benin, Burkina Faso, Côte d'Ivoire, Guinea, Mali, Mauritania, Niger, and Senegal) and Togo, which was placed under French colonial rule after Germany's defeat in World War I.

■ EVOLVING FOREIGN POLICY PRINCIPLES

Three sets of foreign policy principles are essential to any comprehensive understanding of the contemporary foreign policies of Francophone West Africa. The preservation and strengthening of a greater, French-speaking community of nations—*la francophonie*—has served as the bedrock foreign policy principle throughout the independence era. The resilience of this cultural factor is demonstrated by the continued importance of French as one of the official languages of government activity and by the self-classification of local elites as composing part of a larger French-speaking community. The most vigorous proponents of this culturally based foreign policy in the independence years were Ivoirian president Félix Houphouët-Boigny and Senegalese president Léopold Sédar Senghor, the leaders of the two most economically and politically influential countries in Francophone West Africa. Although the once privileged status of French is gradually being eroded in several countries by national-language movements intent on fostering indigenous languages and increasing the learning of English, the commitment of the Francophone West African elite to *la francophonie* remains strong.

Regular Franco-African summits attended by the president of France and his African counterparts demonstrate the foreign policy dimension of *la francophonie*. These summits have been described as the "centerpiece" of Franco-African cultural relations, primarily because they are perceived as "family reunions" designed to strengthen already close personal relationships between the French president and his Francophone African counterparts.[9] The careful nurturing of close, high-level personal ties is the cornerstone of each gathering and is equally important as regards the day-to-day decisionmaking related to French foreign policy toward Africa. Only three Francophone West African leaders—Blaise Compaoré of Burkina Faso (1996), Gnassingbé Eyadéma of Togo (1986), and Senghor of Senegal (1977)—have had the highly coveted honor of serving as the hosts of this Franco-African summit. Although critics assert that very few (if any) real gains, such as increased trade or investment, accrue to the host country, one should not downplay the diplomatic importance of these gatherings. Competition to host this meeting is not unlike that associated with hosting the Organization of African Unity (OAU), the Olympics, or any other international meeting that places the international spotlight on the country in question. President Compaoré successfully sought to make Ouagadougou the site of the 1996 meeting, which conferred a significant amount of prestige on him and anointed Burkina Faso as one of the leaders of Francophone West Africa.

A second foreign policy principle that has been reinforced by the end of the Cold War is the pursuit of regional integration and development. One of the most important rationales for regional integration— promoting self-reliant development to reduce dependence on foreign actors—nonetheless has served as a point of dissension among the

Francophone states due to their links with France. During the 1950s, for example, there were two extreme versions of this argument: Ivoirian president Houphouët-Boigny embraced the strengthening of economic ties with France, leading some to denounce him as "more French than African"; Guinean president Ahmed Sékou Touré emerged as the most critical opponent of what he perceived as the perpetuation of French neocolonialism in West Africa. The majority of Francophone West African elites put themselves between these two positions, albeit with a strong tilt toward the maintenance of ties with France. Despite these differences, all agreed that the productivity of their respective economies had been constrained by a system that favored trade with France at the expense of West African intraregional trade links. It is for this reason that the primary objective of early regional economic schemes was to promote intraregional trade with neighbors who shared a common set of development objectives—irrespective of geographic features, historical ties, or a common cultural heritage.[10] By strengthening ties with like-minded neighbors, the Francophone states expected to create a stronger regional economic entity to bargain with foreign actors.

The cornerstone of economic cooperation in Francophone West Africa is the Union Économique et Monétaire Ouest-Africaine (UEMOA; West African Economic and Monetary Union), which was established on August 1, 1994, and superseded the Union Monétaire Ouest-Africaine (UMOA; West African Monetary Union) and the Communauté Économique de l'Afrique de l'Ouest (CEAO; Economic Community of West Africa).[11] Ultimately seeking the creation of a common market based on the free circulation of goods and people, the UEMOA serves as the Francophone core of the Economic Community of West African States (ECOWAS), a much larger economic community originally established in 1975 that also includes Guinea and Mauritania and the non-Francophone states of Cape Verde, Gambia, Ghana, Liberia, Nigeria, and Sierra Leone.[12] Although there is a clear geographical logic for creating a regional economic grouping that includes both Anglophone and Francophone states, the split between them ensured that several Francophone West African countries with French assistance would seek to counterbalance Nigeria's overwhelming economic influence within the region.[13] As a result, most of the core Francophone members of CEAO perceived it as a competitor to the ECOWAS vision of regional integration. With the death in 1993 of Côte d'Ivoire's Houphouët-Boigny, the most vociferous Francophone opponent of cooperation with Nigeria, the newly restructured UEMOA sought to form a greater partnership with both Nigeria and ECOWAS. This new trend in regional foreign policy was symbolically demonstrated by Nigeria's decision in 1996 to take part for the first time in the Franco-African summit, held in that year in Ouagadougou, Burkina Faso.

A common monetary policy is guaranteed by Francophone West Africa's inclusion in the franc zone, a supranational financial system created in 1947 that links UEMOA member states, Equatorial Guinea, and six other former French colonies (Cameroon, the Central African Republic, the Comoros, Chad, Congo-Brazzaville, and Gabon). Under this arrangement, France serves as a central bank, and a common currency, the Communauté Financière Africaine (CFA) franc, is tied to the French franc and guaranteed by the French treasury.[14] The potential pitfalls of deferring monetary policy to France were sharply felt for the first time in 1994 when French policymakers took the extraordinary step of devaluing the CFA franc by 50 percent. Strongly supported by international financial institutions and other foreign donors, the decision caused instability throughout the CFA franc zone largely because French authorities did not consult with African leaders in advance. The sensitivity associated with France's decision to undertake such a drastic measure with no forewarning was demonstrated at the 1996 Franco-African summit, held in Burkina Faso. The only significant point of dissension at this summit occurred when French president Jacques Chirac sought to allay the fears of his franc zone counterparts by proclaiming that France would never again devalue the CFA franc. The response of the assembled franc zone leaders was both guarded and lighthearted, with President Pascal Lissouba of Congo-Brazzaville taking the lead in demanding that Chirac place this promise in writing—a clear reference to earlier promises obviously not kept when France devalued the CFA franc in 1994.

A third theme of Francophone West African foreign policies that is gaining momentum in the post–Cold War era is a commitment to conflict resolution. In the Cold War era, ideological differences significantly hindered a common approach to conflict resolution. The majority of conservative and pro-West regimes felt threatened by the more radical states such as Sékou Touré's Guinea, Luiz Cabral's Guinea-Bissau, and Modibo Keita's Mali.[15] The post–Cold War era is characterized by the emergence of a multiplicity of conflicts devoid of ideological overtones. These conflicts range from diplomatic disputes over shared border resources, such as that surrounding the discovery at the beginning of the 1990s of off-shore oil reserves along the disputed boundary between Senegal and Guinea-Bissau; the reemergence of once-latent border conflicts, such as the January 1998 border dispute between Benin and Niger over the Island of Lete; internal guerrilla conflicts that transcend national frontiers, such as the intermittent guerrilla insurgencies by Tuareg minorities in both Mali and Niger; military coups, including unsuccessful mutinies in the Central African Republic and Guinea in 1997; the complete collapse of any central authority as civil wars spill over into neighboring territories, as in the case of the spread of the Liberian civil war to Sierra Leone, Guinea, and Côte d'Ivoire; and military clashes as occurred in the 1989 border conflict between Mauritania and Senegal.

The approach of Francophone West African policymakers to resolving these conflicts demonstrates an increased willingness to focus on diplomatic solutions that emphasize the regional dimension of a given conflict. Especially in the case of Liberia, a brutal civil war pitted the Ivoirian- and Burkinabe-supported forces of Charles Taylor's National Patriotic Front of Liberia (NPFL) first against the dictatorship of Samuel K. Doe and subsequently against a Nigerian-led multilateral military force sanctioned by ECOWAS and formally referred to as the Cease-Fire Monitoring Group (ECOMOG). A series of Francophone-inspired diplomatic initiatives, most notably Senegal's decision to include Senegalese troops in the ECOMOG force (1991–1993) and a series of Ivoirian-led peace talks in Yamoussoukro, Côte d'Ivoire, furthered the peace process but ultimately failed to achieve the peace.[16] Success ultimately hinged on a regional Anglophone-Francophone rapprochement between Nigeria, Côte d'Ivoire, and Burkina Faso that was accepted by Taylor and blessed by the United States and France.[17] This rapprochement was signaled in August 1995 by the signing of a peace accord in Abuja, Nigeria. Unlike in the Cold War era, when non-African powers often played the critical role, the resolution of the Liberian civil war demonstrated the rising importance of regional military powers, particularly Nigeria, as the new power brokers of African international relations. Although itself a military dictatorship at the time, Nigeria with the blessing of its neighbors underscored this fact again in March 1998 when a Nigerian-led military offensive reinstated the democratically elected government of President Ahmed Tejan Kabbah in Sierra Leone.

■   FOREIGN POLICY ACTORS

The predominance of big-man interpretations of West African foreign policies was based on two realities of the policymaking environment during the initial decades of the independence era. First,
like their Western counterparts, each of these political systems was
derivative of the widely shared belief that foreign policy constitutes
the *domaine réservé* (privileged realm) of the leader—regardless of
whether he is an elected president, a military leader who took power
in a military coup d'état, or a reigning monarch. This belief led to
highly centralized foreign policy establishments modeled on France
under the constitution of the Fifth Republic, in which the president
is granted a wide array of foreign policy prerogatives.

      The authoritarian nature of most Francophone West African polit-
ical systems also contributed to the intellectual popularity of the big-
man theory of foreign policy. In the immediate postindependence
decades, the majority of the first generation of African leaders systematically suppressed and dismantled centers of power that challenged the foreign policy supremacy of the presidencies. Efforts by
these leaders to secure their authority included the stifling of a free
press, the suspension of constitutions, the banning of opposition parties, the jailing of vocal political opponents, the dismantling of independent judiciaries, and the co-optation or jailing of legislative opponents. The net result was the creation of a highly centralized foreign
policy apparatus that led to the promotion of highly personalized foreign policies.

      Even if one accepts the validity of such personal rule–oriented
explanations, the process of democratization at the bare minimum
has ensured the progressive decline of the importance of personal
rule as once highly centralized foreign policy establishments become
increasingly democratic. As demonstrated by the relatively crude yet
nonetheless useful democracy scores that Freedom House, a conservative think tank, compiles on an annual basis, the process of democratization ensured a progressive increase in political rights and
civil liberties throughout Francophone West Africa from 1986 to
1996 (see Table 3.1). The figures correctly capture the emergence of
Benin and Mali as the democratic leaders of Francophone West
Africa. Especially in the case of Benin, the alternation of power in
1996 from the democratically elected administration of President
Nicéphore Soglo to that of President Mathieu Kérékou revealed the

growing consolidation of democracy. The scores also categorize Senegal and Burkina Faso as liberalizing yet imperfect semi- or partial democracies. Although figures for 2000 have yet to be released, Senegal's alternation of power, as demonstrated by Abdoulaye Wade's victory in the March 2000 presidential elections, suggests the further consolidation of Senegalese democracy. The remaining five countries of Francophone West Africa—Côte d'Ivoire, Guinea, Mauritania, Niger, and Togo—embody varying degrees of authoritarianism.

The foreign policy implication of the Freedom House scores is that democratization has strengthened power centers that can challenge traditional arenas of foreign policy. The countries achieving the best scores on the scale of democratization also embody increasingly

Table 3.1   Levels of Democracy in Francophone West Africa (1986–1996)

Country	Year	Political Rights	Civil Liberties	Democracy Score
Benin	1986	7	7	14
	1996	2	2	4
Burkina Faso	1986	7	6	13
	1996	5	4	9
Côte d'Ivoire	1986	6	5	11
	1996	6	5	11
Guinea	1986	7	5	12
	1996	6	5	11
Mali	1986	7	6	13
	1996	2	2	4
Mauritania	1986	7	6	13
	1996	6	6	12
Niger	1986	7	6	13
	1996	7	5	12
Senegal	1986	3	4	7
	1996	4	4	8
Average	1986	6.4	5.6	12.0
	1996	4.8	4.1	8.9

Source: Freedom House, *Freedom in the World: The Annual Survey of Political Rights and Civil Liberties, 1996–1997* (New Brunswick: Transaction, 1997).

Notes: Political rights (1–7), most to least free; civil liberties (1–7), most to least free; democracy score (2–4), democratic; (5–10), partially democratic; (11–14), authoritarian.

democratic foreign policy establishments. Those achieving the worst scores constitute the most entrenched forms of personal rule. Drawing principally on Senegalese foreign policy making during the administration of Abdou Diouf (1981–2000), the following analysis reveals not only that personal rule progressively declines as Francophone West Africa democratizes but that personal rule–oriented explanations constituted at best exaggerations of more complex and dynamic foreign policy processes.[18]

Like that of many of its Francophone neighbors, the Senegalese constitution reflects a political system based on presidential dominance. Following the model of the French Fifth Republic, the Senegalese president is granted a wide array of foreign policy prerogatives.[19] One must be careful, however, not to equate presidential dominance with the lack of influence on the part of other foreign policy actors. The formulation and implementation of Senegal's foreign policy cannot be explained by mere reference to the personal interests and idiosyncrasies of the first two Senegalese presidents, Senghor and Diouf. Other, often downplayed foreign policy actors must be examined to gain a better understanding.

First, in most of these countries, an officially designated vice president or prime minister often complements the office of the president in the policymaking arena. The Senegalese constitution stipulates that the president is to appoint a prime minister to manage the day-to-day functioning of the government. Unlike his counterparts in other Francophone West African political systems, the Senegalese prime minister is not beholden to the national assembly. The prime minister also maintains a diplomatic cabinet under the guidance of a diplomatic adviser and therefore plays an influential role in the making of foreign policy. The Senegalese political system under Diouf constituted a significant change from that of the early 1960s, when the Office of the President and the Office of the Prime Minister were constitutionally independent of each other. During this period, an intensifying power struggle between President Senghor and Prime Minister Mamadou Dia led to the revision of the constitution in 1963 to create a system based on presidential dominance.

The Ministry of Foreign Affairs usually is the largest and most active of the foreign affairs bureaucracies in Francophone West African policymaking establishments, taking responsibility for much of the day-to-day administration of foreign relations.[20] Depending on his personality and bureaucratic skills, the minister of foreign affairs therefore is potentially a key player within the policymaking network. His direct access to the president combined with his links to the far-reaching foreign affairs bureaucracy provides him with bureaucratic tools to set the foreign policy agenda.[21] In Senegal, for example, former minister of foreign affairs Ibrahima Fall was the driving force behind the Diouf administration's adoption of a more "progressive" stance toward regional African issues, such as the decision to recognize the Marxist regime of Angola, then headed by President Antonio Agostinho Neto.[22] Moustapha Niasse, who succeeded Fall, carried these bureaucratic tools as well.

The Ministry of Defense is another foreign affairs bureaucracy that has played an influential role in Francophone West African foreign policies. In extreme cases, this bureaucracy has served as one of the sources of military coup d'états.[23] In Niger, for example, Colonel Ibrahim Maïnassara Baré achieved the dubious honor of leading the first successful military coup against a democratically elected government in Francophone West Africa since the beginning of the democratization process in 1990. In a throwback to an earlier era of authoritarian rule and practices, Colonel Baré announced that there would be multiparty elections in 1996, presented himself as the "civilian" candidate of the ruling party, and subsequently won grossly flawed elections to the congratulatory toasts of local French diplomats. The events in Niger signaled the reemergence of the military as a critical force in West Africa and the growing stagnation of the democratization process.

In Senegal, strong adherence to the republican ideal of civilian control of the military has not prevented military leaders from playing important behind-the-scenes roles in shaping its history.[24] During the 1963 constitutional crisis between President Senghor and Prime Minister Mamadou Dia, pro-Senghor military forces prevailed over those preferring to depose the president. Under the Diouf administration, Army Chief of Staff General Taverez Da Souza was removed from office in 1988 amid charges that he had convened meetings with other high-ranking officers to discuss the potential necessity of military intervention to end the political disturbances following the 1988 presidential elections. These examples are not unique but instead are indicative of a bureaucratically important institution that increased its influence during the 1980s and the 1990s due to Senegal's internal and external security problems.[25]

The legislative branch of government has played an increasingly influential role in Francophone West African foreign policies.[26] Beginning in the 1980s, the Senegalese national assembly emerged as an increasingly vocal arena of national debate. Largely reduced to the role of a rubber-stamp institution during the Senghor years (there was no opposition between 1964 and 1978), the national assembly has questioned government policies since the lifting of multiparty restrictions in 1981, particularly in the aftermath of the 1993 legislative elections, in which candidates from five opposition parties won a total of thirty-six seats in the 120-seat national assembly. The most important foreign affairs components of the national assembly include the Committee on Foreign Affairs, headed by Daouda Sow, and over twenty friendship groups that promote formal and informal contacts between Senegalese representatives and their foreign counterparts.

The Senegalese case nonetheless demonstrates ongoing constraints that potentially hinder a more effective role for Francophone West African legislatures. The willingness of Senegalese representatives to challenge the executive branch in the realm of foreign policy remains relatively lukewarm, and when a challenge occurs it is largely restricted to issues related to the Senegalese economy, such as the domestic costs and impacts of foreign-sponsored structural adjustment programs (i.e., the vast array of economic and political conditions designed to restructure African economies and political systems in the image of the northern industrialized democracies).[27] Furthermore, the national assembly must cope with a weak constitutional role relative to that of the executive branch, as well as an ongoing negative public image as constituting nothing more than *applaudisseurs* (literally, "applauders" of government policies).

The national assembly's role in foreign affairs is also seriously hampered by the lack of economic resources, especially the lack of a sufficient budget that would allow committees and representatives to hire staffs and independently conduct research and fact-finding missions. "If we want the national assembly to truly play its constitutionally mandated role," explains Representative Sémou Pathé Guèye, "we must put an end to the disastrous conditions under which Representatives work."[28] As is further lamented by Iba Der Thiam, representatives do not even enjoy something as simple as individual offices within which they can work and privately receive members of their constituencies.[29]

The formulation and implementation of foreign policies in Francophone West Africa are also influenced by a wide variety of nongovernmental actors. The print and broadcast media, for example, have flourished in the liberal political environment associated with transitions to democracy during the 1990s. In Senegal, the reporting of the daily government newspaper, *Le Soleil,* is now challenged by the publication of two privately funded daily newspapers, *Le Sud* and *Wal Fadjri,* as well as by a host of sporadically published newspapers such as *Le Témoin* and *Démocraties.*[30] These private newspapers play an important agenda-setting role and, at the very least, offer a more critical perspective of day-to-day issues in foreign policy. For example, the German government's March 1996 decision to include Senegal in the list of nondemocratic countries for which requests for political asylum would be routinely considered was picked up by the press and turned into a public debate, prompting Minister of Communication Serigne Diop to hold a widely reported special meeting with the German ambassador to Senegal.[31]

The growing number of immigrants from Francophone West Africa in Western countries is beginning to have an impact on their foreign policies.[32] Although exact numbers are unavailable, the seriousness with which the Senegalese government treats the growing number of Senegalese living and working abroad is demonstrated by the telling June 1993 decision to rename the Ministry of Foreign Affairs as the Ministry of Foreign Affairs and of Senegalese Abroad. Senegal's tilt toward warmer relations with the United States during the 1980s and the 1990s has certainly been influenced by the large numbers of Senegalese in the United States, who are now capable of mobilizing financial resources for a variety of business undertakings in Senegal. In 1996 the Senegalese government aided in the creation of an investment consortium of Senegalese living in the United States as a unique means of attracting greater investment in Senegal and promoting trade links between the two countries.

Public opinion has also exerted an influential, albeit intermittent, influence in African foreign policies. As witnessed in other African countries, the strengthening of the democratization process portends greater popular input in policy as public opinion becomes critical in the overall policies of the new generation of leaders. In Senegal, it has been argued that public opinion, fueled primarily by broadcasts by Radio France Internationale, was the primary factor that led to bloody clashes between Senegal and Mauritania in 1989.[33] Despite the fact that this conflict was neither desired nor promoted by President Diouf of Senegal or President Ould Taya of Mauritania, both were confronted by violent clashes that spiraled out of control. In a sense, both of these leaders, as well as the foreign policies of their respective countries, became prisoners of public opinion.[34]

Finally, one must also take into account the impact of religious groups and leaders on Francophone West African foreign policies. In Senegal, religious leaders known as marabouts historically have constituted an integral part of the domestic political system and play both informal and formal roles in foreign policy.[35] For example, the marabouts played an informal role in reducing tensions between Senegal and Mauritania in the aftermath of the 1989 border conflict by undertaking an unofficial form of shuttle diplomacy across the river that separates the two countries. In a formal sense, one of President Diouf's closest advisers was Moustaffa Cisse, a marabout who served as the former Senegalese ambassador to Egypt and to Saudi Arabia.

The power of the marabouts comes from the population's belief in the spiritual powers of these personal religious guides. The marabouts enjoy almost complete financial autonomy from state control due to a highly complex system of alms collection by *taalibe* (disciples), who, depending on their charisma and power, are capable of channeling enormous amounts of money into a designated cause. The marabouts are, therefore, capable of mobilizing a potent reaction to undesired foreign policies (and supporting others) with little or no fear of state retribution. In the mid-1980s the Diouf administration was forced to withdraw an invitation to Pope John Paul II to visit the country because leading marabouts threatened to call upon their *taalibe* to occupy the runways at the international airport. Although the pope subsequently visited Senegal several years later in 1991 to the wide acclaim of both Muslims and Christians, the marabouts had served notice that sensitive issues had to be raised with them in advance if the Diouf administration wished to avoid embarrassing public confrontations. Thus, to understand the formulation and implementation of Senegal's foreign policy, and that of other West African countries with sizable Muslim populations, one must take into account the role of religion.

The election of Abdoulaye Wade as president of Senegal in March 2000 promises to further strengthen Senegal's democracy and place it among the ranks of democratic Benin and Mali. Wade's election under the banner of the Parti Démocratique Sénégalais (PDS; Senegalese Democratic Party) ushered in an era of change in which, for the first time since independence, a party other than the Socialist

Party controlled the reins of power. Although it is still too early to assess the impact of Wade's election on Senegalese foreign policy, Wade has promised to oversee the complete restructuring of Senegalese institutions, including strengthening the role of parliament and restricting the powers of the presidency. If carried out, this consolidation of Senegalese democracy will enhance the democratization of the foreign policy establishment. At the bare minimum, it will promote the foreign policy role of the National Assembly and deepen the involvement of a wide variety of nonstate actors in foreign policy making.

■   FOREIGN POLICY RELATIONSHIPS

The combined effects of democratic transition (however imperfect) and the demise of the Cold War have contributed to the gradual transformation of Francophone West Africa's foreign policy relationships. The foreign policies of the democratically elected Soglo administration of Benin (1991–1996) and President Alpha Oumar Konaré of Mali (1992–present) demonstrate the growing trend of democratic transitions fostering a second generation of leaders less aligned to France.

In Benin, Soglo's victory led to the formation of an administration that was interested in promoting closer ties with the United States. Some critics of French policies in Africa note that this is the reason local French diplomats provided significant support to Soglo's predecessor, Kérékou, who emerged victorious in the 1996 presidential elections. Although he ultimately accepted the 1996 election results, Soglo remained sharply critical of the "northern countries" (read France), which he partially blamed for his defeat at the hands of Benin's former dictator. Regardless of France's ultimate role in the 1996 presidential elections, however, Kérékou's reemergence did not signal a return to the same Beninois-French relationship that existed prior to 1991. As already discussed, the strengthening of several competing institutional actors, most notably a vibrant national assembly, has contributed to growing pluralism in Beninois foreign policy.

The demise of the Cold War has similarly fostered the rise of a pluralistic economic environment in which France, Germany, Japan, and the United States compete for economic influence in Francophone West Africa. The emergence of this "cold peace" derives from

Western recognition of the rising importance of the pursuit of economic self-interest and has contributed to international competition in the lucrative petroleum, telecommunications, and transport industries of West Africa. From the perspective of French policymakers, the penetration of U.S., German, and Japanese companies constitutes at best an intrusion and at worst an aggression into France's *chasse gardée*. To West African leaders, however, such competition provides them with greater maneuverability to reduce some of the ties of inherited dependency. For example, the Diouf administration in 1995 withstood intense French pressures to maintain preferential treatment for French petroleum companies and signed contracts with South African and U.S. companies to exploit oil fields discovered off Senegal's southwestern coast. The behavior of the Diouf administration is not unique but rather indicative of a more competitive foreign policy environment that is less receptive to French foreign policy interests.

The diversification of Francophone West Africa's foreign policy relationships is captured by the evolution of foreign assistance from 1965 to 1995 (see Table 3.2). Three trends stand out. Not surprisingly, France has been the largest bilateral aid donor, distributing nearly $1.3 billion to Francophone West Africa in 1995. The upsurge in French foreign aid levels from $433 million in 1985 to more than $1.2 billion in 1990 represented the determination of French policymakers to bail out clients on the verge of financial bankruptcy and to

Table 3.2   Foreign Assistance to Francophone West Africa, 1965–1995
            (millions of U.S.$, official development assistance)

Country	1965	(%)	1975	(%)	1985	(%)	1990	(%)	1995	(%)
France	85	(44)	230	(30)	433	(24)	1237	(33)	1287	(30)
Germany	11	(06)	65	(08)	136	(07)	316	(08)	282	(07)
Japan	0	(00)	3	(00)	50	(03)	211	(06)	313	(07)
United States	34	(18)	45	(06)	267	(15)	171	(05)	150	(03)
Other DACs[a]	5	(03)	71	(09)	262	(14)	515	(14)	455	(11)
Multilateral	58	(30)	293	(38)	547	(30)	1287	(34)	1813	(42)
Bilateral	0	(00)	73	(09)	137	(07)	60	(02)	1	(00)
Total	193	(100)	780	(100)	1831	(100)	3799	(100)	4301	(100)

Source: International Monetary Fund, *Geographical Distribution of Financial Flows to Developing Countries,* various years.
   Note: a. Development assistance countries (OECD countries).

ensure the victory of pro-French elites in confrontations with pro-democracy movements. In Côte d'Ivoire, for example, French aid increased to $416 million in 1990 to ensure that President Houphouët-Boigny and his ruling Parti Démocratique de la Côte d'Ivoire–Rassemblement Démocratique Africain (PDCI-RDA; Democratic Party of Côte d'Ivoire–African Democratic Assembly) would successfully manage the democratization process by winning the October 1990 multiparty elections. Aid was subsequently increased in the aftermath of Houphouët-Boigny's death to ensure that his *dauphin* (chosen successor), President Henri Konan Bédié, would emerge victorious in the highly flawed October 1995 presidential elections.[36]

The willingness of French policymakers to provide financial support for their privileged nations in Francophone West Africa has fostered a cultural foreign policy bond not easily broken. For example, when newly elected French president Jacques Chirac made his first presidential tour of Africa in July 1995, the only two West African stops on his itinerary were Côte d'Ivoire and Senegal—the linchpins of French foreign policy in the region. In a testament to the continued salience of *la francophonie,* Ould Taya of Mauritania and Colonel Lansana Conté of Guinea traveled to Dakar, and Kérékou of Benin, Compaoré of Burkina Faso, Eyadéma of Togo, and former president Ousmane Mahamané of Niger traveled to Abidjan to meet with Chirac during his visit. Only the Malian president, Konaré, refused to make the trip on the principle that Chirac's itinerary implied an unacceptable hierarchy in France's relationships with Francophone West Africa.

The foreign aid figures nonetheless demonstrate the success of West African leaders in currying the favor of other foreign powers. In 1995, this region received 7 percent of its bilateral aid from Japan ($313 million), Germany ($282 million), and the United States ($150 million). Japanese policymakers in particular have pursued an aggressive foreign aid policy in their quest to translate Japan's extraordinary economic power into political influence and leadership on a global scale.[37] Toward this end, Japanese foreign aid to Francophone West Africa has increased approximately sixfold from the relatively modest $50 million in 1985. Once criticized for a neomercantilist approach that relegated Africa to a producer of natural resources for Japan's industrial growth, Japanese foreign policy is beginning to be seen by West Africans as vital to the region's economic development. The emerging Japanese presence in Francophone West Africa is best symbolized by the inauguration in 1995 of a massive Japanese embassy overlooking the ocean in Dakar. A Japanese diplomat once remarked that he could not help but be struck by the symbolism of the potential replacement of traditional Western influence with Asian forms of capitalism as he watched the setting sun from one of the dozens of new offices with large picture windows facing West.[38]

One of the most striking trends demonstrated by the foreign aid figures is the emergence of multilateral organizations, in particular the International Monetary Fund (IMF) and the World Bank, as key players in Francophone West Africa. As of 1995, these organizations were the largest source of foreign aid in terms of both raw totals ($1.8 billion) and as a percentage of overall aid (42 percent) from all sources. Multilateral aid from the IMF and the World Bank has been accompanied by structural adjustment programs (SAPs), which have deepened the political conditionalities imposed on West African states. In turn, the terms of the debate have shifted away from previous questions such as whether Marxism or African socialism is favorable to capitalism and whether single-party or multiparty regimes can better promote the welfare of their respective peoples. The consensus today favors the creation of capitalist, multiparty political systems. The critical dilemma confronting newly elected democratic leaders is the extent to which they will work with international financial institutions. If they wholeheartedly embrace SAPs to ensure the future economic health of their societies, they are bound to alienate important political actors in their political systems and jeopardize their chances of prevailing in subsequent democratic elections. In Benin, for example, Soglo's defeat in the 1996 presidential elections after only one term of office came about because of his strong support for SAPs. Yet if these same leaders refuse to embrace SAPs, they risk losing access to international capital and potentially re-creating the economic conditions that led to the overthrow of their predecessors.

The ability of Francophone West African leaders to decrease the colonial ties of dependency and take advantage of the pluralistic economic environment of the cold peace is demonstrated by the evolution of trade patterns from 1965 to 1995. As indicated by the general trends presented in Table 3.3, Francophone West Africa's overall exports significantly expanded from $600 million in 1965 to nearly $7.7 billion in 1995. France emerges as Francophone West Africa's largest bilateral trading partner, in 1995 importing nearly $1.3 billion (17 percent) of goods from the region. But this figure

Table 3.3   Francophone West African Exports, 1965–1995 (millions of U.S.$)

Country	1965	(%)	1975	(%)	1985	(%)	1990	(%)	1995	(%)
France	252	(42)	672	(31)	924	(18)	1128	(18)	1292	(17)
Germany	42	(07)	170	(08)	298	(06)	350	(06)	428	(06)
Japan	6	(01)	59	(03)	123	(02)	178	(03)	204	(03)
United States	58	(10)	156	(25)	484	(10)	426	(07)	381	(05)
Other DACs	133	(22)	536	(25)	1772	(35)	2044	(33)	2595	(34)
Africa	69	(11)	265	(12)	718	(14)	1127	(18)	1839	(24)
Asia	0	(00)	12	(01)	127	(03)	351	(06)	498	(06)
Middle East	7	(01)	15	(01)	12	(00)	12	(00)	45	(01)
Other	33	(05)	265	(12)	538	(11)	685	(11)	406	(05)
Total	600	(100)	2150	(100)	5000	(100)	6301	(100)	7690	(100)

Source: Organization of Economic Cooperation and Development (OECD), *Direction of Trade Statistics Yearbook,* various years.

represents a significant decline from the early independence era, when France accounted for 42 percent of Francophone West Africa's exports. Together Germany ($428 million), the United States ($381 million), and Japan ($204 million) accounted for 14 percent of Francophone West African exports in 1995. The figures also signal the rising importance of the Asian market (not including Japan) in the post–Cold War era, absorbing $498 million (6 percent) of Francophone West African exports in 1995.

The import patterns of Francophone West Africa also offer interesting insights (see Table 3.4). As was the case with exports, its overall imports significantly expanded—from $622 million in 1965 to nearly $10.3 billion in 1995. France's portion of those imports dropped from 52 percent ($323 million) to 26 percent ($2.6 billion) during that same period. This trend clearly demonstrates the growing pluralism of Francophone West Africa's trading patterns. The most notable difference between import and export patterns is that the United States emerges as the second largest bilateral source of imports in 1995 ($530 million), followed by Germany ($351 million) and Japan ($278 million). The 1995 U.S. figures, the highest for the 30-year period, are perhaps indicative of the Clinton administration's aggressive trade policy in the region—a trend that undoubtedly was strengthened by the U.S. Congress's passage in 2000 of the Africa Growth and Opportunity Act.[39] The importance of the Asian market (not including Japan) once again emerges in the post–Cold War era, serving as the source of 13 percent ($1.3 billion) of Francophone West African imports.

Table 3.4   Francophone West African Imports, 1965–1995 (millions of U.S.$)

Country	1965	(%)	1975	(%)	1985	(%)	1990	(%)	1995	(%)
France	323	(52)	1154	(39)	1442	(29)	2350	(32)	2651	(26)
Germany	38	(06)	168	(06)	278	(06)	364	(05)	351	(03)
Japan	8	(01)	103	(03)	189	(04)	215	(03)	278	(03)
United States	47	(08)	213	(07)	412	(08)	315	(04)	530	(05)
Other DACs	67	(11)	461	(16)	1181	(24)	1581	(21)	1872	(18)
Africa	54	(09)	255	(09)	819	(16)	1328	(18)	2530	(25)
Asia	22	(04)	75	(03)	422	(08)	827	(11)	1346	(13)
Middle East	6	(01)	7	(00)	2	(00)	12	(00)	30	(00)
Other	44	(07)	344	(12)	351	(07)	438	(06)	706	(07)
Total	609	(100)	2780	(100)	5016	(100)	7430	(100)	10294	(100)

Source: Organization of Economic Cooperation and Development (OECD), *Direction of Trade Statistics Yearbook*, various years.

The most surprising trend to emerge from the trade statistics, however, is the growing importance of African markets in Francophone West African trade. As demonstrated in Table 3.3, Francophone West Africa's exports to Africa steadily rose from $69 million (11 percent) in 1965 to $1.8 billion (24 percent) in 1995. Imports from Africa also increased—from $54 million (9 percent) in 1965 to over $2.5 billion (25 percent) in 1995 (see Table 3.4). The fact that nearly 25 percent—a figure that is still rising—of Francophone West Africa's trade is with the African continent clearly suggests the growing fruits of the region's commitment to regional integration and development. Ironically, the 1994 devaluation of the CFA franc, so vigorously opposed by West African elites, appears to have strengthened this trend by making less expensive, regionally produced products more attractive to import. This trend remains consistent across the past three and a half decades, suggesting the prospects for even greater levels of trade cooperation and regional integration in the future. The trend is indicative of the growing realization among West African elites that any enduring solutions to the region's myriad foreign policy challenges must by necessity begin within the region itself.

■   FRANCOPHONE WEST AFRICAN
    FOREIGN POLICIES IN PERSPECTIVE

The Cold War's end and the process of democratization have significantly affected the formulation and implementation of Francophone

West African foreign policies. The evolving commitment of its elites to three foreign policy principles—*la francophonie,* regional integration, and conflict resolution—suggests the beginning of the bridging of the historic gap between Francophone and Anglophone West Africa. Nigeria's attendance at the 1996 Franco-African summit, increased cooperation between the UEMOA and ECOWAS, and the settlement of the Liberian civil war are examples of enhanced cooperation within greater West Africa. It is ironic that growing Francophone-Anglophone rapprochement among West African elites is happening against the backdrop of rising Francophone-Anglophone tensions at the continental level, such as in the OAU and within the international system, as witnessed by growing tensions between Washington and Paris.

The case of Francophone West Africa demonstrates that personal rule theories are incapable of providing complete explanations of African foreign policies in the post–Cold War era. The process of democratization in particular has strengthened the role of new domestic players, the actions of which require additional research. One of the most fruitful avenues in this regard is the role of national legislatures (especially if one includes the transient national conferences that were influential in the process of democratic transition in numerous Francophone West African countries). National legislatures have served as arenas of national debate, particularly in those countries, such as Benin and Mali, that significantly liberalized their political systems during the 1990s but also in those semidemocracies, such as Senegal and Burkina Faso, that permitted an autonomous legislative role. If President Wade is successful in achieving his promised reforms of the Senegalese political system, the Senegalese legislature should play an increasing foreign policy role beginning in 2001. The primary reason behind this newfound legislative role is the creation of democratic political systems that embody the concept of separation of powers among the various branches of government. But it is thus far not clear whether the newly empowered legislatures will largely restrict themselves to the national arena—calling to mind the old maxim that "politics stops at the water's edge"—or if they will continue to have a growing voice in the realm of foreign affairs.

Francophone West Africa also demonstrates the declining importance of Cold War and dependency-oriented explanations of African foreign policies. Aid and trade relationships have been diversified, and foreign powers, not to mention the region's elites, are no longer content to defer to France's foreign policy objectives in the region.

The net result is that Francophone West African elites have greater degrees of maneuverability in foreign policy. After the 1994 devaluation of the CFA franc, even those leaders who favored maintaining close ties with France rather than with other Western powers faced the reality of the end of unparalleled French financial support. The CFA's devaluation underscored the pitfalls of relying too closely on France and emboldened West African elites to diversify foreign policy relationships by courting Berlin, Tokyo, and Washington.

■ NOTES

1. For an overview of the AOF, see Charles Becker, Saliou Mbaye, and Ibrahima Thioub, eds., *AOF: Réalités et Héritages: Sociétés Ouest-Africaines et Ordre Colonial, 1895–1960,* 2 vols. (Dakar: Direction des Archives du Senegal, 1997). See also Joseph Roger de Benoist, *L'Afrique Occidentale Française de la Conférence de Brazzaville (1944) à l'Indépendence (1960)* (Dakar: Les Nouvelles Éditions Africaines, 1982).

2. See Guy Martin, "Francophone Africa in the Context of Franco-African Relations," in John W. Harbeson and Donald Rothchild, eds., *Africa in World Politics: Post–Cold War Challenges* (Boulder: Westview Press, 1995), p. 163.

3. The best work on this topic is Michael Bratton and Nicolas van de Walle, *Democratic Experiments in Africa: Regime Transitions in Comparative Perspective* (Cambridge: Cambridge University Press, 1997). For a specific analysis of Francophone West Africa, see John F. Clark and David E. Gardinier, eds., *Political Reform in Francophone West Africa* (Boulder: Westview Press, 1997).

4. Martin, "Francophone Africa," p. 163.

5. See Jeffrey E. Garten, *A Cold Peace: America, Japan, Germany, and the Struggle for Supremacy* (New York: Twentieth Century Fund, 1993).

6. Stephen Smith, "France-Rwanda: Lévirat Colonial et Abandon dans la Région des Grands Lacs," in André Guichaoua, ed., *Les Crises Politiques au Burundi et Rwanda (1993–1994): Analyses, Faits et Documents* (Paris: Karthala, 1995), p. 452.

7. Antoine Glaser and Stephen Smith, *L'Afrique sans Africains: Le Rêve Blanc du Continent Noir* (Paris: Editions Stock, 1994), pp. 182–185.

8. See Peter J. Schraeder, "Elites as Facilitators or Impediments to Political Development? Lessons from the 'Third Wave' of Democratization in Africa," *Journal of Developing Areas* 29, no. 1 (1994): 69–90.

9. Martin, "Francophone Africa," pp. 164–166.

10. See Kenneth Grundy, "The Impact of Region on Contemporary African Politics," in Gwendolen M. Carter and Patrick O'Meara, eds., *African Independence: The First Twenty-five Years* (Bloomington: Indiana University Press, 1985), pp. 97–125.

11. The UEMOA's membership includes eight nations: six of the former AOF states (Benin, Burkina Faso, Côte d'Ivoire, Mali, Niger, and Senegal), Togo, and, since May 1997, Guinea-Bissau.

12. Assou Massou, "Intégration: Où en est l'UEMOA," *Jeune Afrique,* no. 1930 (January 6–12, 1998): 68–70.

13. See Emeka Nwokedi, "Strands and Strains of 'Good Neighborliness': The Case of Nigeria and Its Francophone Neighbors," *Génève-Afrique* 23, no. 1 (1985): 39–60; and Daniel C. Bach, "Régionalismes Francophones ou Régionalisme Franco-Africain," in Daniel C. Bach and Anthony A. Kirk-Greene, *États et Sociétés en Afrique Francophone* (Paris: Économica, 1993), pp. 219–233.

14. The UEMOA portion of the CFA franc zone is partially managed through a subregional central bank, the Banque Centrale des États de l'Afrique de l'Ouest (BCEAO; Central Bank of West African States), based in Dakar, Senegal, as well as by a regionally focused development bank, the Banque Ouest-Africaine de Développement (BOAD; West African Development Bank), based in Lomé, Togo.

15. See Moustapha Kane, "Le Sénégal et la Guinée (1958–1978)," in Momar-Coumba Diop, ed., *Le Sénégal et Ses Voisins* (Dakar: Sociétés-Espaces-Temps, 1994), pp. 164–188; Ibrahima Thioub, "Le Sénégal et le Mali," in Diop, *Le Sénégal et Ses Voisins,* pp. 95–116; and Ousseynou Faye, "La Crise Casamançaise et les Relations du Sénégal avec la Gambie et Guinea-Bissau (1980–1992)," in Diop, *Le Sénégal et Ses Voisins,* pp. 189–214.

16. See Robert A. Mortimer, "Senegal's Role in Ecomog: The Francophone Dimension in the Liberian Crisis," *Journal of Modern African Studies* 34, no. 2 (1996): 293–306.

17. See William Reno, "The Business of War in Liberia," *Current History* 95, no. 601 (May 1996): 213.

18. For a historical overview, see W.A.E. Skurnik, *The Foreign Policy of Senegal* (Evanston, IL: Northwestern University Press, 1972). See also Diop, *Le Sénégal et Ses Voisins;* and Peter J. Schraeder with Nefertiti Gaye, "Senegal's Foreign Policy: Challenges of Democratization and Marginalization," *African Affairs* 96, no. 385 (1997): 485–508.

19. For example, he is recognized as the commander in chief of the armed forces (Article 39); is empowered to name Senegalese diplomats abroad and accredit those from foreign countries (Article 40); and is authorized to negotiate, ratify, and approve international agreements (Article 75) except in certain specified realms, such as peace treaties and agreements with international organizations, that require ratification by the national assembly (Article 76). See Cheikh Tidiane Thiam, *Droit Public du Sénégal (Vol. 1): L'état et le Citoyen* (Dakar: Les Éditions du CREDILA, 1993).

20. See Maurice A. East, "Foreign Policy-Making in Small States: Some Theoretical Observations Based on a Study of the Uganda Ministry of Foreign Affairs," *Policy Sciences* 4, no. 4 (1973): 491–508. See also O. O. Fafowora, "The Role of the Ministry of External Affairs in the Formulation of Nigerian Foreign Policy: Personal Reminiscences," *Quarterly Journal of Administration* 18, nos. 3–4 (1983–1984): 92–110.

21. Elhadj Mbodj, "Senegal's Foreign Policy." Typed notes of a presentation made at the University of Wisconsin, Madison (no date).

22. Ibid.

23. See William Foltz and Henry Bienen, eds., *Arms and the African: Military Influences on Africa's International Relations* (New Haven: Yale University Press, 1985).

24. See Momar-Coumba Diop and Moussa Paye, "Armée et Pouvoir au Sénégal," paper presented at the CODESRIA-sponsored seminar The Military and Militarism in Africa, Accra, Ghana, April 21–23, 1993, pp. 8–9.

25. Abdoulaye Ndiaye, "Généraux Civils," *Jeune Afrique,* no. 1934 (February 3–9, 1998): 44–45.

26. For a historical overview, see Victor T. Le Vine, "Parliaments in Francophone Africa: Some Lessons from the Decolonization Process," in Joel Smith and Lloyd D. Musolf, eds., *Legislatures in Development: Dynamics of Change in New and Old States* (Durham: Duke University Press, 1979), pp. 125–154.

27. For an overview, see Thomas M. Callaghy and John Ravenhill, eds., *Hemmed In: Responses to Africa's Economic Decline* (New York: Columbia University Press, 1993).

28. Quoted in Papa Mor Sylla, "Le Travail des Députés: Entre les Séances-Marathon et le Repos Prolongé," *Le Soleil,* July 27, 1995, p. 5.

29. Ibid.

30. See Abdou Latif Coulibaly, "Rôle de la Presse dans la Sauvegarde et la Consolidation de la Démocratie au Sénégal," *Afrique Espoir,* no. 12 (December 1994): 15–19.

31. See the series of articles and op-ed pieces in *Le Soleil, Le Sud,* and *Wal Fadjri* during the week of March 11–18, 1996.

32. See Joel Millman, *The Other Americans: How Immigrants Renew Our Country, Our Economy, Our Values* (New York: Viking Penguin, 1997), especially chapter 6 on Senegalese immigrants in New York.

33. See Ron Parker, "The Senegal-Mauritania Conflict of 1989: A Fragile Equilibrium," *Journal of Modern African Studies* 29, no. 1 (1991): 155–171; and Anthony G. Pazzanita, "Mauritania's Foreign Policy: The Search for Protection," *Journal of Modern African Studies* 30, no. 2 (1992): 281–304.

34. It has also been argued that negative public reactions to the deaths of Senegalese peacekeepers taking part in ECOMOG operations in Liberia played a significant role in President Diouf's decision to withdraw these troops in 1993. See Mortimer, "Senegal's Role in Ecomog," p. 300.

35. See Leonardo A. Villalón, *Islamic Society and State Power in Senegal: Disciples and Citizens in Fatick* (Cambridge: Cambridge University Press, 1995).

36. For a summary, see Jennifer A. Widner, "The 1990 Elections in Côte d'Ivoire," *Issue* 20, no. 1 (1991): 31–40. See also Yves Fauré, "Democracy and Realism: Reflections on the Case of Côte d'Ivoire," *Africa: Journal of the International African Institute* 63, no. 3 (1993): 313–329.

37. See Jun Morikawa, *Japan and Africa: Big Business and Diplomacy* (Trenton, NJ: Africa World Press, 1997).

38. Personal interview, Dakar, Senegal, 1996.

39. This idea is further expanded in Peter J. Schraeder, "Cold War to Cold Peace: Explaining U.S.-French Competition in Francophone Africa," *Political Science Quarterly* 115, no. 3 (2000): 1–25.

4

Foreign Policy Making in Central Africa: The Imperative of Regime Security in a New Context

John F. Clark

Despite all the dramatic changes in African politics since the dawn of the post–Cold War era, foreign policy making in central Africa is marked more by continuity than change. As in the pre-1989 period, the domestic needs of personalistic regimes continue to dominate the process of foreign policy decisionmaking. In addition, the process of foreign policy making has been more constant in central Africa than elsewhere because there has been less fundamental political change. What has changed in the new period is the context, both local and international, in which crucial decisions are made. The changes in the context of decisionmaking have generated a new variety of foreign policies that are distinctive even though the processes and substantive goals have changed little. In this chapter I outline the overall process of foreign policy making for central African states, describe the new context in which it is now operative, and illustrate its functioning with examples from Angola, the Central African Republic (CAR), the Congo Republic, the Democratic Republic of Congo (DRC), and Gabon.

■ THE DOMESTIC IMPERATIVE

Foreign policy making in central Africa can most usefully be explained as a direct outgrowth of domestic political needs. The fundamental fact of political life that ensures continuity in the basic patterns of foreign policy making before and after the end of the Cold War is the preeminence of regime security. This imperative is the first priority of any government in the region, and it has driven, and continues to drive, both foreign and domestic policy. Moreover, regime security has rarely been assured for most central African states since independence. This assertion should not be uncritically accepted, but it can reasonably be argued. In one sense, the much-proclaimed instability of regimes in African states has been overstated; even in volatile central Africa, many regimes of specific leaders lasted for at least a decade, and some for over thirty years, as Table 4.1 illustrates. During the 1980s, rulers such as Omar Bongo (Gabon), Mobutu Sese Seko (Zaire), and Denis Sassou-Nguesso (Congo) seemed to be providing stable authoritarian rule in their countries.

In a deeper sense, however, all of these regimes were unstable no matter how long the rulers in question reigned. Angola, of course, has since independence been continually wracked by civil war between the Popular Movement for the Liberation of Angola (MPLA) government forces and those of Jonas Savimbi's National Union for the Total Independence of Angola (UNITA). The MPLA once depended for its survival on the presence of Cuban troops and Soviet weapons and military advisers. Similarly, the regimes of Omar Bongo (Gabon) and André Kolingba (CAR) depended largely, though to a lesser extent, on the presence of French military forces and bases to ensure their continuation in power.[1] Although the Congo Republic, known as the People's Republic of Congo from 1970 to 1992, did not allow French bases on its territory, Sassou's government nonetheless availed itself of French paratroopers in putting down an attempted coup d'état in 1987. Sassou also relied on arms and advisers from Cuba and the Eastern bloc. The regime of

Table 4.1 Regime Longevity

State	Ruler	Duration in Power
Angola	Eduardo dos Santos	1979–present (MPLA since 1975)
Congo-Brazzaville	Denis Sassou-Nguesso (I)	1979–1992
Central African Republic	André Kolingba	1981–1993
Gabon	Omar (Albert-Bernard) Bongo	1967–present
Zaire (now Democratic Republic of Congo)	Mobutu Sese Seko	1965–1997

Mobutu Sese Seko in Zaire (now the DRC) was likewise dependent on foreign support, notably from the United States and, toward the end, France. His regime was nearly overthrown twice by poorly planned and executed invasions from Angola in 1977 and 1978.[2] As the reach of the state into society continually eroded beginning in the early 1980s, the social basis for Mobutu's regime, always weak, completely dissolved.[3] There were attempted coups d'état in all five of these states during the 1980s and 1990s.

The politico-economic basis for all these regimes was the distribution of rents derived from natural resource extraction, although the CAR was handicapped in this regard compared to the others. Specifically, oil revenues have provided the economic basis for the regimes in Gabon, the Congo Republic, and Angola; copper, cobalt, and uranium revenues were a key basis in Zaire-DRC.[4] These regimes co-opted potential political opponents by allowing them access to state resources. This neopatrimonial strategy mollified the political opposition without rooting the regimes deeply in society.[5] Only the succession of regimes in the CAR since independence has lacked a "mineral" basis for neopatrimonialism, which may explain why it was even less stable than the others. In any case, none of the regimes has rested on a meaningful social contract between the citizens and the state. Rather, the divide between elites depending on economic rents, on the one hand, and the urban lumpenproletariat and rural peasants, on the other, widened in postcolonial times. In periods when favorable terms of trade for commodities have declined, these regimes have faltered. Thus none of the regimes gained a solid basis for stability even if individual rulers remained at the helm over many years.

Another enormous source of regime instability for these five states has been ethnic or ethnoregional identities and antagonisms. For instance, attempted coups d'état, as in the Congo Republic in 1987, have often been generated largely by ethnic jealousies of those in power. Likewise, the two invasions originating from Angola that shook Zaire in 1977 and 1978 had a (pro-Shaba) regional identity basis.[6] The counterpart of this phenomenon is that all of these regimes have relied more or less explicitly on the loyalty of ethnic or regional constituencies to keep them in power. The most typical pattern was for personal rulers to rely heavily on kinsmen or coethnics at the centers of power, often in informal positions, while publicly enunciating policies of ethnic and regional equity. By appointing cabinets with the widest possible ethnic and regional representations, these rulers sought to superficially uphold the principle of regional equity. These cabinet members typically enjoyed considerable access to state resources but virtually no real power, which was exercised by loyalists in the presidential circle and in elite presidential guards or special military forces.[7] Sometimes these rulers have consciously sought to create or reinforce regional identities to support them, as has President Bongo with regard to the Haut-Ogooué region in Gabon.[8]

To the extent that any of their regimes was ever secure, these states have engaged in the more ambitious program of state building. This imperative, like that of regime security, is another key to understanding foreign policy making in the region. One of the most compelling recent theories of international relations has stressed the importance of state building as a critical determinant of foreign policy everywhere in the developing world.[9] In central Africa, such a project could be undertaken only when regime security could be taken for granted, which was not often. In times of crisis, moreover, actions destructive to the state were often necessary to keep specific rulers in power. For instance, when the Congo Republic's Sassou faced challenge from opposition forces in late 1990 and early 1991, he quickly recruited some 5,000 new members for Congo's already bloated civil service. This initiative was designed to buy the president support in urban areas, though its longer-term effect was to undermine the country's already fragile state finances. In Zaire, Mobutu attempted to stir up ethnic antagonisms in the Shaba and Kivu regions during 1992–1994, and again during 1996, as a tactic to divide political forces opposing him and divert the country's attention from the political stalemate in Kinshasa.[10] These actions weakened the power of the state in society while serving to temporarily divide the forces opposing Mobutu. Indeed, by the early 1990s Mobutu had long abandoned any dreams of developing the Zairian state or economy and was merely seeking to cling to power.[11]

Despite these examples, state building was just as frequently the long-term result of regime maintenance. To the extent that states prospered and ethnoregional antagonism was diverted into other political outlets, threats to regime security diminished. For these reasons, some fraction of the income generated from natural resources was devoted to social development. After all, an environment of declining standards of social welfare has often provided support and justification for coups d'état. Another common justification has been blatant ethnic or regional favoritism on the parts of regimes in power. This explains why African leaders really have sought to create a national (statewide) political consciousness; an example is Mobutu's program of authenticity in the 1970s. Mobutu's policies such as renaming the country and ordering a return to the use of indigenous African names for persons and places were aimed at creating such a consciousness, and they did so with some success, as even Mobutu's critics have acknowledged.[12] The Marxist-Leninist rhetoric used in the Congo Republic and Angola represented a parallel effort to replace local loyalists with a transregional, transethnic ideological consciousness. These needs explain the apparent paradox of personal rulers who rely on their kinsmen to occupy the most important security positions while simultaneously appealing for national unity.

Whereas such domestic concerns in central African politics are undeniable, their influence on foreign policy is less apparent. This is because central Africa does not have the consensus that exists in the West, where regime security can be taken for granted and there are long histories of national integration. Most ordinary Congolese, for instance, resent external (Rwandan and Ugandan) interference in their country's affairs. Opposition parties in most of central Africa would readily accept the military assistance of outsiders to gain and retain power. The first priority of leaders of central African states, as with those of early modern European states, has to be the taming of internal challengers for power.[13]

■   THE LOGIC OF FOREIGN
    POLICY MAKING IN CENTRAL AFRICA

Such considerations help us understand why most common foreign policy models designed to explain decisionmaking in developed states are inadequate to explain the decisions in African states. Among the models for developed states, none has been as useful and popular as that of Graham Allison, originally outlined in 1969.[14] The utility of Allison's two models, those of bureaucratic politics and organizational process, are of minimal value for central African states because of the limited role of bureaucratic agencies in foreign policy making. The various Marxist, quasi-Marxist, and business conflict approaches are also limited in their explanatory powers because there is no real bourgeoisie in central Africa.[15] The elite class that has appeared is the bureaucratic bourgeoisie, which does sometimes have distinct interests, including foreign policy interests.[16] Yet there is little evidence that such a class, even if it is influential, has gained control over the typical African state.

How, then, can one try to understand how foreign policy is made in central Africa? Among Western-based models, the rational actor model, which served as Allison's straw man, seems to have the most relevance if regime interests are substituted for national interests. Most foreign policies have resulted from the decisions of presidentialist rulers, influenced by a few close advisers, who seek to implement foreign policies to preserve their regimes.[17] Those rulers who do not devote their primary efforts to regime maintenance are not likely to remain in power for long. Past leaders in central Africa, such as Jean-Bedel Bokassa and Mobutu Sese Seko, sought to preserve their power using every conceivable method. But when they got distracted from the overall goal of regime maintenance, their rule was jeopardized, as Bokassa's example illustrates. Although bureaucratic agencies and other sectors of society try to have an impact on foreign policy making, their role is circumscribed by the personalized nature of power. It is only when public protests by middle classes threaten the survival of these rulers that some of them make foreign policy decisions (such as mortgaging future oil revenues with Western companies) to keep them quiescent.

■ FOREIGN POLICY PROCESSES

If foreign policy decisions preserve personal regimes, what are the processes that determine these decisions? First, personal ties among leaders are likely to exercise an unusually high degree of influence over foreign policy decisions. Although personal ties are hardly insignificant among Western leaders, as the Reagan-Thatcher or Clinton-Blair relationships demonstrate, the importance of such ties between leaders of the developed states is limited by well-established institutional linkages and the perception of overlapping national (not regime) interests.

The bases for strong personal ties between the different central African leaders have been varied. Simply serving in power together over long periods of time has been the source of many personal ties in the region. For instance, although many African leaders disdained Mobutu, he eventually gained acceptance from his neighbors. Angola's Eduardo dos Santos accepted Mobutu as a mediator in the Angolan civil war in the late 1980s even after UNITA had military bases on Zairian territory. Congo's Sassou and Angola's dos Santos have a long-standing personal relationship that was partly cemented in the late 1970s and early 1980s, when their shared reliance on Marxist-Leninist symbols to maintain their dictatorships gave them a natural bond. Other sources of personal amity are much less visible to the political scientist seeking rational explanations for every relationship but are important nonetheless. In this category, the bonds of Masonry lodges are a perhaps surprising source of both amity, between leaders such as Bongo and Sassou, and conflict: Rivalry between lodges pitted former Congolese president Pascal Lissouba against Sassou.[18] Another important tie between Bongo and Sassou is the fact that Bongo married Sassou's daughter, Edith, in 1990.

The second major process determinant of foreign policy is ethnic considerations. Just as rulers have depended on ethnic ties at home, so they have sought support from ethnic groups abroad. Ethnic considerations, in fact, are often yet another source of personal fealty and collaboration between leaders. In the early independence period, the good personal relations between the Congo Republic's president, Fulbert Youlou, and the DRC's president, Joseph Kasavubu, were sometimes attributed to their shared Bakongo ethnicity and the rough congruence of ideologies.[19] Yet ethnicity is important not only because of the personal relations that it may affect: Any Mukongo leader in Brazzaville, Kinshasa, or Luanda would immediately take into account the natural allies that he would have in the neighboring countries among his Kongo kinsmen.

When rulers come from small ethnic groups, they often try to build larger constituencies on fabricated regional identities. When the ethnoregional bases of support for different rulers overlap, they have a natural basis for international collaboration. The collaboration of Gabon's Bongo and the Congo Republic's Lissouba is instructive in this regard. Bongo is a member of the Téké, who represent only a tiny percentage of Gabon's population, but a substantial portion of them live in the Congo Republic; Lissouba belongs to the Nzabi people, who, similarly, represent a tiny percentage of Congo's population but constitute a substantial portion of the Gabonese population. During the early 1990s, Bongo sought to build a regional coalition of ethnic forces that lumped the Téké with Gabon's Nzabi, whereas Lissouba tried to build a regional coalition that linked the Nzabi with the larger Téké group in Congo. By expressing political support for each other, these presidents strengthened the fragile ethnoregional blocs of support that they sought to hold together in their own countries: The alliance gave Lissouba support among Congo's Téké and Bongo support among Gabon's Nzabi. This collaboration endured until Bongo was forced to abandon his colleague during the Congo Republic's civil war.

Finally, along the same personal lines, Mobutu supported Juvènal Habyarimana in Rwanda during the civil war and, after the latter's defeat, allowed the rump of Habyarimana's Armed Forces of Rwanda (FAR) to organize in the refugee camps on the border with Rwanda between 1994 and 1996. These forces provided military support to Mobutu during the civil war of 1996–1997 until they were routed by a combination of Rwandan army soldiers of the Rwandan Patriotic Front and local Tutsi (Banyamulenge) militias from within Zaire.[20] Mobutu's support for Habyarimana during the war reflected the deep personal relationship between the two leaders, which had developed over many years. After Habyarimana's death and the emergence of the RPF to power in Rwanda, Mobutu failed to disarm the ex-FAR militia and tried to expel indigenous Zairian Tutsi from their homes.

■ FOREIGN POLICY GOALS

What are the most substantive needs of the foreign policy makers? Substantive needs can be divided into those emanating from the extraregional world and those within the region. From the larger world, rulers seek to secure arms, military training, and foreign aid. Arms support provides physical protection for presidential leaders, and economic assistance provides patronage to fend off regime opponents. The conservative former French colonies, Gabon and the CAR, sought such support primarily from France, both with good results. Zaire under Mobutu sought security assistance from the United States, China, and France, duping each into believing that its interests corresponded with his own regime security needs. In the 1970s and 1980s, Congo and Angola played the Marxist card, acquiring large amounts of arms from the Eastern bloc. All these states received significant amounts of economic aid from the international financial institutions (IFIs) and, in Angola's case, from individual bilateral partners.

From the 1960s through the 1980s, there was one major contradiction in receiving foreign arms and economic aid. Since foreign aid undermined the nationalist credentials of regimes in power, it was both a threat to immediate regime security and a subversion of the state-building goals that leaders sometimes pursued. Thus Mobutu, in his most nationalist phase in the 1970s, liked to emphasize his regime's links with China while downplaying those with the United States and France; likewise, Sassou relied on French military-training assistance while trumpeting the utility of Eastern bloc cooperation. As a result of this contradiction, central African leaders have frequently denied their dependence on Western military aid. For instance, several regimes have been silent on Israeli's assistance in training their praetorian guards.

Leaders in the region have sought the goodwill of their immediate neighbors, hoping to dissuade them from directly intervening in their affairs. In the absence of such direct intervention, there are always expectations that neighbors will not allow opponents to mobilize from their territory or provide material aid to political opponents. At the maximum, they also expect neighbors to cooperate in ejecting armed opponents from their territory.

During the 1970s and 1980s, such concerns were prominent in the foreign policy thinking of the leaders of Angola, Congo, and Zaire. For a long time, UNITA, the primary opponent of Angola's MPLA regime, operated from Zairian territory with Mobutu's explicit support. Angola, in turn, sometimes allowed opponents of Mobutu to organize on its territory, including the forces that invaded Zaire in 1977 and again in 1978. Less well known, but falling in the same category, was the mutual hostility between Congo and Zaire from the mid-1960s through the 1980s, and the mutual sponsoring of opposition groups in each country. For instance, in 1970 a coup attempted against Congolese president Marien Ngouabi was mounted from Zairian territory.[21] Finally, both Congos have also allowed forces seeking the independence of the Angolan region of Cabinda to operate from their territory. Such policies represent perhaps the most serious and immediate threat to regime security and, in the case of those seeking Cabindan independence, to the territorial integrity of central African states. Thus the region's rulers have seen containment of these threats as their very highest priority.

When negotiations fail to secure the goodwill of neighboring states, counterintervention to bring more cooperative governments to power is the logical next step. The recent behavior of Angola's MPLA government illustrates the point. First, during the 1996–1997 civil war in the DRC, Angola intervened on Kabila's side, along with Rwanda and Uganda, to help him gain power. Then, during the 1997 civil war in the Congo Republic, Angola intervened decisively to end the stalemate in that country between the rival militias of President Lissouba and former president Sassou, essentially putting Sassou back in power. The first instance of intervention stemmed from the fact that UNITA rebels had been operating from Zairian territory for over twenty years and that Mobutu had either turned a blind eye or even encouraged their activities. Hence, dos Santos and his MPLA colleagues must certainly have hoped that Kabila would repay the favor by expelling UNITA from its territory. The Angolan government tried to help Laurent Kabila for the same reason—to deprive UNITA of bases on contiguous territory.

The intervention of the Angolan army in the civil war in the Congo Republic in October 1997 may be attributed essentially to the same reason: the desire of the Angolan government to deprive UNITA of bases on the soil of neighboring countries.[22] President Lissouba, perhaps in a misguided effort to win French favor, allowed UNITA to move its headquarters to the Congolese city of Pointe Noire after its expulsion from the former Zaire. Subsequently, flows of arms from Europe were dispatched to UNITA via Pointe Noire and into Angola.[23] Moreover, Lissouba allowed armed groups fighting for the independence of the Angolan enclave of Cabinda, the Front for the Liberation of Cabinda (FLEC), to use Congolese territory. Previous Congolese governments had collaborated much more fully with Angolan authorities to try to suppress such groups. Finally, there was the long personal friendship that existed between two old comrades in arms, dos Santos and Sassou-Nguesso. During the Cold War period, "Marxist" Congo had been a constant friend to the MPLA regime in Luanda, allowing Congolese territory to serve as a rear base for the flow of Cuban troops and Soviet arms into Angola. After they rose to power, dos Santos and Sassou worked together against South Africa and shared an anti-imperialist stand on many world issues. Although the ideological basis for their relationship had long evaporated by 1997, the personal friendship remained.

■ THE CHANGING FOREIGN POLICY MAKING CONTEXT

How did the context of foreign policy making change in the 1990s, and what new foreign policy patterns emerged? Some scholars have argued that recent events have rendered the old paradigms of foreign policy making for African states, based on the personal predilections of leaders, obsolete.[24] In central Africa, although the context has changed significantly, the basic priorities and means of foreign policy making have not. The changes in the context have led to new variations distinct to the era but based on the underlying characteristics of the Cold War era—a focus on regime survival, the dominance of "big men," and dependence on foreign actors.

Some of the changes include the recent wave of "democratic" transitions that convulsed Africa between 1990 and 1994 and the end of the Cold War, which largely brought an end to superpower sponsorship of regimes in the region. Another important area of change is in France's support for regimes in the region, though the nature of this change is complex and contested. At the beginning of the 1990s, France seemed to abandon its long-standing practice of supporting its regional clients, but its subsequent behavior proved that this was far from the case.[25] Another change in France's behavior is that it has become more focused on the economic benefits accruing from its engagement with Francophone Africa. Some have also suggested an overall decline in the influence of France in Africa's affairs, represented most spectacularly by Paul Kagame's ascent to power in Rwanda in 1994.[26] Finally, the erosion of norms that supported nonintervention has contributed to a new pattern of regionalized conflict and greater security links between central and southern Africa. Yet despite their significance for central Africa, these changes have not affected the imperative of regime security for its rulers, and none of them has quite the effect on foreign policy that one might expect.

Although there is an assumption that democratization has weakened the prerogatives of the big men in foreign policy, as it has in other national policy contexts, there is no such trend in central Africa, since political change has not yielded liberal environments. Of the five countries, there was no regime change in Angola, Gabon, and Zaire-DRC as a result of the political openings of the early 1990s. Each of the three rulers stayed in power by a different, but equally effective, method: dos Santos allowed a relatively free and fair election, monitored by the UN, knowing that he stood to win; Bongo orchestrated fraudulent elections with the help of secret French security; and Mobutu divided the opposition and perpetually delayed the elections until he was overthrown.[27] In Gabon and Zaire, opposition forces did gain representation in the national assembly or (in Zaire's case) transitional parliament, but in neither case did these forces exercise significant influence over foreign policy.

In addition, one should not mistake regime transition, even by an election, for real democratization. In the CAR and the Congo, there were regime transitions through elections, but neither of the elected regimes proved to be genuinely democratic in its methods and behavior.[28] Moreover, opposition forces were generally excluded from participation in cabinets, and opposition forces in parliament did not play any significant role in foreign policy making. What is significant about the recent era of political reform, however, is that it has created a new internal context for foreign policy making. That is, it has rendered the regimes far more vulnerable than before to coup d'état or civilian overthrow. External powers and the IFIs have also made their continued assistance dependent on progress toward political reform. More generally, external forces, public and private, are encouraging internal opposition forces to put pressure on the existing regimes to undertake political reform. In addition, all five states came under severe economic pressures as their economies deteriorated and as oil and mineral prices on world markets plummeted. As a result, all these regimes became more desperate for external sources of aid and for gaining the goodwill of neighbors that could potentially support internal opposition forces. Overall, central African states became more externally dependent on the IFIs and great powers than they had been before. More important, democratization made them all more vulnerable and sensitive to physical attacks emanating from neighboring states.

Although the end of the Cold War has had an impact on central Africa, it hardly ended intraregional rivalries or extraregional intervention. The present political stalemates in Angola and the DRC reflect the same dynamic as the rivalries of the 1970s and 1980s, which were driven as much by personal and ethnic considerations as by ideological ones. Moreover, even though the Anglophone-Francophone rivalry has to some degree replaced the Soviet-U.S. rivalry in Francophone Africa, local rivals are still able to find new external sponsors for their causes.[29] U.S. and French oil companies are competing for influence in the three oil-producing states (as well as in Chad), and French and U.S. capital continues to compete for influence in the DRC, as it has for decades. In addition, France and the United States now find themselves on opposite sides of civil wars and international confrontations in the region. For instance, France continued to back the Habyarimana regime in Rwanda even beyond the death of Habyarimana in April 1994, whereas the United States was tacitly supportive of the RPF invasion, led by Kagame. France and the United States were similarly on opposite sides of the conflict that engulfed Zaire-DRC in 1996–1997.

Finally, there are two important issues regarding changes in French regional influence. First, it is not clear that French political interests evaporated with France's setback in Rwanda in 1994. France remains the steady backer of Bongo in Gabon, and it maintained support for the regime of Ange-Félix Patassé in the Central African Republic during the mutinies in 1996 and 1997. Besides, several networks in French government and business circles supported the return to power of Denis Sassou-Nguesso in 1997, even if others remained loyal to Lissouba. Some analysts saw Kabila's rise to power as a major reversal of French influence in the DRC because of the support from Rwanda and Uganda.[30] When, however, Kagame and Yoweri Museveni turned against Kabila in August 1998, France saw an opening to reassert its influence in the region. Before he was assassinated in January 2000, Kabila made overtures to France in an attempt to find external support. His successor, Joseph Kabila, has continued this trend.

There are three other cases of continuing French influence in the region. Although the Congo Republic's three nominally Marxist presidents, who ruled from 1969 to 1991, denounced France's neocolonial economic policies, they quietly cooperated with the French in return for economic and military aid. With the advent of multiparty politics in the Congo, there have been public demands for the new government to reduce this dependence on France, particularly in the oil sector. But when Lissouba attempted such a policy by trying to reduce the role of the local subsidiary of Elf-Aquitaine, France reduced aid and, more important, withdrew political support. As a result Lissouba made the decision in 1994 to placate France by allowing it to maintain its privileged place in the Congolese oil industry and economy at large.[31] Thereafter Lissouba followed an essentially pro-France course in foreign policy, supporting Mobutu's regime to the bitter end. This position led to an initial relationship of hostility between Lissouba and Kabila when the latter assumed power in May 1997.

The following month war broke out in the Congo Republic when Lissouba attempted to arrest former president Sassou, who was to have been a candidate for president in the elections scheduled for July 1997.[32] France soon made it clear that it would do nothing to aid Lissouba militarily and took an officially neutral stance in the war. Lissouba was greatly puzzled and angered by the French position given that France had repeatedly supported the elected government in the CAR in the face of army mutinies and that Lissouba had been elected in fair elections. When Lissouba went to France in August 1997, he was snubbed by the French government; Lissouba's supporters claimed that both the French government and private French capital interests were supporting Sassou's bid to retake power by force.[33] In desperation, Lissouba soon abandoned his previous course and sought assistance from Kabila, then known to be anti-French. Specifically, Lissouba slowly distanced himself from the mediation that was taking place in Libreville, Gabon, which was dominated by pro-French leaders including Gabon's President Bongo. At the time of one critical meeting in Libreville in August 1997, Lissouba instead flew to Kinshasa for talks with Kabila, who was outside the Libreville process. Lissouba's ultimate failure to enlist sustained support for his regime from outside meant that Angola's forces quickly tipped the balance to Sassou's favor when they intervened in October.

Foreign policy decisionmaking in the CAR was similarly conditioned by the country's dependence on France. The new regime of Patassé, elected in September 1993, was rocked by army mutinies on three occasions—in April 1996, May 1996, and again in January 1997. On each occasion, French troops already within the country were mobilized to engage the mutinous troops and put down any attempted coup d'état, making Patassé directly dependent on direct French support.[34] As a result, when Patassé learned that the French intended to close their two bases in the CAR, he retaliated by refusing to allow the French to dispatch planes at night from their bases, accusing them of aiding Sassou in the Congo's civil war. When France announced in July 1997 that it would close its military bases for economic reasons, Patassé vehemently denounced the decision and began to seek other external allies. He immediately aligned himself with Lissouba and

Kabila, both of whom were completely hostile to France, and he even made overtures to the United States, offering that country the right to establish bases in the CAR.[35] Fearing that he had lost his external protector, despite French reassurances that their defense treaty with the CAR remained intact, Patassé turned on his former patron and desperately sought new ones.

The need to satisfy French concerns also determined President Bongo's behavior in war in the Congo Republic. At the outbreak of the war, Bongo offered to serve as a mediator. As the regional collaborator of Lissouba and as the son-in-law of Sassou, he had the confidence and goodwill of both sides in the war and a personal relationship with both of the Congolese antagonists. In the early 1970s Bongo had intervened on Lissouba's behalf when Lissouba was imprisoned and sentenced to death by the radical Ngouabi regime. At the same time, Bongo's regime has maintained some of the closest relations with France.[36] As the war escalated in the Congo Republic, Bongo decided on the course of action that would protect his own power. In the event, he allowed Gabonese territory to be used as a staging ground for the shipment of arms to Sassou's forces in the Congo.

Two recent trends in central Africa have also gained salience in the post–Cold War context. First, there has been an erosion of the shaky norm of nonintervention in the political affairs of neighbors. Although the practice of hosting and supporting groups hostile to neighboring regimes has existed since independence, the norm of nonintervention in the UN and OAU charters exercised significant restraint on the region's decisionmakers before the 1990s. For instance, although Mobutu allowed Savimbi to move some of his operations from Namibia to Zaire in the late 1980s, he did not allow Zairian territory to become a full-scale launching pad for a major invasion of Angola. Much of the "hosting" of foreign forces intervening in neighboring states was by default because existing regimes had little control over their own territory. In addition, unlike previously, invasion by a national army was a rare occurrence. Yet in the 1990s, all of these activities became much more common. For instance, the Angolan military forces were actively involved in overthrowing Mobutu in Zaire in 1996 and Lissouba in the Congo Republic in 1997. In the latter case, the Angolan forces were the deciding factor in the civil war. In August 1998, units from the national armies of Angola and Zimbabwe intervened in the second civil war in the DRC, and armies from Uganda and Rwanda fought on the opposite side.

Second, the international politics of central Africa has now become far more connected to that of the Great Lakes region and to the southern African region, whereas the connections to West Africa have grown more fragile. The DRC has long been involved in affairs of the Great Lakes because of its colonial and cultural ties with Rwanda and Burundi. But with the exodus of over 1 million refugees, mostly Hutu, from Rwanda into Zairian territory in 1994, the fate of the two countries' contemporary political trajectories was intertwined more directly for the remainder of the 1990s. Mobutu was linked with Habyarimana through their personal ties, and their mutual reliance on French support came under attack in the early 1990s. Mobutu's unwillingness to disarm former members of the FAR on Zairian territory put Kagame and Mobutu at odds. Meanwhile, Uganda's Museveni, who had been scornful of Mobutu's corrupt, ineffective rule for years, was ready to join Kagame in sponsoring those who would eventually overthrow Mobutu's decrepit regime.[37] When Kabila's rule became less satisfactory for Museveni and Kagame, the two rulers again intervened in the DRC with the intention of removing Kabila from power.

Central Africa's increasing ties with southern Africa predate the end of apartheid in South Africa in 1994, but that event greatly accelerated the trends that were already unfolding. During the Cold War only Angola, as a member of the Front Line States (FLS) and the Southern African Development Coordination Conference (SADCC), was deeply integrated into the politics of southern Africa. Zaire traded with neighboring states in southern Africa, and Mobutu maintained ties with the apartheid regime, particularly to facilitate effective diamond marketing. South Africa also quietly cultivated ties to the "conservative" Francophone African states, such as Gabon and the CAR.[38] Both the conservative and "radical" states (Angola, Congo Republic) began to establish much closer links to industrialized South Africa after the signing of the Angola-Namibia Peace Accords in December 1988. South Africa's former antagonists, Angola and the Congo Republic, were soon negotiating with their former nemesis, and the Congo Republic finally established diplomatic relations with South Africa in 1993. These warmer relations allowed the conservative regimes in Libreville, Bangui, and Kinshasa to finally make public and formal their ties to South Africa. Investments from South Africa had begun to flow into Angola, Zaire, the Congo Republic, and Gabon even before Nelson Mandela was elected president of South Africa in 1994.

The new political relationship between southern and central Africa has thus far been manifest in two distinct ways. On the one hand, there is much greater diplomatic contact and potential for economic integration than before. When he was in power, Mandela sought to use his enormous political prestige to negotiate peaceful settlements to conflicts in central Africa. Mandela and his successor, Thabo Mbeki, attempted to mediate in the civil war in the DRC in 1997 and 1998. After Kabila rose to power, he joined SADC in 1997, raising the possibility of integration of the power grids and transportation networks of the two regions. On the other hand, Zimbabwe and Namibia intervened in the second Congolese civil war. Such interventions promise to link the two regions for ill as well as for good.

■ CONCLUSION

The changes in the context of foreign policy making in central Africa in the 1990s are significant. But one should not conclude that the changes have been mostly beneficial or that they have altered the underlying logic of foreign policy making. Whereas the imperative of regime preservation has not changed, the environment for accomplishing this task has become more difficult. The end of the Cold War robbed the regimes in Angola and the Congo Republic of their ideological legitimacy of anti-Western, socialist solidarity in the face of imperialism and apartheid. The regime in Brazzaville quickly evaporated in 1990–1991; that in Luanda has hung on, despite its moral bankruptcy and corruption, because its chief political opponent, UNITA, seems to have the same weaknesses. The other three regimes depended on French support, which declined in the early 1990s, leading to political upheavals in all three. Far from stimulating a more liberal political context and a peaceful environment, the recent changes have rendered all the regimes weaker and their foreign policies more desperate and violent.

As the foregoing discussion demonstrates, the imperative of external support for regime maintenance persisted in central Africa into the 1990s with the new volatility of regimes only heightening the need for such support. After the Soviet Union disappeared as a potential external backer, rulers in the region tried to encourage the perception of a Franco-U.S. rivalry in a bid to attract increased support from the two powers. At the same time, the new volatility has caused the region's states to be more interventionist than ever before in one another's affairs. Angola has tried to take advantage of the fall of Mobutu, and then Lissouba, to drive UNITA far away from its borders. In general, little has changed for most of the governments in central Africa except the context in which their game is played. Since the game is more dangerous than ever, the old determinants of personal links, the need for external support, and ethnicity continue to be key to understanding the strategies of regime security.

■ NOTES

1. On Gabon, see David E. Gardinier, "Gabon: Limited Reform and Regime Survival," in John F. Clark and David E. Gardinier, eds., *Political Reform in Francophone Africa* (Boulder: Westview Press, 1997), pp. 147–148; and Samuel Decalo, *The Stable Minority: Civilian Rule in Africa* (Gainesville: Florida Academic Press, 1998), pp. 175–272. On the CAR, see Thomas O'Toole, "The Central African Republic: Political Reform and Social Malaise," in Clark and Gardinier, *Political Reform*, pp. 112–119.

2. On the two invasions, see Crawford Young, "Zaire: The Unending Crisis," *Foreign Affairs* 57 (Fall 1978): 169–185.

3. John F. Clark, "The Extractive State in Zaire," in Leonardo Villalon, ed., *Critical Juncture: The African State Between Disintegration and Reconfiguration* (Boulder: Lynne Rienner, 1997), pp. 109–125.

4. On Gabon, see Douglas Yates, *The Rentier State in Africa: Oil Rent Dependency and Neocolonialism in the Republic of Gabon* (Trenton, NJ: Africa World Press, 1996); on the Congo, John F. Clark, "Petro-Politics in Congo," *Journal of Democracy* 8, no. 3 (July 1997): 62–76.

5. For a concise and useful discussion of the neopatrimonial strategy, see Michael Bratton and Nicolas van de Walle, *Democratic Experiments in Africa: Regime Transitions in Comparative Perspective* (Cambridge: Cambridge University Press, 1997), pp. 61–68.

6. See Young, "Zaire: The Unending Crisis."

7. This was precisely the policy adopted by Mobutu, for instance. See John F. Clark, "Ethno-Regionalism in Zaire: Roots, Manifestations and Meaning," *Journal of African Policy Studies* 1, no. 2 (1995): 33–34; and Crawford Young and Thomas Turner, *The Rise and Decline of the Zairian State* (Madison: University of Wisconsin Press, 1985), p. 149.

8. See Chris Gray, "Regional Identity in Congo (Ex-Zaire) and Gabon: From Colonial Invention to African Imagination," paper presented at the International Studies Association–South Conference, Miami, Florida, October 1997.

9. Mohammed Ayoob, "Subaltern Realism: International Relations Theory Meets the Third World," in Stephanie Neumann, ed., *International Relations Theory and the Third World* (New York: St. Martin's Press, 1998), pp. 31–54.

10. See Clark, "Ethno-Regionalism in Zaire."

11. See Clark, "The Extractive State in Zaire."

12. Colette Braeckman, *Le Dinosaure: Le Zaire de Mobutu* (Paris: Fayard, 1992), pp. 190–192.

13. For comparisons between African states and those of early modern Europe, see Ayoob, "Subaltern Realism," pp. 31–54; and Thomas Callaghy, *The State-Society Struggle: Zaire in Comparative Perspective* (New York: Columbia University Press, 1984).

14. Graham T. Allison, "Conceptual Models of the Cuban Missile Crisis," *American Political Science Review,* 63, no. 3 (September 1969): 689–718.

15. The Marxist approaches to foreign policy are already well known to most political scientists. On the business conflict model, see Ronald W. Cox, ed., *Business and the State in International Relations* (Boulder: Westview Press, 1996).

16. See Irving Leonard Markowitz, "Introduction: Continuities in the Study of Power and Class in Africa," in Markowitz, ed., *Studies in Power and Class in Africa* (New York: Oxford University Press, 1987).

17. See Bratton and van de Walle, *Democratic Experiments in Africa,* pp. 63–65; and Robert Jackson and Carl Rosberg, *Personal Rule in Black Africa: Prince, Autocrat, Prophet, Tyrant* (Berkeley: University of California Press, 1982). Although the structuralist analysis of Bratton and van de Walle downplays the influence of individual will or leadership style in democratic transitions and consolidations, they acknowledge, following the classic work of Jackson and Rosberg, that the prerogatives of personalist presidents have been the key to policymaking, domestic and foreign, in African states.

18. "Congos: Les Drères Ennemis," *La Lettre du Continent,* no. 282 (May 22, 1997): 1.

19. In the context of Congo-Brazzaville, Youlou would always have been identified as a Lari, never as a Mukongo. Although the Lari are considered by most ethnographers to be a Bakongo subgroup, the Lari possess a distinct ethnopolitical identity in the Congo Republic and are frequently the political antagonists of other Bakongo groups.

20. For one particularly thorough account of the civil war by a Pentagon insider, see William G. Thom, "Congo-Zaire's 1996–97 Civil War in the Context of Evolving Patterns of Military Conflict in Africa in the Era of Independence," paper presented at the African Studies Association Conference, Columbus, Ohio, November 1997.

21. Samuel Decalo, Virginia Thompson, and Richard Adloff, *Historical Dictionary of Congo* (Lanham, MD: Scarecrow Press, 1996), p. 82.

22. For more details on the Congolese civil war, see John F. Clark, "International Aspects of the Civil War in Congo-Brazzaville," *Issue* 26, no.1 (1998). For discussions of Angola's motives in intervening, also see *Africa Confidential,* October 24, 1997; and Raymond W. Copson, "Congo Brazzaville Conflict: Issues and Implications," *CRS Report for Congress,* November 21, 1997, p. 4.

23. This information was provided by a source in the U.S. State Department in an interview in July 1998.

24. See, for instance, Peter Schraeder's Chapter 3 in this volume.

25. See Clark, "Introduction," and individual chapters in this volume.

26. See Schraeder's contribution in this volume.

27. See Gardinier, "Gabon."

28. On the CAR, see O'Toole, "The Central African Republic"; on the Congo Republic, see John F. Clark, "Congo: Transition and the Struggle to Consolidate," in Clark and Gardinier, *Political Reform,* pp. 62–85.

29. See Peter Schraeder, "Cold War to Cold Peace: Explaining the U.S.-French Tensions in Francophone Africa," paper presented at the 1998 ISA conference, Minneapolis, March 1998. Also see John F. Clark, "Francophone and Anglophone Alignments and Rwanda's Crises," paper presented at the 38th Annual Conference of the African Studies Association, Orlando, Florida, November 1995.

30. See, for instance, the discussion in René Lemarchand's Chapter 5.

31. Calixte Baniafouna, *Congo Démocratie: Les Déboires de l'Apprentissage,* vol. 1 (Paris: l'Harmattan, 1995), pp. 213–114.

32. For a short synopsis of the war, see John F. Clark, "Democracy Dismantled in the Congo Republic," *Current History* 97, no. 619 (May 1998): 234–237.

33. "Congo—Radio Criticizes French Assistance to Cobra Militia," Foreign Broadcast Information Service–Sub-Saharan Africa (FBIS-SSA), August 29, 1997; and "Congo—Lissouba Accuses France of Backing Sassou," FBIS-SSA, September 11, 1997.

34. On the various mutinies and the specifics of the roles played by French troops see *West Africa,* April 29, 1996, p. 667; May 27, 1996, p. 812; and June 3, 1996, p. 852. See also "France: Defense Minister on Role in Africa," Foreign Broadcast Information Service–Western Europe (FBIS-WEU), January 9, 1997; and "Central African Republic: French Troops Attack Rebels in Bangui," FBIS-SSA, January 5, 1997.

35. "Central African Republic: Patasse Urges Closure of French Military Bases," FBIS-SSA, October 8, 1997.

36. David E. Gardinier, "Gabon: Limited Reform and Regime Survival," in Clark and Gardinier, *Political Reform in Francophone Africa;* and Samuel Decalo, *The Stable Minority: Civilian Rule in Africa* (Gainesville: Florida Academic Press, 1998).

37. See Margaret A. Novicki, "Interview with President Yoweri Museveni," *Africa Report* 38, no. 4 (July-August 1993): 25.

38. See Cyril K. Daddieh, "South Africa and Francophone African Relations," in Larry A. Swatuk and David R. Black, eds., *Bridging the Rift: The New South Africa in Africa* (Boulder: Westview Press, 1997), pp. 184–185.

5

Foreign Policy Making in the Great Lakes Region

René Lemarchand

The capture of Kigali by Paul Kagame's Rwanda Patriotic Front in July 1994 did more than bring to an end the third biggest genocide of the century. It triggered a power shift of seismic proportions throughout the central African Great Lakes region. The aftershocks within and beyond the boundaries of the successor states will be felt for years. Nowhere in the continent has ethnic conflict taken on a more savage edge than in the Great Lakes region. Nowhere else does ethnic and political exclusion pose a more daunting challenge. This observation applies especially to the barely reconstructed state systems of Rwanda, Burundi, and the Democratic Republic of Congo (former Zaire). U.S. Secretary of State Madeleine Albright emphasized the centrality of the Great Lakes to the U.S. foreign policy agenda in an address to the Organization of African Unity (OAU) on December 9, 1997: "Africa matters, and right now no place matters more in Africa than the Great Lakes. The region's natural and human resources as well as its strategic location make it either a catalyst or a stumbling block to African unity."[1]

Although commentaries about the future of the region have stressed the "catalysts of cooperation within Africa's new bloc"[2] (comprising Rwanda, Burundi, Congo, Uganda, Ethiopia, and Eritrea), closer scrutiny of the evidence suggests a more nuanced interpretation. Though sharing certain common characteristics, the leaders in these states do not always see eye to eye on how to deal with their enemies at home and abroad. Their similarities also do not imply, as Secretary Albright claimed, "a common vision of empowerment for all their citizens, for their nations, and for their continent" or a commitment to the "consent of the governed."[3] To impute such commendable motives to these leaders invites skepticism, raising questions as to whether official U.S. perceptions have anything to do with the harsh realities facing these rulers.

Before turning to their foreign policy goals, and how these are shaping the geopolitics of the region, let us take a closer look at the circumstances of their rise to power, their ethnic identities, and how recent events within their respective countries have shaped their perceptions of international actors. It is at this level, where history interacts with ethnicity and ethnicity transcends national boundaries, that one finds a significant convergence of outlook among the new leaders. Central to their outlook is not the consent of the governed but precisely the opposite—exclusion of the majority for the sake of ensuring the physical survival of the minority.

■ THE NEW LEADERS: A REVISIONIST PERSPECTIVE

The first and most obvious common feature among the new leaders is that they all came to power through the use of force. Paul Kagame, former Congolese president Laurent Kabila, and Yoweri Museveni fought their way to power on the crest of externally supported rural insurgencies and with considerable support from each other. Meles Zenawi in Ethiopia and Isaias Afewerki in Eritrea similarly fought their way to power in a joint campaign against the former regime of Mengistu Haile Mariam. Pierre Buyoya is the exception, taking power through a bloodless palace coup on July 15, 1996, thirty-two months after being voted out of office by the late Melchior Ndadaye, Burundi's first Hutu president.

Tutsi refugee support was a critical factor in giving Museveni's National Resistance Army (NRA) the upper hand in its fight against President Milton Obote, leading to the NRA's victorious march to Kampala in January 1986. Four and a half years later Museveni returned the favor. Uganda's military and logistical assistance proved decisive when the time came for the Rwandan Patriotic Front (RPF) to fight its way into Rwanda. That Uganda's role was critical is not too surprising given that the RPF was at the time little more than a clone of the NRA. The late Major General Fred Rwigyema, the RPF's first leader, once served as deputy commander of the NRA and as Uganda's deputy minister of defense. Major Paul Kagame, who took over the command of the invading force after Rwigyema's death on the day of the Rwanda invasion in 1990, was at one time the head of military intelligence in the NRA.

The ties of solidarity between Kagame and Museveni were thus forged in the crucible of battle. Although Kabila did not have the same intimate ties with Kagame and Museveni, he was indebted to both.[4] His ability to stitch together a credible coalition of insurgents under the umbrella of the Alliance of Democratic Forces for the Liberation of the Congo (ADFL) depended on significant assistance from Rwanda. Kabila was able to defeat the Zairian armed forces with the help provided by units of the Rwanda Patriotic Army (RPA), ethnic Tutsi from the Kivu region (the so-called Banyamulenge), and the auxiliary support of troops from Angola.

What holds the trio together is not just their shared experience as rebels and allies in their fight against a common enemy but their sense of being heavily dependent on each other, militarily and politically. This mutual dependence is also true of Buyoya in Burundi, whose fortunes are linked to those of his neighbors to the west and the north. Even more important in creating strong solidarity among Kagame, Buyoya, and Museveni is their sense of belonging to the same embattled minority subculture, to the same pastoralist interlacustrine diaspora. Whether Tutsi (Kagame), Tutsi-Hima (Buyoya), or Hima-Munyankole (Museveni), they share the same cultural self-awareness and therefore see themselves as the spokesmen of threatened minorities. Deeply distrustful of what they see as the tyranny of the majority implicit in Western forms of democracy, they regard as their first obligation to ensure the survival of their respective communities. Fear of annihilation is nowhere more evident than in Rwanda and Burundi. In both states the perception of an impending bloodbath continues to shape the attitude of the Tutsi minority. Similar fears are also widely shared by Tutsi communities indigenous to North and South Kivu in the Congo, now collectively referred to as Banyamulenge.[5]

This is not to suggest that ethnicity supersedes all other factors, making for automatic unanimity on foreign policy issues. The situational qualities of the phenomenon preclude definitive judgments about its impact on regional policies. To see in the coming to power of the "Hamitic trio" ominous proof of the reemergence of a Hima empire, as some Hutu opposition figures are wont to claim, belongs to the realm of fantasy, much like the reference to a precolonial Hima empire. To stress their cultural self-awareness, therefore, does not mean that Museveni and Buyoya must necessarily see eye to eye on most regional issues. As long as they see the immediate threats to their security originating from Hutu insurgents on their borders, they mobilize ethnicity as a major source of cohesion, but it becomes irrelevant the moment attention shifts to secondary issues.

A third major characteristic of these leaders is their profound aversion to external interference in domestic and regional affairs. That they are conspicuously resistant to outside pressures was made abundantly clear during the crisis leading to Mobutu's demise. Kagame's searing criticisms of the UN for its inability to stop the genocide and of the humanitarian NGOs for playing into the hands of the Hutu extremists organized in the *interahamwe* in the refugee camps in eastern Congo fell on receptive ears in Uganda and Burundi. Much the same suspicion surrounding the agenda of the international community was seen in Kabila's less than cooperative attitude toward the UN investigation of the massacres of Hutu refugees committed by Kagame's RPA in eastern Congo. Similar suspicion was equally evident in Buyoya's recalcitrance to yield to external prodding in support of a negotiated solution to the Hutu-Tutsi crisis, not to mention his barely contained anger over the role of regional leaders (including Tanzania) in imposing economic sanctions against Burundi. Each of these leaders saw the international community's interference as little more than a smoke screen for a political agenda designed to prop up their enemies.

The outcome was an undeniable sense of regional solidarity, particularly among the leaders of Rwanda, Uganda, and Burundi. This sense of common purpose was rooted in part in the circumstances of their rise to power, in part in their shared cultural identities, and, above all, in their shared distrust of the international community's good intentions.

■ UNITY IN DIVERSITY

Their common affinities should not obscure the factors and circumstances that are specific to each state. Just as there are doubts about whether their "common vision of empowerment for all their citizens" constitutes a source of unity among the new leaders, focusing exclusively on their common attitude toward the international community can mask the diversity of policy objectives. Only in Rwanda has the capture of power by Tutsi refugee warriors been accompanied by genocide of unprecedented magnitude, resulting in the loss of an estimated 1 million human lives, mostly Tutsi. The sheer scale of the carnage coupled with the extraordinary passivity of the international community explains Kagame's pathological distrust toward the UN and international humanitarian organizations. Why did the UN look the other way while the killings were going on? Why were the warnings issued by UN Assistance Mission in Rwanda (UNAMIR) Commander Romeo Dallaire concerning the probability of an impending genocide ignored by the Department of Peace-Keeping Operations (DPKO), then headed by Kofi Annan, at UN Headquarters? By what moral blindness could the humanitarian NGOs in eastern Congo lean over backward to provide assistance to the killers—the former Forces Armées Rwandaises (FAR) and the *interahamwe* militia—in the Hutu refugee camps while so little was being done to help out the tens of thousands of Tutsi returnees?

Kagame believes that French military backing of the Habyarimana regime prolonged the war and increased battlefield casualties. Moreover, France's initiative in getting Operation Turquoise under way, under the fallacious pretext of saving human lives, made it possible for hundreds of *interahamwe* to get away with murder, again. If the latter were so successful in conducting cross-border raids into Rwanda after their exodus into eastern Congo, part of the credit must go to their French suppliers of arms and ammunition. That some of the gunrunning networks extended to Zaire, China, and South Africa does little to exonerate the French from their sustained military support of the Habyarimana regime.[6]

For Rwanda there is no alternative to ethnic exclusion as long as the Hutu opposition appears to condone or becomes complicit in the crimes of the *interahamwe*. Externally there is no other choice but to exterminate the exterminators operating from foreign bases, even if this approach involves collateral damage among innocent civilians. Anyone seeking to interfere with this objective, be it the UN, NGOs, the World Bank, or the European Union, does a disservice to Rwanda's security interests.

There is no equivalent in Burundi for the way in which the genocide has shaped Rwanda's policies at home and abroad. Nor is there any parallel in Bujumbura to the intense suspicion displayed by Kigali toward Paris. These differences were evident in President Pierre Buyoya's trips to Paris and in French support to Buyoya in getting regional actors to lift economic sanctions on Burundi.

A highly contentious issue among regional actors with regard to Burundi was the question of the embargo. Whereas former Tanzanian president Julius Nyerere consistently advocated maintenance of the embargo as a way of forcing Bujumbura to come to terms with Hutu opposition, Uganda's President Museveni had been most reluctant to do so. At the same time Museveni made thinly veiled overtures to Buyoya's rival, former president Jean-Pierre Bagaza, one of the Tutsi leaders least disposed to make concessions to the Hutu. Museveni's position seemed to reflect, in part, his longtime friendship with and heavy indebtedness to Bagaza, dating back to when Bagaza was president of Burundi and Museveni a guerrilla fighter. Kagame, meanwhile, agreed in principle with the decision to impose sanctions, fearing that doing otherwise might antagonize his powerful neighbor to the east, but looked the other way when truckloads of commodities made their way into Burundi in violation of the embargo.

The foreign policies of the new leaders bear the mark of significant power asymmetries among them. The critical element in the regional power equation is the rise of Rwanda as the central actor in the Great Lakes. That a minute, impoverished, and overcrowded state like Rwanda emerged as something of a regional hegemon almost overnight is a commentary on the relative size and professional competence of its army and the considerable material support it received from Uganda. Rwanda's centrality also draws attention to Kagame's astuteness in drawing maximum advantage from the presence in eastern Congo of a large pool of potential allies (the Banyamulenge), and to the prominent place occupied—for a time—by Banyamulenge elements in the officer corps of the ADFL military (the so-called *afande* [officers], as distinct from the *kadogo* [the little ones]).

Kagame's capacity to project his military power effectively into neighboring states was convincingly demonstrated by the devastating incursions of the RPA into the Congo in 1996–1997, first against the refugee camps, then against the Mobutist army, and finally in the cleansing operations against fleeing bands of hapless refugees. In the first incursions, the RPA joined forces with Banyamulenge units trained in Rwanda. The result was the enhancement of Rwanda's regional stature out of all proportion to its size and resources. If there is such a thing as a regional pecking order, Kagame and Museveni must be seen as the dominant figures and Buyoya as the lesser one. With these observations in mind, let us now turn to the security problems faced by Rwanda, Burundi, and Uganda in the wake of the genocide and examine how the threats have shaped their perceptions of who their enemies are at home, in neighboring states, and in the wider international community.

■ THE SECURITY IMPERATIVE: REGIONAL DIMENSION

The Rwanda genocide has created an enduring fear of physical elimination among the Tutsi minorities in Rwanda, Burundi, and eastern Congo. This is the central consideration behind Kagame's regional security concerns. Much of the mutual incomprehension that has developed between Kigali and the international community in the wake of the genocide is traceable to the failure to appreciate the all-pervasive nature of this fear. Although Kagame never ceased to draw attention to the mortal threats posed to the security of his people by Hutu former FAR and *interahamwe* militias in the camps, camp security, not regional security, was the primary concern of humanitarian NGOs.

"The friends of our friends are our friends, the friends of our enemies are our enemies." Most of the foreign policy choices faced by Museveni, Kagame, and Buyoya are reducible to this axiomatic truth. Translated into ethnic terms the formula might read, "The friends of the Tutsi are our friends, and the friends of the Hutu are our enemies." As a guiding principle its relevance came into view as early as 1990, in the wake of the RPF invasion. At no time were enemies and friends more clearly identifiable than when France, Belgium, and Zaire responded to President Juvènal Habyarimana's request for military assistance by immediately dispatching troops to Kigali. From the first days of the invasion a pattern emerged that continued to shape Kagame's foreign policy lens: His perceptions of the enemy centered not just on the Habyarimana clique and its northern supporters but on their external allies, primarily France and Zaire.

In the wake of the dramatic and complex sequence of events triggered by the genocide and the subsequent flow of a million Hutu refugees, former FAR, and *interahamwe* into eastern Congo, the line between friends and enemies was drawn ever more sharply. In addition, Kigali added the UN and the humanitarian NGOs to its list of enemies. The French were further discredited after they launched Operation Turquoise from eastern Congo in July 1994. This military intervention, ostensibly designed to save human lives, was perceived by the RPF as a thinly disguised attempt to prop up Mobutu. In the context of the intervention, the French cozied up to Mobutu and promised to intercede on his behalf with the international community in return for his strategic support for Turquoise. The French continued to provide arms and ammunition to the former FAR well after the genocide got under way. To this day Kagame views France as his international bête noire, and France's direct and indirect responsibility in the genocide is by now widely recognized.

Zaire under Mobutu did not fare much better. The part played by the Mobutist state in supplying arms and ammunition to the former FAR and *interahamwe* and providing them with a staging ground for cross-border raids into Rwanda is well established. So is the rapid deterioration of Hutu-Tutsi relations within the so-called Banyarwanda community of North and South Kivu after July 1994 and the subsequent unleashing of Hutu-instigated violence against ethnic Tutsi. The withdrawal of citizenship rights from the Banyarwanda community of North and South Kivu by the 1981 Nationality Act affected both Hutu and Tutsi and generated enormous tension between "native tribes" and Banyarwanda. The massive exodus of Hutu into Goma in July 1994, however, paved the way for a swift polarization of identities between Hutu refugees and their kinsmen indigenous to the Kivu, on the one hand, and Tutsi elements, on the other.

As cross-border raids into Rwanda increased in frequency and intensity, along with attacks against Tutsi civilians in North Kivu, the need for a massive search-and-destroy operation against the refugee camps became increasingly evident in Kigali. By then, however, the UN and humanitarian NGOs figured prominently on the list of Rwanda's external enemies. Kagame views the UN as being part of the problem, never part of the solution. This perception is due to the failure of the UN to take appropriate steps to stop the genocide and its unwillingness to recognize the danger posed to the security of Rwanda by thousands of unrepentant perpetrators of the genocide who regrouped in refugee camps in eastern Congo. Humanitarian NGOs are viewed in the same light.[7] Not only did they make no effort to discriminate between the perpetrators of genocide and the civilian refugee population but by allowing relief assistance to pass through the former's hands, they significantly strengthened the influence of the *interahamwe* in the camps.

The inability of international actors to comprehend the fears of the Kigali authorities in the face of mounting threats to their security is nowhere more pithily described than in Steve Stedman's searing commentary on the failure of preventive action in the Great Lakes.

> The failure of comprehension was twofold: first, an inability to understand the flesh and blood, visceral world-view of a regime that had won a narrow victory against a genocidal enemy that still survived and with the help of outside actors was regrouping to continue its genocidal war; and, second, and more troubling, the absolute galling failure of outsiders, drunk on the wine of reconciliation, to consider for a moment the views, concerns, and continuing fears of the victims of the genocide. Instead, outside governments and the UN Secretariat ignored the victims and instead condescendingly instructed them on what they needed. The European Community, for instance, created a fantasy version of what was important after the genocide, making its assistance contingent on respect for human rights and progress towards "national reconciliation." Similarly, in a sentence redolent of American pop-psychologist, Dr. Laura Schlesinger, whose advice to the victimized usually amounts to "get over it," the Secretary General of the UN could pronounce from New York in April 1995: "The indignation and deep sense of injustice felt by many Rwandese after the genocide is certainly understandable, but it cannot be allowed to frustrate the healing process that must take place if Rwanda is to be restored to peace and harmony."[8]

Stedman's indictment captures a fundamental dimension of Kagame's foreign policy agenda—a deep distrust of the UN and international NGOs. This distrust is combined with an iron-willed determination to punish Rwanda's "genocidal enemies," even if this means sending military units into the Congo to do what neither the UN nor the NGOs were willing or able to do.

What is left out of the picture, however, is no less essential. Hutu activists have a visceral hatred of the ruling military RPF ethnocracy, which they feel is equally guilty of genocidal crimes. Furthermore, Kagame's rise to power was accomplished not through the ballot box but through the brazen violation of Rwanda's sovereignty, the deliberate use of violence against civilian populations, and massive military and logistical support from Uganda. This view of the Kagame government as the incarnation of Satan became even more widespread after the ethnic cleansing of refugee populations in the Congo in 1996 and 1997. Thus if Kagame's Manichean vision of Rwanda's enemies at home and abroad is inseparable from the experience of

genocide, Hutu perceptions of Kagame likewise have been profoundly influenced by the sheer brutality of his military interventions in Rwanda and the Congo.

■   THE 1996 WATERSHED:
    KILLING FOUR BIRDS WITH ONE STONE

Kagame's November 1996 decision to launch a massive search-and-
destroy operation in eastern Congo marks a watershed in the geopolitics of the region. Directed against a Hutu refugee population of
well over a million, it stands as the high point of military cooperation among Rwanda, Uganda, and Burundi and, more important, as
the critical triggering event behind Kabila's meteoric rise to power
and Mobutu's no less spectacular fall from grace.

Seen retrospectively, the events of 1996 bring to light another
important dimension in the geopolitics of the Great Lakes: the contradiction between short-term military victories and long-term political problems. It is indeed a commentary on the sheer unpredictabil-
ity of regional dynamics that a strategy designed to deal a telling
blow to the Hutu activists in the camps created the conditions of
even more serious threats to the security of both Rwanda and Burundi and raised grave doubts about Kabila's statesmanship. As I
have noted elsewhere,[9] behind the wreckage of the refugee camps
and ensuing human tragedy there was an underlying grand design,
for which Kagame and Museveni deserve full credit. The immediate
objectives were essentially four:

1. Destroy the refugee camps of North Kivu and thus bring to a
   halt the armed incursions into Rwanda mounted by former
   FAR and *interahamwe.*
2. Extend the search-and-destroy operations to the campsites in
   and around Uvira, in South Kivu, where some 150,000 Hutu
   refugees from Burundi had found shelter since 1995. Such an
   attack dealt a crippling blow to Leonard Nyagomna's Conseil
   National pour la Defense de la Démocratie (CNDD), the leading "activist" faction of the Hutu rebellion in Burundi.
3. Eradicate Ugandan rebels operating in North Kivu, including the
   loose coalition of forces around the Alliance of Democratic Forces
   (ADF) and the West Nile Bank Liberation Front (WNBLF).

4. Pave the way for Kabila's victory and in so doing repay Mobutu in kind for his military assistance to the Habyarimana government and subsequent covert support for the *interahamwe* militias.

On each count the Kagame-Museveni plan succeeded beyond all expectations, at least in the short term.

A brief inventory of the tactical benefits resulting from Kagame's cross-border blitz would include the following:

• The campsites of North Kivu were thoroughly dismantled and many of the *interahamwe* killed along with civilians. Whereas no more, and possibly fewer, than 500,000 Hutu refugees marched back into Rwanda (and not 700,000, as claimed by the Kigali authorities and the U.S. embassy), the remaining 500,000 were left to their own devices as they wandered into the forests in search of food and shelter. Of these it is not unreasonable to assume that at least half, if not more, died of hunger and disease; the RPA units subsequently massacred thousands of others.

• By grossly inflating the number of Hutu returnees and by claiming, contrary to all the evidence, that all had returned of their own free will after being "liberated" from the clutches of the *interahamwe,* the Rwanda government could plausibly argue that there was no longer any need or justification for a multinational force to create safe havens for the refugees. The only refugees left behind were those implicated in the genocide, or so the argument went. Only the most disingenuous of analysts could claim otherwise.

• In South Kivu the attacks on Uvira and Bukavu deprived the CNDD of its main sanctuary while leaving the survivors no other choice but to walk across northern Burundi into Tanzania. The Burundian army killed thousands before they reached their destination.

• In the northern parts of North Kivu, units of the National Resistance Army (NRA) joined hands with the RPA to cleanse the area of ADF-WNBLF elements, thereby decisively weakening the Zairian-Sudanese connection behind the two major Ugandan opposition movements.

• In Zaire, the anointing of Kabila as the leader of the ADFL prepared the ground for a spectacular reversal of regional alliances. None of the regional actors had more reasons for rejoicing than Kagame. After playing a decisive role in transforming Kabila from a nearly forgotten terrorist-cum-trafficker into a major political figure, Kagame could now expect a free hand in policing the border area between North Kivu and Rwanda and could eventually reclaim the areas as part of Rwanda's precolonial domain. In late 1996, shortly after the destruction of the camps, President Pasteur Bizimungu, armed with maps of the region, invoked Rwanda's glorious precolonial past—but with utter disregard of historical facts[10]—to lay claim to a large chunk of North Kivu (Rutshuru, Masisi, Gishari). Perhaps even more surprising than this sudden display of Rwanda irredenta was that it failed to elicit as much as a whisper of protest from Kinshasa.

On the negative side of the ledger, however, and with the benefit of hindsight, the following considerations are worth bearing in mind:

• If the destruction of the refugee camps was meant to eliminate the security threats posed by the former FAR and *interahamwe,* the results have been less than optimal. Many of the killers were able to infiltrate back into Rwanda by joining the flow of refugees. Others were able to regroup in North Kivu and join hands with Mayi-Mayi elements recruited among non-Banyamulenge elements.

• The trend among those Hutu activists from Rwanda and Burundi currently operating in the Congo has been to develop tactical alliances, so as to better coordinate their strikes against civilians, while seeking to enlist maximum support from elements indigenous to North and South Kivu.

• The mopping-up operations (which some would not hesitate to describe as outright genocide) conducted by the RPA in the Congo have done irreparable damage to Kagame's image by placing him in the company of *genocidaires.* In addition, a number of unanswered questions remain about the exact role played by members of the U.S. embassy in Kigali in the weeks immediately following Kagame's incursions, including what kind of assistance, if any, was given to the RPA as it went about the grim task of wiping out thousands of hapless refugees.

• In terms of his domestic policies it became patently clear that Kabila was not the savior that he was cracked up to be. Besides having gone further than Mobutu in repressing opposition forces and civil society organizations, his continued reliance on Banyamulenge elements in the government and the army generated enormous resentment across a broad spectrum of the Congolese population, most notably in North and South Kivu.

• The circumstances of Kabila's rise to power reduced him to a client of Rwanda, heavily indebted to Kagame's RPA. It is hard to imagine that without the military backing of the Rwanda army he could have emerged as the spearhead of a local rebellion that quickly snowballed into a massive crusade. By then, however, important diplomatic realignments had taken place that paved the way for the emergence of the United States as the new leader's major regional ally.

■   THE UNITED STATES AS A REGIONAL ALLY

In the aftermath of Kagame's strike into Zaire, the mutuality of interests among the new leaders became evident. Kigali and Bujumbura derived immediate benefits from the shooting up of the camps, since it meant the elimination of the sanctuaries and training grounds from which the Hutu guerrillas operated with impunity. Kampala gained from the dismemberment of the ADF-WNBLF networks. Angola reaped rich dividends from the dismantling of UNITA's bases in Zaire. The odd man out was Daniel arap Moi of Kenya, longtime Mobutu ally, largely discredited by his failed attempts at mediation and protection of some major *interahamwe* figures.

Such striking mutuality of interests stood in sharp contrast with the growing disagreements in the international community, most notably between the United States and the European Union (EU), over the handling of the refugee crisis in eastern Congo. At the root of the discord lay France's plea for a multilateral force into the Congo to create safe havens for refugees to avoid yet another human tragedy. Most EU members, and Canada, endorsed the French proposal. The United States, however, reluctantly expressed interest but then withdrew its support. The critical factor behind the U.S. decision to pull out was the announcement by Kigali that some 700,000 Hutu refugees had voluntarily returned to their homeland, thus rendering nugatory recourse to an international force. The case for not intervening was straightforward: Since there were virtually no refugees left in the Congo, why bother to send a multinational force?

By distancing itself from the French proposal, Washington won the immediate sympathy of Kigali and its regional allies. Had a multilateral force been sent to eastern Congo the RPA would have been faced with a major obstacle in the conduct of its ethnic cleansing operations. The *genocidaires* would have regrouped under the protective wing of the multilateral force and resumed their deadly raids into Rwanda, the partnership between Kabila and his Rwandese patron would have been exposed, and the overthrow of Mobutu would have taken longer. From Kagame's perspective it was much to the credit of the U.S. reversal on supporting the multinational force that the worst had been avoided.

The U.S. decision had a certain redemptive quality. Until then, the reluctance of the State Department to use the term genocide had done little to ingratiate it with Kigali. The same is true of the efforts of Susan Rice, then U.S. assistant secretary of state for African affairs and head of the peacekeeping operations in the National Security Council, to push for a withdrawal of UN troops from Rwanda. On May 3, 1994, at the height of the carnage, the U.S. position on Rwanda was formalized into broader policy guidelines through Presidential Decision Directive 25, which in effect precluded military intervention in arenas where the stakes of conflict were unrelated to U.S. national interests. That a cop-out of such colossal proportion could have happened while genocide was going on was neither forgotten nor forgiven by Kagame.

After President Clinton's three-hour pilgrimage to Kigali on March 24, 1998, Kagame seemed willing to forgive if not to forget. Clinton's act of contrition, phrased in a language free of diplomatic double-talk, was well received in Kigali, Kampala, and Bujumbura: "We did not act quickly enough after the killing began. We should not have allowed the refugee camps to become safe haven for the killers. We did not immediately call these crimes by their rightful name: genocide. We cannot change the past. But we can and must do everything in our power to help you build a future."[11] Interestingly, not a word was said of the ethnic cleansing of thousands of Hutu refugees in eastern Congo.

The regional dimension of U.S. policy was inscribed in rather more nebulous terms in the communiqué issued after President Clinton met in Entebbe (Uganda) with Pasteur Bizimungu of Rwanda, Meles Zenawi of Ethiopia, Benjamin Mkapa of Tanzania, Daniel arap Moi of Kenya, Kabila, and Museveni. All six were invited to "pursue a dialogue on democratization." While recognizing that "there is no fixed model for democratic institutions," the communiqué stressed the need to "explore alternative approaches to the democratic management of cultural diversity."[12] What emerged through this carefully calibrated rhetoric was a pro forma commitment to democracy in return for more debt relief and financial assistance for the participants in the "dialogue on democratization."

In no other part of the continent were domestic issues so closely intertwined with foreign policy choices. Security concerns informed the domestic and regional options of Rwanda, Burundi, and Uganda. In all three states, security at home depended on their capacity to counter the threats posed by opposition movements with roots in neighboring territories. In order to deal effectively with Hutu "terrorists" Rwanda enlisted the cooperation of Kabila in North and South Kivu, used as staging grounds for armed raids into Rwanda. And to put teeth in the alliance, Kagame maintained a substantial Tutsi presence in commanding positions in Kabila's army. Museveni and Buyoya embraced Kabila with much the same motives.

The security imperative dictated choices that were often difficult to reconcile with the expectations of the international community. Nowhere was this dilemma more evident than in the circumstances forced upon former president Kabila: On the one hand, whenever he gave in to Western demands for democratization and cooperation with the UN he would incur the wrath of his patron, Kagame, and would find himself dangerously isolated. On the other hand, the price exacted by his subservience to Rwanda was a rapid erosion of his domestic legitimacy.

Burundi was caught on the horns of a dilemma with relation to the choice of meeting the demands of the opposition for effective political participation or holding back on liberalization. On one hand, by surrendering to regional pressures to engage the opposition in a dialogue toward national reconciliation, Buyoya ran the risk of being overthrown by Tutsi hard-liners in the army. On the other, whenever he refused to heed calls for a dialogue with Hutu opponents, he exposed the country to economic strangulation. With very little room to maneuver in the face of a sharply polarized ethnic arena, Buyoya had no other option but to accept the push for talks with opposition groups in return for lifting the embargo.

■ AFRICA'S FIRST WORLD WAR

The Rwanda-sponsored insurrection against Kabila in August 1998 greatly widened the scope of violence and the military involvement of neighboring and more distant states. Since the war began, the battlefield casualties have expanded to include not just Hutu and Tutsi, Ugandans and Congolese, but Chadians, Angolans, Zimbabweans, and Namibians. As the Congo has dissolved into a regional war it is the people of the Congo who are paying the heaviest price in human lives lost, massive displacements of civilian populations, refugee flows to neighboring states, property looted or confiscated, and infrastructures destroyed.

The insurrection grew out of Kabila's decision to cut his ties with his former Tutsi allies. By yielding to the mounting anti-Tutsi sentiment surrounding the presence of "foreigners" in the army and the government, the Congo's new king turned the king-makers into his bitterest enemies. The crunch came on July 27, when he dismissed a number of troops of Banyamulenge and Rwandan origins stationed in eastern Congo. This action took place only weeks after sacking the army chief of staff, James Kabare, a Rwandan Tutsi with years of service in Kagame's RPA. The sense of outrage felt by Kagame struck a responsive chord among several Congolese opposition figures whose distaste for Kabila far exceeded their grievances against Rwandans and Banyamulenge. Like Kabila in 1996, they knew that the road to Kinshasa passes through Kigali, and like Kabila, they quickly realized the need for an authentically Congolese vehicle to validate their claims. Thus came into existence the Congolese Rally for Democracy (CRD), the political arm of the rebellion.

The eastern rebellion had all the earmarks of a replay of the 1996 anti-Mobutist insurrection, when Kabila proclaimed himself leader of a ramshackle coalition of politico-military factions whose only source of cohesion was their hatred of the Mobutist state. The CRD suffers from much the same internal tensions that once plagued the ADFL. Although the leadership of the movement is in Congolese hands, the real power lies with military men, many of them of Rwandan and Ugandan origins. There is little coordination, and more often than not considerable friction, between the political wing of the CRD and the military factions on the ground. In 1998, as in 1996, Rwanda provided the initial push behind the insurgency as well as the military and logistical support needed to ensure its success, and in both cases the points of ignition were Goma and Bukavu, the provincial capitals of North and South Kivu.

This is about as far as the parallel can be drawn. The crucial difference between 1996 and 1998 is that in 1998 Angola backed Kinshasa, providing Kabila with the providential backing that prevented the rebels from capturing Kinshasa after their daring raid on Kitona and Inga in August of that year. Furthermore, whereas in 1996 Mobutu found himself utterly isolated diplomatically, in 1998 Mobutu's successor had the support of at least six states—Angola, Zimbabwe, Chad, Namibia, Sudan, and Congo-Brazzaville—of which at least three had a military presence in the Congo (Angola, Zimbabwe, and Chad).

Kagame's decision to execute against Kabila the very same coup that brought the collapse of the Mobutist state has proven extraordinarily counterproductive, at least in the short run. For one thing, it triggered the horrendous carnage of ethnic Tutsi in many parts of the country as well as among Africans bearing a physical resemblance to the conventional Tutsi body map. Thousands are said to have died in an outburst of xenophobic rage encouraged by the Kinshasa media. Meanwhile, Kabila's domestic popularity increased dramatically. The discredit he had earned for himself as a result of his disastrous handling of the opposition evaporated almost instantly, giving way to the image of a nationalist hero fighting outside aggression. Prior to August 2 his domestic and foreign policies met with little sympathy among most African states; after Rwanda and Uganda cast their lot with the rebels, however, Angola, Zimbabwe, Namibia, and Chad expressed immediate and unconditional support for his decision to fight the rebellion by every means available. Congo-Brazzaville and Sudan followed suit a few weeks later.

Ironically, the strength of Kabila's diplomatic backing was inversely proportional to his military capabilities, and since none of his allies appeared willing to engage the rebels on their turf, the prospects for a quick end to the conflict became extremely dim. Kabila's army was simply no match for the 6,000 Rwandan and Ugandan troops stationed in eastern Congo and assisted by thousands of Rwanda-trained Banyamulenge. The ability of the rebellion to project its military force was the only explanation for its rapid expansion into nearly one-third of the Congo's national territory as far north as Kisangani, Kindu in the Maniema, and Kalemie in North Shaba.

Further tilting the balance of forces against Kabila were the domestic difficulties faced by Angola, Congo-Brazzaville, and Zimbabwe. In Angola the all-out offensive unleashed by UNITA in Cuito made it imperative for President dos Santos to recall hundreds of troops previously stationed in the Congo. Just as the UNITA offensive got under way, in Congo-Brazzaville the pro-UNITA Ninja and Zulu militias—respectively identified with President Sassou Nguesso's main opponents, former president Pascal Lissouba and Bernard Kolelas—went on the rampage, sowing chaos in many parts of Brazzaville and killing scores of people. In Zimbabwe the economic costs of military involvement in the Congo (estimated to range between $.5 million and $1 million a day) came home to roost, causing widespread antiwar demonstrations in the capital city. Adding to the sense of frustration felt by many Zimbabweans over the costs of the war was the realization that certain key members of the government and the military reaped huge benefits from commercial contracts with the Congolese government.

The war also exacted a heavy price among the rebels and their external patrons. In Uganda the war effort decisively weakened Museveni's hand in dealing with threats from the Sudan. Unable to give his full military support to his longtime ally, the Sudan People's Liberation Army (SPLA), Museveni remained as vulnerable as ever to the raids of the Lord's Resistance Army (LRA), the Sudan-based Ugandan rebel movement. His credibility was seriously damaged by the involvement of his brother, Major-General Salim Saleh, in shady business dealings in eastern Congo. With his foreign policy floundering, Museveni's domestic foes became increasingly critical of his military adventurism in the Congo. Rwanda did not fare much better. Accused by his critics, at home and abroad, of seeking to establish a Hamitic empire in the Great Lakes, Kagame had to contend with continuing threats to his security from former FAR and *interahamwe* elements, many of whom received military training in Kinshasa.

Beneath the surface of the Congolese rebellion there developed intense rivalries within the factions and leadership. A split occurred in the CRD, pitting a Rwanda-supported faction against a Uganda-supported one. In addition, other movements emerged in the Equateur region and in South Kivu, such as Jean-Pierre Bemba's Movement for the Liberation of the Congo (MLC). In eastern Congo, there emerged a flurry of pro-government armed groups fighting the rebellion, such as the former Mobutu army Forces Armées Zairoises (FAZ), *interahamwe,* and the Mayi-Mayi, a loose assemblage of bush warriors whose bases of support are among the Nande and Hunde of North Kivu. In this highly fragmented and fluid arena the conflict took on a peculiarly savage edge as local skirmishes and assassinations were followed by revenge killings and widespread massacres of civilians. It is no exaggeration to say that except for the Banyamulenge, the vast majority of the populations of North and South Kivu—numbering approximately 8 million—were profoundly antagonistic to the rebels, most of them seen as Rwanda's "gurkhas."

Further complicating the power equation was the underlying struggle for the mineral wealth of the Congo. Competition among rebels and their allies over access to gold and diamond deposits and marketing those resources pitted individuals and factions against each other. A multiplicity of smuggling networks flourished in the interstices of the rebellion, and like so many camp followers, European and Levantine fly-by-night operators traveled to the "liberated" areas on gold- and diamond-buying missions. Ugandan and Rwanda army men became deeply ensconced in the informal war economy. Some peddled influence and protection for material rewards; others engaged in thievery and looting on a grand scale.

■ NOTES

1. Secretary of State Madeleine Albright's address to the Organization of African Unity (OAU), Addis Ababa, December 9, 1997.

2. Dan Connell and Frank Smyth, "Africa's New Block," *Foreign Affairs* 77, no. 2 (March-April 1998): 80.

3. Albright, address to the OAU.

4. Kabila's background as a Marxist-Leninist thug emerges with striking clarity from the collective letter to the editor of the *Wall Street Journal* by the four former hostages kidnapped by him in 1975. Kabila's status as a terrorist was bestowed upon him by the State Department in 1975, when he kidnapped, beat, and held hostage three U.S. students and one Dutch researcher who had been conducting studies at Jane Goodall's famed scientific camp in Tanzania. After months of life-threatening terror, during which they were used by Kabila to further his political and military objectives, the young hostages were finally released after their families paid a $460,000 ransom. *Wall Street Journal,* March 5, 1998.

5. The original meaning of Banyamulenge was the people of Mulenge, a high-lying plateau area in South Kivu. They were essentially Tutsi from Rwanda who migrated into South Kivu before the advent of colonial rule. Today the term is commonly used to designate all Tutsi from North and South Kivu, regardless of the time of their arrival in the region. For an excellent analysis of the Banyamulenge phenomenon see Jean-Claude Willame, *Banyarwanda et Banyamulenge: Violences Ethniques et Gestion de l'Identitaire au Kivu* (Paris: l'Harmattan, 1997). See also F. Reyntjens and S. Marysse, *Conflits au Kivu* (Paris: l'Harmattan, 1997); and F. Reyntjens and S. Marysse, *Conflits au Kivu: Antecedents et Enjeux* (Antwerp: Center for the Study of the Great Lakes Region of Africa, 1996).

6. For a thorough inquest into France's role in Rwanda see the recently published report of the French parliamentary commission headed by

Paul Quilles, *Mission d'Information sur le Rwandaa: Enciuete sur la Tragedie Rwandaise (1990–1994),* tome 1, vols. 1 and 2 (Paris: Assemblée Nationale, 1998).

7. For a persuasive critique of the political implications of NGO activities in Africa, see Alex De Wall, "Democratizing the Aid Encounter in Africa," *International Affairs* 73, no. 4 (October 1997): 623–640. Most of the arguments set forth by De Wall, including the notion that "aid resources are filtered through institutions of power [and are therefore] readily manipulable by political authorities" (p. 628), are consonant with the official thinking of Kigali.

8. Stephen John Stedman, "The Failure of Preventive Action: The Great Lakes Region of Africa, 1995–1997," paper presented at the Center for Preventive Action Fourth Annual Conference on Progress and Pitfalls in Preventive Action, New York, Council on Foreign Relations, December 1998, p. 6.

9. René Lemarchand, "Patterns of State Collapse and Reconstruction in Central Africa: Reflections on the Crisis in the Great Lakes Region," *Afrika Spectrum* (Hamburg) 32, no. 22 (1997): 173–193.

10. For an excellent critique of the greater Rwanda thesis see David Newbury, "Irredentist Rwanda: Ethnic and Territorial Frontiers in Central Africa," *Africa Today* 44, no. 2 (April-June 1997): 211–222.

11. *New York Times,* March 26, 1998, p. A12.

12. Ibid.

6

The Foreign Policies of the Horn: The Clash Between the Old and the New

Ruth Iyob

There has never been a simple way to describe the foreign policies of the states of Africa's Horn. Whereas the balance of power and quest for hegemony have characterized regional relations, there have been other foreign policy mixes that have provided a measure of depth and complexity to interstate relations. One of the things that permits us to speak of "the Horn," besides its hornlike perch on maps of continental Africa, is that its geography determines its politics as much as anything in its history or social makeup. For one, the peoples of the Horn face one another *in the first instance* rather than outsiders who usually had to cross water to get at them. Although there were always outsiders who did just that, the chief sources of threat usually came from within the region. For another, except perhaps during the colonial interlude from 1855 to 1941, geopolitical contests over land, water, ports, human and raw materials, were always of greater interest to the Horn's contending powers than to outsiders. And finally, the political and economic weaknesses of the Horn's core powers of Ethiopia and Sudan circumscribed their imperial ambitions. All this speaks to the primacy of Horn-generated elements in the region's foreign relations, but it remains that powerful external forces have had lasting impact on its domestic and foreign politics.

Of much greater impact are the historical narratives, ideological streams, sociopolitical constructions, communal perceptions, and identities created by the people of the region in the process of interactions

with each other over the centuries. This chapter explores how different factors have played themselves out in the modern arena of interstate relations on the Horn. The African Horn is defined by its geographic location and by a continuous struggle for regional hegemony
among the states of the area.[1] Five countries of varying sizes, state
capabilities, and strengths—Ethiopia, Sudan, Somalia, Djibouti, and
Eritrea—make up the region. In the early 1990s, the spillover of conflicts in Ethiopia, Sudan, and Somalia drew Kenya and Uganda into
the politics of the Horn.

The "security complex" of the Horn is represented by an enduring pattern of conflict between incumbent regimes and opponents
operating from neighboring countries.[2] Between the activities of
armed opposition groups and the articulation of foreign policies based
on threats to national security lies a realm in which formal policies
define the visions espoused by states and societies of the Horn. This
latter realm contains societal norms and state-based institutions that
make up what international relations theorists have called the "idea
of the state" and "organizing ideologies" that furnish the impetus for
relations of cooperation, competition, or confrontation.[3] The old
axiom "The enemy of my enemy is my friend" forms the basis for
interstate alliances between states and among nonstate actors in the
Horn. Diplomatic practice is also characterized by the language of
international statehood, equality, human rights, and local vernaculars
whose repertoire reflects relations of slavery, serfdom, and inferior-
ity for the historically subordinate as well as the supposed manifest
destiny of rulers.[4]

In this chapter I seeks to decode various impulses that guide foreign policy making in this volatile region. As the Horn has yet to co-
here into a distinct subregion with its members acknowledging cooperative as well as conflicting relations, any attempt to study the
complex relations among actors remains an unenviable archaeological exercise where frequently what is hidden or missing is more important than what is visible and audible. The social and political
mythologies have, throughout the ages, developed such a familiar
resonance that when the empirical is marshaled to prove otherwise,
the convention is to resort to the more palatable and simpler versions. All this, then, provides a narrative that reaches into the recent
and distant past to decode present relations of hostility, hierarchy,
and dissidence.

■ THE DISCOURSE OF FOREIGN POLICY:
   FACTS, FICTION, AND SOTTO VOCE POLITICS

The discourse of foreign policy in the Horn is characterized by official versions, expressed in bilateral and multilateral agreements and
treaties, and unofficial understandings between incumbent regimes
and insurgent movements. Whereas the formal sphere is characterized by the use of universally acknowledged terms of references and
protocols, the informal is encoded with symbols reflecting shared
historical experiences and sociocultural affinities linking disparate
groups in fluid alliances. The formal lexicon of interstate relations
disallows the local vernaculars, which are often laced with racial and
religious undertones. Thus there is a wide gap between documented,
official communications and the informal codes. Two related examples from Sudan and Ethiopia suffice to demonstrate the synthesis of
different languages based on state institutions and societal legacies.

On the one hand, the obdurate refusal of northern Sudanese
elites to allow the emergence of a postcolonial ideology of "Su-
danism" to supplant "fictional notions of Arabism and Africanism"
has remained the key obstacle to the resolution of the north-south
conflict that began in 1955.[5] On the other, Ethiopia's historical ruling elites have produced modern Africa's most enduring idea of the
state, replete with myths of biblical lore, the glories of ancient
Axum, and the splendor of Gondarine courts, to justify postcolonial
conquest. Ethiopia's nineteenth-century southward conquests were
couched in heroic terms of *neftegna* (settler) expansion that pushed
the empire's frontiers to Oromo and Somali lands, institutionalizing
relations of domination through slavery and serfdom and sowing the
future seeds of resistance. A regional analyst captured the "meta-
physics" of empire with reference to Ethiopian-Somali relations,
which applies equally to policies on the "Southern Problem" formulated by Sudanese regimes:

> Empires, which have based themselves on an attributed divine au-
> thority of some mystical *voiksgeist,* do not seem to accept the no-
> tion of fixed borders. Instead they conceive of what we may call
> "perimeters" provisionally demarking their sphere of effective
> control from that of the "barbarians." The perimeter is to be re-
> spected by the barbarian but will be pushed back at an appropriate
> time by the power of the empire. In the interim, imperial designs

on imperial territory are to be respected by third states. This meta-
physics, confounding to the outsider but self-evident to believers,
permits the empire to simultaneously demand respect for the
perimeter at will, and to retain the right to denounce with full
righteous indignation, territorial moves by another state in its own
intended area as "aggressive" or "expansionist."[6]

Both the post-1945 Sudanese and Ethiopian states have been engaged in protracted and costly wars with subordinated communities
seeking to affirm their right to self-determination. Although the cul-
tures and histories of southern Sudan, Ogaden, Eritrea, and Oromoia
differ, they sought variously to reform and escape hegemonic military and other institutions legitimated by some sort of divine genealogy.[7] The two states claimed lineage to the ancient empires of Kush
and Axum as a way of "civilizing" peripheral populations through
coercion and assimilation. During the seventeenth and nineteenth
centuries, the ruling imperial elites expressed a sense of manifest
destiny, embedded in a hegemonic past rooted in two religions:
Tewahdo, or Ethiopian Orthodox Christianity, and Sunni Islam. Rulers
and religious clerics synthesized the rituals of these traditions into a
political and religious orthodoxy that enabled them to become the
nation at the helm of the larger multicultural empire.[8]

The Abyssinians of the northern central highlands in Ethiopia
and the Arabized Muslims of northern Sudan emerged as the dominant elites competing for the glory of God and empire. Religion and
conquest thus formed the two pillars upon which rested "the idea of
the state that both provides the major bindings holding the territorial-
polity-society package together, and defines much of its character
and power as an actor in the international state-system."[9] Ethiopian
emperors and the Sudanese Khalifas fought infidels, made new con-
verts to their respective religions, and incorporated new possessions
into the perimeter of their respective empires. Their battles for supremacy in the nineteenth century were nearly constant, at times
temporarily halted by, and at other times enhanced by, new European empire builders.[10]

The colonial interlude was a critical juncture for the formation
of new nations and states. But the emergence of states capable of exercising full sovereignty in the Horn took a very long time. This lag
was due partially to the permeability of the region to external influences and the recalcitrance of the ruling elites of the two core states
to acknowledge the legitimacy of newer states seeking to redress

historical injustices and resource inequities. It is for this reason that memories of long-standing grievances and visions of empires have informed the interaction between societies and regimes, particularly those opposed to the status quo. There has also been an endurance of social norms that militate against equality of citizenship for marginalized groups. The precolonial and postcolonial involvement of external actors altered the balance of power between dissidents and the state on the one hand and between rival states on the other. Localized grievances became national crises spilling over borders of nation-states and entangling them in webs of conflicts.

The conflicts of the Horn, such as between northern and southern Sudan, Ethiopia and Eritrea, and Ethiopia, Kenya, Djibouti, and Somalia reflect a pattern of relations of domination and subordination within states as well as between states. The distinction between domestic and regional factors is difficult to discern because kinship and religious ties transcend national borders, which have yet to be demarcated and ratified by the postcolonial states.[11] Some social scientists have examined intrasocietal and interstate relations by focusing on disputes over ownership of territories or resources. But delinking social history from the process of state formation in the region has resulted in a misreading of the nature of external, or foreign, policy, a misreading that stems partly from what Clapham has characterized as the swing between "extremes of heroism and pragmatism" in third world policymaking processes. According to Clapham:

> Heroism points to the implementation in foreign policy of moral themes, which reflect the national aspirations of African peoples for independence, against colonialism, racial discrimination. . . . Pragmatism points to the maintenance of relationships, however unheroic, . . . which seem necessary for the maintenance and expansion of the economy, and which it would be expensive and potentially disruptive to change.[12]

The other reason for the misreading is the recent origin of the majority of Africa's modern states, where policymaking remains a privilege of rulers concerned with maximizing personal gains. In these circumstances, the absence of transparent processes produces outcomes based on noninstitutional criteria such as kinship, distrust, and fear. These outcomes, in turn, contribute to the gap between the formal-institutional discourse at the top and the informal and normative vox populi, which fuels cleavages between peoples and states.[13]

A clear analysis of interstate relations in the Horn requires consideration of social history, societal norms and attitudes, and the socialization of policymakers.

■ THE PAST IN THE PRESENT

There are four main factors that shape the relations between states in the Horn and inform the making of foreign policies: traditions of statehood, legacies of slavery, colonial experience, and the ideas and principles of the postcolonial state. The core states with a history of imperial traditions, Ethiopia and Sudan, differ from Somalia, which attained statehood through decolonization, and southern Sudan, which aspires to statehood on the basis of its distinct colonial history.[14] Eritrea, which seceded from Ethiopia in 1991 following a half-century of rebellion, is much more similar to southern Sudan, but it also displays striking differences based on the kinship ties of half of its population to Ethiopia.[15] The legatees of imperial Ethiopia and Sudan used military capabilities and traditional institutions to constantly nurture a common identity buttressed by coercive measures; those who maintained their traditions of decentralized indigenous rule were treated like truant factions. Akin to loose confederations of village-city-states, their response to coercion was either evasion or creative adaptation.

In the heyday of the Axumite and Kushitic empires, Somalia and southern Sudan constituted distant areas that the ruling power centers used as sources of gold, ivory, incense, and slaves. But local leaders intermittently challenged imperial control through their version of common identity based on resistance. As imperial states gradually faced growing challenges to their hegemony, there emerged kingdoms and states whose rulers constructed identities using a melange of myths and facts to recapture their history. Thus the past began to emerge as a new version of the present.[16] Precolonial Sudanic and Ethiopian kingdoms competed with each other as they tried to convert more believers and incorporate their lands into imperial holdings. Christian Ethiopia's alignment with the Europe of the Crusades was an important early feature of the foreign policy of what became the most well-known African empire; Ethiopia gained fame in Europe as the land of "the mythical Prester John."

The colonial experience left a lasting legacy either by separating subject peoples from the ruling centers and thus liberating them from traditional obligations or by institutionalizing preexisting relations of domination. Whereas the impact of colonialism is still debated today, discussion on the impact of slavery in the Horn has until recently been muted.[17] There is increasing recognition that the legacy of slavery with its inequities and indignities has shaped state-society relations. This repugnant past has reemerged to distinguish the informal processes of foreign policy making that are rarely acknowledged in the formal diplomatic lexicon.[18] For example, despite its pretensions to Pan-African leadership, Haile Selassie's regime could never shake its ingrained contempt for its own black citizens. Similarly, an officially encouraged and well-documented continuation of chattel slavery characterizes the seemingly endless north-south conflict in Sudan.[19]

In light of the Horn states' crisis of identity, stemming from the contest for hegemony by Christianity and Islam and African and Arab civilizations, it is important to inquire how these four factors affected postcolonial ideas of the state and membership in regional and international state systems.[20] By the twelfth century Ethiopia had already begun to interact with Europeans, beginning with the Portuguese, who sought to engage the "Negus" in their search for a passage to India in the twelfth, fifteenth, and sixteenth centuries. Portugal was followed by Rome in the seventeenth century and finally, after 1855, by Britain, Russia, and France.

The early alliances (confirmed much later in the Tripartite Treaty of 1906) with Western powers allowed Ethiopia to play the Catholic countries (Portugal, France, and Italy) against the Protestant countries (Britain and Sweden) with the Coptic element (czarist Russia and Egypt) thrown in for good measure.[21] Islamic Sudan relied on the distant Ottoman Porte (through its Egyptian interlocutors) to placate Ethiopia, which used the Nile card—a threat to cut off the flow of the Blue Nile—effectively.[22] In 1906, the British, then protectors of Egypt and Sudan, got a similar assurance in the Tripartite Treaty with Ethiopia. Egypt's rulers, who had also played the European powers against the Ottomans, were not interested in strengthening the Sudanese state and preferred to maintain a weaker and dependent state in their southern flank. Thus three pillars of foreign policy of the Horn started to take shape by the sixteenth and seventeenth centuries:

permeability to the West-East competition, the Christian-Islamic divide, and the competition for regional hegemony by the Horn's two major powers.

Ethiopia and Sudan claimed ownership of the Nile. They occupied the heartland to the coastal areas of the African Red Sea and archaeological sites that provided them with a consciousness of their ancient empires. The advent of technologically superior empire builders during colonialism intervened to destroy the regional balance of power between Ethiopia and Sudan. Thus colonialism facilitated the weakening of the less than benign tyranny of the old empires. Although more than a century would pass before the end of imperial politics, antihegemonic resistance movements played critical roles in shaping regional politics.

Due to their strong military institutions, Ethiopia and Sudan had colonial histories markedly different from those of their neighbors.[23] Sudan was belatedly incorporated into the Anglo-Egyptian Condominium in 1898, and Ethiopia's subordination to European rule was limited to Italy's brief occupation from 1935 to 1941. Italy's brand of imperialism on a shoestring, known as *il colonialismo straccione* (a pauper's colonialism), had succeeded in effectively controlling the area north of the Mareb River from 1869 to 1890, creating the Eritrean colony in January 1890. The British played a critical role in Italy's success in wresting away Ethiopia's access to the sea through the port of Massawa, where business was conducted through Ottoman and Egyptian intermediaries. British rule of southern Sudan remained dependent on the collusion of northern Sudanese, who regarded themselves as the natural owners of the south.

Somalia's inhabitants fell prey to Britain, France, and Italy and the encroachments of the Ethiopian empire, which had effectively competed for the control of Ogaden. Although Emperor Menelik II acceded to Italian claims to Eritrea, Ethiopia's rulers of the twentieth century came to regard access to the Red Sea as the cornerstone of their foreign policy; this goal supplanted the earlier zeal for southward expansion. They were supported in transforming this ambition into reality by the Western powers' view of Ethiopia as the "core state" in the Horn, the one with the capacity to "compel its neighbors to shape their security policies."[24] If Christianity and empire building characterized the policies of Ethiopian states in the precolonial era, in the twentieth century, access to the Red Sea established Ethiopia's credentials as the regional hegemon of the Horn of

Africa.[25] Thus geography and history, shaped by internal and external configurations of power, gave rise to the hierarchical architecture
of the states of the Horn.

■   THE OLD, THE NEW, AND THE BORROWED
    IN THE HORN: CONTESTED VISIONS OF STATEHOOD

The states of the Horn can be divided into two categories: Ethiopia
and Sudan, which predate European colonialism, and Somalia, Djibouti, and Eritrea, which attained sovereignty after colonization. The
Ethiopian and Sudanese states carried with them precolonial conceptions of statehood and governance based on hegemonic relations of
conquest. Somalia, Djibouti, and Eritrea were, however, shaped primarily by their colonial experience and the diverse ideologies that
nationalist movements used to unify their countries. The various
state identities ranging from monoethnic, multiethnic, secular, theo-
cratic, Pan-African, and Pan-Arab were to profoundly affect postindependence relations.

These ideologies shaped each nation's policies and affected interstate relations. Regional conflicts stemmed from the attempts by
states to mobilize kinship and religious affinities across borders and
culminated in threats to political order in neighboring states. For instance, Pan-Ethiopianism served as the guiding ideology of Emperor
Haile Selassie's vision of expanding Ethiopia's postcolonial borders
to secure control over Eritrea. Pan-Ethiopianism spawned a thirty-
year guerrilla war. Likewise, northern Sudanese elites sought to expand Arab and Muslim influence in southern Sudan using historical
claims of domination in a conflict that remains unresolved.

In Sudan, the Anglo-Egyptian Condominium privileged the north
over the south. Nevertheless, anticolonial Sudanese nationalists of the
1950s and 1960s espoused a secular nationalism that appealed to
southerners who sought socioeconomic and political reforms to combat the inequitable legacies of the past.[26] This minimal basis for a
unified coexistence unraveled as the promise of equality in an independent Sudan remained unmet. In addition, as the north's hegemony
increased through Arabization policies, chances of national unity receded.[27] Since armed unrest broke out in 1963, the Sudanese civil
war has symbolized the enduring crisis of identity that exists in varying degrees throughout the Horn. The "southern problem" represents

the starkest remnant of the negative legacy of the Arab-African encounter with its origins in the spread of Islam and the Arab slave trade.[28]

The ways in which precolonial relations of domination and subordination resurfaced in the postcolonial period provide the first fault lines in the construction of sovereign entities based on a colonial history and the right to exercise self-determination. Resorting to rule by military force instead of democratic concessions almost invariably led to internal dissent. As the cases of the postcolonial Sudanese and Ethiopian imperial states demonstrate, internal discord gradually evolved into protracted armed insurgencies.[29] In the postcolonial era, these armed movements became liberation fronts with sufficient capabilities to counter the military and diplomatic might of the incumbent regimes. Operating from neighboring states' territories, these guerrilla groups constituted security threats to ruling elites and to the sovereignty and physical integrity of nations.

Somalia, the oldest of the new states, embraced the organizing ideology of Pan-Somalism, which was predicated on the reunification of the idealized Somali nation within the newly created state. Since its ascension to independence in 1960, the new state has envisioned the return and reincorporation of Ogaden, Kenya's Northern Frontier District, and French Somaliland in the jurisdiction of a greater Somalia. This transnational ideology was an attempt to redress grievances suffered at the hands of European and Ethiopian empire builders. Its irredentist underpinnings also tested the fragile postcolonial order based on the sanctity of colonial borders.[30]

The transnational vision of statehood posed the most severe challenge to Ethiopia, Djibouti, and Kenya. Portrayed as an irredentist threat by all its neighbors, Somalia drove its neighbors into a defensive alliance. Isolated in its own region, Somalia in turn sought to break out of its encirclement through alliance with external patrons such as the People's Republic of China (PRC) and the Soviet Union. In the process, Pan-Somalism became a domestic and foreign policy that allowed the country to fall prey to the authoritarian rule of a strongman like Siad Barre. The Somali nationalists' crusade against their more powerful neighbor, Ethiopia, and their ideal of a unified state became hostage to the depredations of a vicious patrimonial elite. The failure of the Somali state's policymakers to translate their idea into a viable and sustainable policy led to the transmogrification of Somali nationalism and the dissolution of the postcolonial unitary state. Somali society, which for thirty years, 1960–1990, had been unified in this quest, collapsed in 1991, and the state institutions and nationalist ideology that had underpinned the sovereign Somali state's *raison d'existence* unraveled, leaving behind a political vacuum. As its northern half, the former British Somaliland, made a de facto breakaway, dissident politicians-turned-warlords competed for control of fiefdoms in the rest of Somalia. In turn, its inhabitants witnessed the piecemeal destruction of their country and their own transformation into an emotionally exiled people dispossessed of both nation and state.

A different set of national concerns drove the leaders of Ethiopia and Sudan. The governments of both sides emphasized historic ties to justify the postcolonial incorporation of Eritrea and southern Sudan into the traditional centers of power Addis Ababa and Khartoum, respectively. Retention of power over these areas became central pillars of the Ethiopian and Sudanese states' foreign policy, thus providing the two oldest and traditionally rival states with a common stand against separatist insurgencies. Bad governance and harsh domestic policies, stemming from a traditional exercise of manifest destiny based on assumptions of ethnocultural superiority by the ruling elites in Addis Ababa and Khartoum, led to growing disaffection and alienation of the Eritrean and southern Sudanese populace from their rulers.

Nationalist leaders in Eritrea and southern Sudan sought alternatives to the status quo of juridical sovereignty that conferred immunity on postcolonial states to forcefully dominate unwilling populations. Thus while the principle of territorial integrity was invoked by sovereign states, armed dissidents countered with demands predicated on their rights to self-determination. Fears of meeting the fate of Eritrea in Ethiopia and of southerners in Sudan led to a consensus on delayed independence by the leaders of Djibouti. Its survival as a microstate wedged between Ethiopia and Somalia (and later also Eritrea) has led to a policy based on countering any threats with military and diplomatic support from the former colonial metropole, France.

■ FOREIGN POLICY MAKING IN THE HORN:
MANIFEST DESTINY VERSUS SELF-DETERMINATION

Postcolonial interstate relations in the Horn are largely driven by the efforts of regional states to establish ownership of the area's key resources, such as seaports, oil deposits, grazing and agricultural land,

and the Nile's waters. Various confrontations emerged where states attempted to control resources valued by communities, in particular communal grazing, rivers, and trading areas. A recurrent response by the fiercely independent nomads, pastoralists, and agropastoralists of the Horn has been the mobilization of clans and communities in defense of their "homelands" and patrimonies, leading to the creation of armed opposition groups. Due to the porousness of borders, conflicts over scarce resources assumed regional overtones as neighboring states nurtured their neighbors' dissidents.[31] What began as small bands of armed men, such as the Eritrean Liberation Front and Anya-Nya of southern Sudan, over time developed into impressive formations with military and diplomatic capabilities that enabled them to act as political actors negotiating for a share of resources in return for formal recognition.

Ethiopian-Sudanese relations were dictated by the presence of Eritrean dissidents in Sudan and of southern Sudanese in Ethiopia. Refugee flows in both directions, as a result of government campaigns to reestablish control over border areas, also fed the insurgent groups' search for recruits. Civilian refugees who lived in encampments became an indirect source of international revenue for the host country. Thus interstate clashes over resources and state-society frictions evolved into larger conflicts involving large-scale militarization that derailed nation building and economic development. These clashes also led to the creation of millions of displaced persons whose fate remains entangled with the rebels' strategies of guerrilla warfare and whose survival depends on the vagaries of host-country policymaking and the charity of international aid organizations.[32]

The roots of the conflicts in Eritrea, southern Sudan, and Ogaden can be traced to the attempts by the older imperial states to perpetuate precolonial relations of dominance. Although European colonial rule in the Horn was quite brief, it carved new entities from older social fabrics that opposed the claims of Addis Ababa and Khartoum. Seeking respite from the hegemonic control of imperial Ethiopia and Arabized northern Sudan, the inhabitants north of the Mareb River and south of the Sudd tried to develop new and alternative political institutions based on more equitable relationships. In Sudan and Ethiopia, resistance to state-based hegemonic claims emerged first as political opposition to centralized autocracy and demands for more inclusion in state bureaucracies. Such demands for reform were rejected by elites who underestimated the capacity of marginalized populations to seek redress for past grievances. Numerous opportunities were missed to negotiate solutions that would accommodate both state and societal interests. Due to their vulnerability to secessionist movements, relations between Ethiopia and Sudan from 1956 until 1991 were predicated on the consensus of their respective leaders to contain and eliminate separatist insurgencies in Eritrea and southern Sudan.[33]

Excluded from equal citizenship and bearing the brunt of hegemony, dissident elites in Eritrea and southern Sudan organized their own communities to take ownership of their territories. Self-determination accompanied by calls for communal self-reliance became a political demand for shared rights in resource allocation and utilization.[34] For example, in the late 1980s, Eritrean guerrillas made it extremely costly for the Ethiopian state to use the two Red Sea ports (Massawa and Assab), and southern Sudanese rebels targeted areas where international companies were conducting oil explorations. The occupation of Massawa by the Eritrean People's Liberation Forces (EPLF) one year prior to the demise of the Mengistu regime signaled a change in the military balance between insurgents and government forces. The Southern Sudan People's Liberation Movement/Sudan People's Liberation Army (SPLM/SPLA) intermittently interrupted oil explorations and cut oil pipelines but did not establish complete control over key areas. The Khartoum regime has used internal schisms in the SPLM/SPLA to weaken its adversaries. For the immediate future, much will depend on whether the reformed Islamists, who triumphed in 2000, will devise creative strategies to deal with the ongoing southern civil war.[35]

The pre-1991 regime in Mogadishu differed from its counterparts in Addis and Khartoum because it based its legitimacy on Pan-Somalism and made overtures to Pan-Arabism. Most of Somalia's neighbors were understandably apprehensive of the threat of Pan-Somalism to established borders. Perceived fears of Somali irredentism gradually robbed Pan-Somalism of any merit it may have had to redress injuries suffered by the Somali peoples during the colonial era. Equally important, the support of Arab countries, especially Egypt, Libya, and Saudi Arabia, and, prior to 1974, Soviet support for the Somali Republic discredited Pan-Arabism, which most of the Horn countries increasingly saw as a source of instability.[36]

As the Somali Democratic Republic faced numerous defeats at the hands of the regime in Addis Ababa, some Somali dissidents in safe havens inside Ethiopia organized to overthrow the Siad Barre regime while others planned insurrections from Rome and Cairo. Ethiopian sponsorship of Somali armed groups demonstrated the decline of Pan-Somalism and its replacement with the objective of getting rid of the dictatorship of Siad Barre.[37] An entente between the Ethiopian and Somali leaders was reached, and the Somali National Movement (SNM) was forced to evacuate Ethiopia. The SNM leadership then opted to take the war inside Somalia, and its activities in the north set off the series of clashes in 1988 that led to the collapse of the regime and Siad Barre's flight from Mogadishu in January 1991.

Somalia's claim to ethnic homogeneity had also led outsiders to discount interclan friction as a potential factor of instability. As a consequence, the world was taken by surprise by the spiraling violence that led to the ill-fated U.S. intervention, Operation Restore Hope, in December 1992. The rupture of the idea of the Somali state from its institutional base tore apart the fabric that had held postcolonial Somali society together. Outward-oriented Somali nationalism could no longer provide the viable bond that gave Somalis a sense of purpose and coherence. When the idea of Pan-Somalism collapsed along with the sense of national purpose, Somalis were transformed into Hobbesian individuals seeking protection from the would-be Leviathans rising from the ashes. Clan affiliation and lineage became the critical modes of survival, thereby forcing leaders to mobilize on the basis of kinship in order to seize control of key areas and resources. In the Somali case, the ideologies of Pan-Africanism, Pan-Arabism, and Pan-Islamism could not fill the gap left by the erosion of the idea and institutions of the nation.[38]

In contrast to Ethiopia and Sudan, where ethnicity and religion were primary referents in national politics, the Eritrean and southern Sudanese insurgents sought to construct a nationalist ideology that countered the ruling elite's invocation of transnational ideologies, such as Pan-Arabism and Pan-Africanism, to justify a coercive unity.[39] In the Horn, Pan-Africanism became the ideology of the various nationalist movements jostling for recognition and support from international and regional organizations.[40] However, failure to obtain the patronage of the OAU usually led to at least verbal subscription to Pan-Arabism and to the solicitation of aid from Middle Eastern sources interested in securing a foothold in this geostrategic area. In the process, the equation of Pan-Arabism with Islamism highlighted differences between the Arabized and non-Arabized populations of the Horn, thus further polarizing ethnic and religious differences and camouflaging the root conflicts over resources.

The Ethiopian state used Pan-African tenets to buttress its own visions as a bulwark against Arab and Islamic invasions. The post-1945 Ethiopian state, crafted by the modernizing autocrat Emperor Haile Selassie, formulated an active foreign policy based on gaining and consolidating its control of access to the Red Sea and establishing its hegemony in the region. Before 1974, Haile Selassie's reconstructed "Christian" empire, with its romanticized linkages to biblical Israel, was quickly transformed into an ally of the United States and a bastion of anti-Arabism.[41]

As Africa's first century of sovereign existence ended, the postcolonial status quo of adhering to the principle of noninterference in other nation-states' affairs gave way to new formulations of collective security by a cadre of leaders. Reviving alliances forged earlier, guerrilla leaders-turned-statesmen of Eritrea and Ethiopia redefined security concerns in order to counter the threat of Islamic fundamentalism emanating from Khartoum. Backed by statesmen such as Uganda's Yoweri Museveni, whose international diplomatic networking attracted Western aid to counter Khartoum's Pan-Islamic visions, these new leaders were joined by Paul Kagame of Rwanda in the assault on the normative postcolonial order of the continent. The visionary Somali state of the 1960s had failed to persuade African leaders to speak on its behalf as it sought to redress colonial and imperial grievances; the new leaders of the 1990s intervened militarily to oust and replace Zaire's strongman, Mobutu. Although this alliance of new leaders fell into disarray in the last half of the 1990s, the concerted efforts of five years did bring about another desired aim—the isolation of the Islamic Sudanese state and the displacement, in early 2000, of Khartoum's indefatigable theologian and ideologue Hassan al-Turabi.[42]

The breakup of the alliance between Eritrea, Ethiopia, Rwanda, Uganda, and the Democratic Republic of Congo (DRC) was accompanied by costly wars pitting former rivals, then allies against one another and turning them into implacable foes. The former leader of the DRC, Laurent Kabila, accused his eastern neighbors of violating his nation's sovereignty and integrity and turned southward for assistance to combat invasions by his former allies. In what amounted to a regional war, the southern African states—Zimbabwe, Angola, and Namibia—confronted the East African states of Rwanda and Uganda.[43]

To the north, the Ethio-Eritrean alliance dissolved in the face of a border dispute that broke out in 1998 and led to the region's deadliest war; the antagonists fought from the trenches as well as mounting aerial bombing campaigns. The Federal Republic of Ethiopia (FDRE) accused the state of Eritrea of violating its territorial integrity, to which the latter responded that it was protecting its sovereignty. The norms and principles that had held the African state system together since 1960 had been shattered by the concerted action and policies of the post–Cold War leaders. As the new century dawned, the old order was in shambles and a new one was not yet in sight. Not a trace remained of the fraternal amity of the new leaders that had so charmed outside observers, old animosities raged, and the old norm of "the enemy of my enemy is my friend" reigned once again.

In the meantime, as Somalia struggled to reemerge from anarchy and warlordism, Djibouti sought to carve out a new role for itself in the region to ensure its survival in the face of Ethiopian hegemony and Somali irredentism. The newest and brashest state of all—Eritrea—entered into the fray with the messianic zeal of a reformer and found itself having to prove its mettle as a political entity in the complex web of the politics of the Horn. As the old norms receded or were superseded by the new imperatives of regionalism, Islamism, and statism, relations between the states of the Horn shifted, giving way to redefinitions of the national interests of both older and newer states. The restoration of Eritrean-Sudanese diplomatic relations in 2000 was accompanied by an Ethio-Eritrean competition to gain allies among Somali warlords. The power vacuum in Somalia and the sheer numbers of the contestants for power presented policymakers and observers with a concrete manifestation of the dilemma of the Horn. The demand for self-determination by the peoples of southern Sudan raged on without resolution.[44]

The perennial questions posed in the Horn are how to maintain security and stability without sacrificing the jealously guarded sovereignty of states and the protection of peoples from human rights violations by their own governments or marauding rebels. Will the southern Sudanese opt for secession or another federation with Khartoum? Will Somali factional leaders finally come together to craft a viable system of administration that meets the needs of Somalia's stateless inhabitants? Will Somalia be balkanized following the model of Somaliland? Can Djibouti lead the way to the reconciliation of Somali factions and provide a needed arena for the negotiations of new covenants? How will the war raging between the oldest and the newest state in the Horn be resolved? Will the new alliances between Eritrea and Sudan lead to the peaceful resolution of the southern Sudan problem?

Evolving alliances and counteralliances need to be understood within their historic context and the imperatives of state survival in a region whose postcolonial existence has been marked more by crises and confrontation than by the peaceful resolution of old and new conflicts. As the twenty-first century dawned, interstate relations in the Horn reflected the weight of past and recent history on the postcolonial framework of the international and regional state system. Any understanding of the foreign policies of this region thus requires exploration of the relationship between older and newer states, their idea of the state, definitions of security, and their role in regional and extraregional affairs extending beyond their national boundaries.

■ CONCLUSION

The Horn of Africa continues to be an arena in which the continent's oldest states are pitted against its newest. The older core states of Ethiopia and Sudan are striving to find ways to retain control over territory that their leaders claimed and incorporated in the past. The newer states, which emerged during the last half of the twentieth century, are trying to affirm and consolidate their sovereignty on the basis of the rules of the post-1945 international state system. The social fabric of the societies of the Horn, however, remains patterned by the norms, mythologies, and institutions that have justified exclusion based on ethnicity, religion, and regionalism. There is thus an inevitable clash between the older and newer states as they interact in a modern international state system premised on the legal equality of all its members. The *diplomatese,* that is, the language of interstate discourse, is couched in terms of sovereignty and fraternal relations, but the sotto voce discourse continues to operate on informal understandings among kinfolk and coreligionists.

If the analytical lenses of foreign policy in the Horn are widened to include more than governmental decrees, we may be able to decipher recurrent patterns resulting in either conflict or cooperation. The twentieth century witnessed the enduring alliance between different regimes of the oldest states and the violent unraveling of ententes between new and old ones. The degree to which the organizing principles of the new states nurture democratic governance will determine whether the conflicts within and between states will be resolved or perpetuated for decades to come.

Despite the ominous clouds of war that continually hang over the Horn, the consciousness of inhabiting shared space has always endured as states have tried to calibrate internal governance with multiple regional pressures. Urgent questions that remain unanswered are how to resolve conflicts that pit northerners against southerners in Sudan, nationalists against clan-based power brokers in Somalia, and constitutionalists against party hard-liners in Eritrea and how the Ethiopian state will handle the smaller and newer states of Djibouti and Eritrea. Similarly, the issue of whether southern Sudan will opt for independence or limited autonomy is compounded by uncertainties about the motives and strategies of northern elites about the future of Sudan. Those who would try to end the costly war that broke out between Ethiopia and Eritrea in 1998 must first address the issue of how to rebuild trust between the peoples and ruling elites of these two countries. Djibouti's role as a mediator in conflicts raging to its north and south also needs to be understood as an attempt to ensure its survival without incurring the wrath of the Ethiopian army and the fragmented but equally destructive Somali warlords. Whether Somalis can reconstitute their state and reconfigure a more effective organizing ideology will depend on whether their survival as a polity is aided or eroded by neighbors whose interests lie in weakening or strengthening the collapsed state.

Understanding the grounding of contemporary intercommunal distrust and the identification of national interests by ruling elites of the Horn will remove the veil from the intricately complex modes of interaction between the states and societies of the Horn. The bifocal lenses afforded by the "bottom-up approach" bring into focus the past as it illuminates the present and both past and present as they will shape the future.[45]

■ NOTES

1. To date there is no consensus among the members of the subregion and scholars on how the area is defined. See Jeffrey Lefebvre, "Middle East Conflicts and Middle-Level Power Intervention in the Horn of Africa," *Middle East Journal* 50, no. 3 (September 1996): 387; John Markakis, *Resource*

Conflict in the Horn of Africa (London: Sage, 1998), p. 5; and John Prendergast, "Building for Peace in the Horn of Africa: Diplomacy and Beyond," special report, U.S. Institute of Peace, June 28, 1999, p. 2.

2. Safe havens for insurgencies from the Horn are not limited to African areas but also extend to the Middle East. See Lefebvre, "Middle East Conflicts and Middle-Level Power Interventions," p. 39.

3. For examples of recent work integrating concepts from international security studies with foreign policy studies in Africa, see Christopher Clapham, *Africa and the International System: The Politics of Survival* (Cambridge: Cambridge University Press, 1996), pp. 15–31. See also Barry Buzan, *People, States and Fear: An Agenda for International Security Studies in the Post–Cold War Era* (Boulder: Lynne Rienner, 1991), pp. 57–90.

4. In Sudan, the northerner habit of calling southerners *'abd* (colloquial Arabic for "slave") is common and reflects the former's sense of superiority in North-South relations. John Garang, on March 3, 1984, at the founding of the SPLM/SPLA, combined both the diplomatic and vernacular language when he admonished Sudanese society for excluding the southerners from meaningful citizenship. He pointed out that in the existing social and economic hierarchy, "no one should say these are those who carry the buckets of waste products (human waste) or this is from the South, this is a Fur and this is a Sudanese National . . . we are all nationals. . . . We want to make the voice of the Sudan." See Mansour Khalid, ed., *John Garang Speaks* (London: KPI, 1987), p. 143. John Sorenson captured this same phenomenon in Ethiopia and the pervasive use of the term *barya* (Tigrigna and Amharic for "slave") in his work on the interface of history and identity. For details, see *Imagining Ethiopia: Struggles for History and Identity in the Horn of Africa* (New Brunswick, NJ: Rutgers University Press, 1993), p. 291. Hamdesa Tuso brings into play the imperial denigration of Oromos as *Galla* and *aramane* (pagan), thereby institutionalizing their inferior status in both "state official communication as well as *Habesha* social circles." See "Indigenous Processes of Conflict Resolution in Oromo Society," in I. William Zartman, ed., *Traditional Cures for Modern Conflicts: African Conflict "Medicine"* (Boulder: Lynne Rienner, 2000), p. 80. Somali society, which until recently has been portrayed as egalitarian, has also demonstrated this same phenomenon in the use of *ooji* and *addon* (slave) or *tiin jareer* (hard-hair) to refer to slave ancestry. The term *habash* refers to "Abyssinian slave" or the Oromos, who were the "internal source of slaves." For details see Catherine Besteman, *Unraveling Somalia: Race, Violence and the Legacy of Slavery* (Philadelphia: University of Pennsylvania Press, 1999), pp. 52–53, 115–116.

5. M. A. Mohamed Salih, "Political Narratives and Identity Formation in Post-1989 Sudan," in Mohamed Salih and John Markakis, eds., *Ethnicity and the State in Eastern Africa* (Uppsala: Nordiska Afrika Institutet, 1998), p. 83.

6. W. Michael Reisman, "Somali Self-Determination in the Horn: Legal Perspectives and Implications for Social and Political Engineering," in I. M. Lewis, ed., *Nationalism and Self-Determination in the Horn of Africa* (London: Ithaca Press, 1983), pp. 152–153.

7. Tsegaye Tegenu, *The Evolution of Ethiopian Absolutism: The Genesis and the Making of the Fiscal Military State, 1696–1913* (Uppsala: Acta Universitatis Upsalensis, no. 180, 1996). For background on the making of the empire of Ethiopia, see Donald Donham and Wendy James, eds., *The Southern Marches of Imperial Ethiopia: Essays in History and Social Anthropology* (Cambridge: Cambridge University Press, 1986).

8. Colin Gordon, ed., *Power/Knowledge: Selected Interviews and Other Writings 1972–1977, Michel Foucault* (New York: Pantheon Books, 1980), pp. 123–132.

9. Barry Buzan's tripartite model, which he uses to "guide exploration into the nature of the state and national security," is also critical to a more comprehensive understanding of the linkage between the legitimacy of ideas and the relationship among populations, territory, and institutions of governance. See *People, States and Fear,* pp. 45–65.

10. Robert O. Collins, *The Waters of the Nile: Hydro-Politics and the Jonglei Canal, 1900–1988* (Princeton: Markus Weiner, 1996), pp. 56–62.

11. A. C. McEwen, *International Boundaries of East Africa* (Oxford: Oxford University Press, 1971), pp. 103–105; and L. I. Griffiths, *The African Inheritance* (London: Routledge, 1995).

12. Christopher Clapham, ed., *Foreign Policy Making in Developing States: A Comparative Approach* (Westmead, Farnsborough, Hants, England: Saxon House, Teakfield, 1977), pp. 99–100.

13. The underlying tensions between formal and informal discourse are highlighted during times of war or economic competition. Abyssinian Ethiopians' disdain and scorn for "Arabs" were featured in every official discourse against Eritrean secessionists and Somali irredentists in the 1970s and 1980s. Muslims were quickly dismissed as ignorant nomads by Christian agriculturalists, and Somali pastoralists denigrated farming communities as *boon* (of low status). The Arab-African divide loomed large in the Horn as the disparate groups sought to either assert Arab identity (northern Sudanese and Somalis), make a counterclaim of Semitic kinship with Israel (Ethiopians), or balance an African identity with Arab heritage (Eritreans).

14. I. M. Lewis, *A Modern History of Somalia: Nation and State in the Horn of Africa,* 3rd ed. (Boulder: Westview Press, 1988); and Robert O. Collins, *Land Beyond the Rivers: The Southern Sudan, 1898–1918* (New Haven: Yale University Press, 1971).

15. For analysis of the emergence of Eritrean statehood see Ruth Iyob, *The Eritrean Struggle for Independence: Domination, Resistance, Liberation, 1941–1991* (Cambridge: Cambridge University Press, 1995).

16. For information on the ancient empires see Stuart Munro-Hay, *Aksum: An African Civilization of Late Antiquity* (Edinburgh: Edinburgh University Press, 1991); Derek A. Wesley, *The Kingdom of Kush: The Napatan and Meriotic Empires* (London: British Museum Press, 1996) and Stanley Burstein, *Ancient African Civilizations: Kush and Axum* (Princeton: Markus Wiener, 1998).

17. For discussion of the African slaves in distant areas see Joseph E. Harris, "Soliaman Bin Haftoo: Ethiopian Imposter in India?" *Journal of Ethiopian Studies,* no. 7–8 (1969–1970): 15–18; Vasant D. Rao, "The Habshis:

India's Unknown Africans," *Africa Report* (September-October 1973): 35–38; C. S. Grisman, "West Africans in Eritrea," *Nigerian Field* 20, no. 1 (1954). For a study of Israeli foreign policy that highlights the "memories of the Arab slave trade," see Arye Oded, *Africa and the Middle East Conflict* (Boulder: Lynne Rienner, 1987), pp. 82–88.

18. Shawn E. Marmon, ed., *Slavery in the Islamic Middle East* (Princeton, NJ: Markus Wiener, 1999), particularly the contributions by John Himwork and Michel Le Gall; James L. Watson, ed., *Asian and African Systems of Slavery* (Berkeley: University of California Press, 1980); Alexandre Popovic, *The Revolt of the African Slaves in Iraq in the Third and Ninth Century* (Princeton, NJ: Markus Wiener, 1999); Patrick Manning, *Slavery and African Life: Occidental, Oriental, and African Slave Trades* (Cambridge: Cambridge University Press, 1990); Bernard Lewis, *Race and Slavery in the Middle East* (New York: Oxford University Press, 1990).

19. For documentation, see, for example, U.S. House of Representatives, Committee on International Relations, Subcommittee on International Operations and Human Rights, session "Slavery in Mauritania and Sudan," March 13, 1996. Also see Human Rights Watch, "Children of Sudan: Slaves, Street Children, and Child Soldiers," September 1995; "Africa's Invisible Slaves," *Boston Phoenix,* June 30, 1995; and "The Islamic Gulag," *UTNE Reader* (March-April 1996).

20. The "idea of the state" as used here is an application of Barry Buzan's model elaborated in Clapham's *Africa and the International System, p.* 45.

21. For a historical background on early Ethiopian foreign policy making, see Sven Rubenson, *The Survival of Ethiopian Independence* (New York: Holms & Meir, 1976).

22. Historian Robert O. Collins provides an analysis of the origins of the emergence of what I have called here the Nile card in *The Waters of the Nile,* pp. 1–25.

23. For a comparative analysis of the impact of colonial rule on the African state see Crawford Young, *The African Colonial State in Comparative Perspective* (New Haven: Yale University Press, 1994).

24. Francis Deng, Sadikiel Kimaro, Terrence Lyons, Donald Rothchild, and I. William Zartman, *Sovereignty as Responsibility: Conflict Management in Africa* (Washington, DC: Brookings Institution, 1996), p. 133.

25. Sir Halford J. Mackinder, *Democratic Ideals and Reality: A Study in the Politics of Reconstruction* (Suffolk: Penguin Books, [1919] 1944, p. 39).

26. For a discussion of Ethiopia as the regional hegemon see Iyob, *The Eritrean Struggle for Independence,* pp. 20–28 and 41–46.

27. Dunstan M. Wai, *The African-Arab Conflict in the Sudan* (New York: Africana, 1981), pp. 127–139; Francis Deng, *War of Visions: Conflict of Identities in the Sudan* (Washington, DC: Brookings Institution, 1995), pp. 101–134; and Tim Niblock, *Class and Power in Sudan: The Dynamics of Sudanese Politics* (Albany: State University of New York Press), pp. 204–232.

28. Arab scholars have produced a version of an African-Arab "fraternal" accord, which focuses on the shared historical experience of European

colonialism and provides a rosier picture than reality warrants. See, for example, Hilmi S. Yousuf, *African-Arab Relations* (Brattelboro, VT: Amana Books, 1986). For contrasting views see Arye Oded, *Africa and the Middle East Conflict* (Boulder: Lynne Rienner, 1987), pp. 82–116.

29. Buzan's study of security provides a very useful model of states: 1) primal nation-state, where the nation precedes the sovereign state; 2) the "state-nation," where the state uses its enormous powers to create a nation; 3) the "part-nation-state," which is linked to its populations living beyond its boundaries; and 4) the "multination state," which is made up of either a federative or an imperial state. The "imperial state" is defined as a state dominated by one of the nations that make up the multinational state. If we use this model, both Ethiopia and Sudan are imperial multinational states, Somalia is a part-nation-state, and Djibouti and Eritrea demonstrate the features of the state-nation. For details see Barry Buzan, *People, States and Fear,* pp. 75–77.

30. Saadia Touval, *Somali Nationalism: International Politics and the Drive for Unity in the Horn of Africa* (Cambridge: Harvard University Press, 1963); and David Laitin and Said Samatar, *Somalia: Nation in Search of a State* (Boulder: Westview Press, 1987), p. 129.

31. John Markakis, "Ethnic Conflict and the State in the Horn in Africa," in Markakis and Katsuyoshi Fukui, eds., *Ethnicity and Conflict in the Horn of Africa* (London: James Currey, 1994), pp. 217–236.

32. Jonathan Bascom, *Losing Place: Refugee Populations and Rural Transformations in East Africa* (New York: Berghahn Books, 1998).

33. See Harold Marcus, *Ethiopia, Great Britain, and the United States, 1941–1974: The Politics of Empire* (Berkeley: University of California Press, 1983), p. 52.

34. Terrence Lyons provides a comparison of different interpretations of self-determination in the Horn in "Crisis on Multiple Levels: Somalia and the Horn of Africa," in Ahmed I. Samatar, ed., *The Somali Challenge: From Catastrophe to Renewal?* (Boulder: Lynne Rienner, 1994), p. 20.

35. Ian Fischer, "Oil Flowing in the Sudan, Raising the Stakes in Its Civil War," *New York Times,* Sunday, October 17, 1999.

36. For a discussion of the opposing African and Arab ideas of the state see Clapham, *Africa and the International System,* p. 129. See also James Mayall, "Self-Determination in the OAU," in I. M. Lewis, ed., *Nationalism and Self-Determination in the Horn of Africa* (London: Ithaca Press, 1983), pp. 87–88.

37. Most accounts seem to highlight the colorful warlords and their arsenals. It should be noted that there were calls by civilians for a national conference as early as May 1990. Signatories to the founding document of the Manifesto Group were jailed by the regime, leaving no other alternatives but armed rebellion.

38. Ken Menkhaus, "Traditional Conflict Management in Contemporary Somalia," in I. William Zartman, ed., *Traditional Cures for Modern Conflict* (Boulder: Lynne Rienner, 2000), pp. 192–196.

39. S.K.B. Asante, *Pan-African Protest: West Africa and the Italo-Ethiopian Crisis, 1934–1941* (London: Longman, 1977).

40. Touval, *Somali Nationalism,* pp. 181–182.

41. Negussay Ayele, "The Foreign Policy of Ethiopia," in Olajide Aluko, ed., *The Foreign Policies of African States* (London: Hodder and Stoughton, 1977), p. 52. Pan-Arab assertions of reinforcing rather than competing with Pan-African interests are consistently reiterated by North African statesmen and diplomats in terms that do not reflect African resentment of Arab paternalism. Boutros Boutros-Ghali's assertion that "more than seventy percent of Arab lands are in Africa" is an example of one perspective that causes Afro-Arab hostilities. See "The Foreign Policy of Egypt," in Aluko, *The Foreign Policies of African States,* p. 42. See also Mohamed Omer Beshir, *The Southern Sudan: From Conflict to Peace* (London: C. Hurst, 1975), p. 137.

42. For a perspective analysis of the short-lived Museveni-Kagame-Kabila-Afwerki-Zanawi alliance, see Phillip Gourevitch, "Continental Shift," *New Yorker,* August 4, 1997, pp. 43–55.

43. For an overview, see International Crisis Group, "Africa's Seven-Nation War," May 21, 1999.

44. Robert O. Collins, "Africans, Arabs, and Islamists: From the Conference Tables to the Battlefields in the Sudan," *African Studies Review* 42, no. 2 (September 1999): 105–123.

45. For details on the bottom-up and other approaches to ongoing conflicts, see Christopher Clapham, "Being Peacekept," in Oliver Furley and Roy May, eds., *Peacekeeping in Africa* (Aldershot: Ashgate, 1998), pp. 304–317.

7

Foreign Policy Decisionmaking in Southern Africa's Fading Frontline

Gilbert M. Khadiagala

The changes stemming from the end of apartheid and the Cold War in the 1990s did not offer significant vistas to southern Africa's states, previously organized as the Frontline States (FLS) and the Southern African Development Coordination Conference (SADCC). After three decades of preoccupation with issues of decolonization and economic survival, the postapartheid, post–Cold War era presaged a shift in priorities to national renewal and development. The global push for political pluralism and economic liberalism seemed to solidify these transformations, becoming widely accepted as the new principles for regime security and regional integration. In addition, the expectations of foreign policy decisionmakers in the region coalesced around the perception that a democratic and prosperous South Africa would furnish the leadership for the construction of collective institutions.

Nearly a decade since these changes began, the foreign policy choices of southern African states are constrained by weak state structures, economic despair, and social dislocations. Instead of constituting fundamental shifts in content and context, foreign policies remain narrowly focused on national concerns of survival in an external environment dominated by a host of emerging security threats. The 1990s promised an era of pluralism when there would be a decline of ossified structures of presidentialism and single-party rule, but the tentative experiments in democratization have neither yielded regime security nor affected the structures of foreign policy making. Although functional cooperation has proceeded farther than in most of Africa, new conflicts have overshadowed the broadening of institutional ties.

This chapter weaves these themes into the argument that there is considerable readjustment in foreign roles and expectations of states north of the Limpopo due to the persistence of old challenges and the emergence of new ones. The external burdens of destabilization have been replaced by the gradual weakening of state authority and legitimacy in a regional environment that exhibits the legacies of economic inequalities and a global context that is less generous than before. Thus although foreign policy is still the medium through which some states assert their primacy and identity, the number of avenues for exerting influence has declined for the majority. In Chapter 8, Denis Venter analyzes the dynamics of South Africa's foreign policy, revealing the task of balancing multiple internal and international constituencies.[1] In examining the foreign policy postures of South Africa's neighbors, I build on and complement some of the regional questions raised in Venter's analysis.

■ THE DOMESTIC-REGIONAL NEXUS OF FOREIGN POLICY MAKING

Efforts to create closer links between domestic and regional structures have always characterized foreign policy making in southern Africa. These links were important because the decolonization conflicts that began in the 1960s and economic dependence on white minority regimes constrained the choices of independent states that were struggling with the postcolonial concerns of nationhood and development. As state security and legitimacy came to rest on regional events, specifically the raging guerrilla wars and struggles against economic and military pressures, African elites framed foreign policy in regional terms. Even when foreign policies veered beyond the region, the FLS (Angola, Botswana, Mozambique, Tanzania, Zambia, and Zimbabwe) nonetheless saw foreign policies as tools of managing a hostile regional environment. As a consequence, the coexistence of patterns of collaboration and conflict over the years bequeathed distinctive institutions and behaviors unique to southern Africa.[2]

A siege mentality reflective of regional threats pervaded the foreign policy behavior of the FLS and informed domestic institution building. Tanzania and Zambia, providing the core of the FLS alliance, illustrated the ties between the domestic structures and regional foreign policy objectives of decolonization. Led by Julius Nyerere and Kenneth Kaunda's African socialist one-party states, Tanzania and Zambia epitomized the pattern of a strong presidency in the articulation and leadership of foreign policies. Mobilizing state institutions around African socialism lend Nyerere and Kaunda considerable domestic legitimacy and the organizational room to maneuver for the cause of southern Africa's liberation. Unencumbered by domestic institutional restraints, the foreign policy establishments in Tanzania and Zambia mirrored the aspirations and imprimatur of the two leaders. Globally, Nyerere and Kaunda cast themselves as victims of white minority regimes, roles that allowed outsiders to provide them with all forms of support.[3]

Angola and Mozambique, the first beneficiaries of FLS collaborative efforts for decolonization in the 1970s, followed remarkably similar behavioral and institutional patterns of foreign policy making. While espousing more radical socialist policies than their allies, the Popular Movement for the Liberation of Angola (MPLA) and the Front for the Liberation of Mozambique (FRELIMO) anchored their foreign policies to the goal of ending minority rule. The Marxist-Leninist credentials of Angola and Mozambique legitimized their one-party states without significantly altering the style and content of their foreign policies. As the costs of liberating Namibia and Zimbabwe escalated, Angola and Mozambique sought external military and economic assistance to help them be effective actors in the regional struggles for self-determination.

Elsewhere in southern Africa, the legacy of traditional monarchies and neopatrimonialism led to foreign policy decisionmaking that privileged presidential rule and executive domination with no competition from countervailing institutions. With varying degrees of success, Botswana, Malawi, Lesotho, and Swaziland forged a compromise between the geographical and economic dependence on minority regimes and the political pressures stemming from the demands of decolonization. With the decolonization of Zimbabwe in 1980, the FLS moved to incorporate the more economically vulnerable regional states into an inclusive alliance, SADCC, that sought economic integration and dependence reduction through sectoral coordination.

SADCC's creation also marked a shift in the regional leadership from the geographically distant Tanzania to the more centrally located Zimbabwe, a shift that gradually affected the flavor and direction of regional foreign policies.[4]

Namibia's independence in 1990 marked the start of changes in the context of foreign policy making because with the end of decolonization and South Africa's destabilization, some of the security concerns of the FLS lost salience. As the original security threats declined, the foreign policy establishments had to find new preoccupations; this task applied even more to states that had devoted disproportionate energies to regional issues at the expense of domestic ones. Questions about the trade-off between national and regional interests became even more glaring with the end of the Cold War and the multiple economic and political pressures on African states for reform. The Frontline States had contributed to decolonization at enormous costs to their political economies, in the end barely able to keep their nations from social and economic disintegration. Furthermore, whereas the exclusive, one-party decisionmaking structures had been conducive to the siege and frontline mentality of the liberation era, the new demands for pluralism and democracy seemed to challenge these established practices. With its liberal democratic constitution that enshrined political competition, the rule of law, and separation of powers, Namibia appeared to set the pace for a new southern Africa whereby foreign policy, like other matters of state, would be routinely deliberated in transparent institutional arenas shorn of the secretive practices of presidencies.

The trend established by Namibia was demonstrated in Zambia, where Frederick Chiluba's Movement for Multiparty Democracy (MMD) initiated a crusade for pluralism and good governance that became popularly identified with Africa's "second liberation." Starting in 1990, the MMD led protests for change. They culminated in multiparty elections in October 1991 that ended Kaunda's twenty-seven years of authoritarian rule. One of the MMD's platforms was to shift attention away from regional concerns to domestic issues, which, it claimed, Kaunda had ignored. As one critic observed: "Liberation was Kaunda's pet project, and he kept it up until all those countries were free. Unfortunately, these preoccupations gave the impression he was neglecting his own country and preferring to play on the world stage."[5] In this respect, therefore, Kaunda's defeat symbolized the start of a new phase in which state actors sought an appropriate balance between domestic and regional priorities.

Equally significant for the region was the internal and external pressure that forced Robert Mugabe of Zimbabwe to hold multiparty elections in 1990. Although the dominant Zimbabwe African National Union–Patriotic Front (ZANU-PF) still won, a new opposition movement was born, laying claims to the rule of law, transparent public institutions, and respect for human rights.[6] By the same token, Mozambique made a successful transition to multiparty politics following years of civil war between FRELIMO and the Mozambique National Resistance Movement (RENAMO). Mozambique's negotiated settlement implemented through international generosity ushered in a period of stability rooted in tolerance and mutual respect. In contrast to Angola, which continued to witness prolonged strife, FRELIMO and RENAMO shifted their conflicts from the battlefield into the regularized institutions of state and society.[7]

Democratization in Mozambique contributed to the pressures for constitutional reforms in Malawi. In 1993 President Kamuzu Banda reluctantly agreed to hold a national referendum on the reintroduction of democratic pluralism; an overwhelming 64 percent voted in favor. Subsequently, Bakili Muluzi's United Democratic Front (UDF) won the presidential and parliamentary elections of May 1994.[8] These momentous changes culminated in South Africa's transition to a multiracial democracy with the inauguration of the Government of National Unity (GNU) in April 1994. In undoing the legacy of apartheid through national reconciliation and power sharing, Nelson Mandela's South Africa reinforced the image of a southern Africa committed to national stability through democratic evolution. Like the regional transformations following the independence of Angola and Mozambique in the 1970s, the South African transition seemed to embrace the foreign policy objectives that the FLS and SADCC had fought for for decades.

■ FORGING A POSTAPARTHEID
   REGIONAL FOREIGN POLICY

❑ *Economic Dimensions*

Although regional conflicts established the close links between domestic and regional policies, economic interdependence provided a more enduring basis for regionalism. Thus as a vehicle for economic regionalism, SADCC became the regional nexus for collective foreign policy making. In the postapartheid era, attempts by regional states to manage the new South Africa led to the formation of a comprehensive organization, the Southern African Development Community (SADC), in 1992.

In a departure from the sectoral coordination that had been SADCC's primary goal, SADC aimed to deepen cooperation and prosperity through a trade and monetary integration scheme. Since 1994, SADC has broadened its membership to fourteen states—Angola, Botswana, Lesotho, Malawi, Mauritius, Mozambique, Namibia, South Africa, Swaziland, Tanzania, Zambia, Zimbabwe, the DRC, and the Seychelles. SADC defined trade liberalization and monetary integration as the elimination of trade barriers, the creation of a common market with free movement of factors of production, and the creation of a common currency by the turn of the century. In 1996 an SADC trade protocol proposed a free-trade area with a low to zero tariff for most goods by 2004 that would generate business opportunities to realize economies of scale, improve productivity, and enhance competitiveness. Under Article 37 of the protocol, it would come into effect after two-thirds of the fourteen members had ratified it. By 1999, key states—South Africa, Mozambique, and Zambia—had yet to do so. In declining to ratify the trade protocol, Mozambique has argued that in the absence of effective regional policy measures, the protocol would endanger the viability of small and medium enterprises.[9]

Integrating South Africa into SADC fulfilled the goal of anchoring South Africa firmly in the region before domestic priorities distracted the majority-ruled government. By this thinking, South Africa was to become the natural "economic growth pole" as a growing market for primary products and an exporter of capital, skills, and services in what Julius Nyerere described as "southern Africa's ASEAN."[10] Building SADC as a focal point of regional policy extended to efforts to forge a common approach to the outside world. This goal also coincided with South Africa's pledge to use its leverage to increase SADC's bargaining position with multilateral institutions and other regional economic blocs.[11] Meetings between SADC and the European Union (EU), beginning in September 1994 in Berlin, Germany, seemed to demonstrate SADC's determination to use such engagements to boost its collective clout with a powerful multilateral actor and strengthen the formal mechanism for dialogue between Europe and southern Africa on a broad spectrum of issues.[12] Over the years, there has been a proliferation of what SADC calls "smart partnerships," such as the Southern African International Dialogue (SAID) forum, southern Africa's versions of the World Economic Forum, and the U.S.-SADC forum, all replicating the SADC-EU model. These conferences bring together business, government, and labor leaders from the region and beyond to discuss issues ranging from how to spread the benefits of economic liberalization to enhancing economic prosperity and open markets.[13] For instance, in September 1999 the United States and SADC signed an agreement to promote U.S. investment in southern Africa, assess the impact of HIV/AIDS and its further growth, and develop capacities to manage the environment in SADC member states.[14]

Managing South Africa within SADC, however, did not eliminate the deeper conflicts over the future of competing organizations, in particular the Southern Africa Customs Union (SACU), dominated by South Africa, and the Common Market for East and Southern Africa States (COMESA). The initial foreign policy position of the African National Congress (ANC) was to propose negotiations with SACU members Botswana, Lesotho, Swaziland, and Namibia for changes that would enable SACU to become a "vehicle for the promotion of mutually beneficial cooperation and integration in Southern Africa."[15] SADC, in contrast, sought the incorporation of all SACU member countries in SADC's proposed regional free-trade area.[16] At the start of negotiations for restructuring SACU in 1993, Trade and Industry Minister Trevor Manuel stated that South Africa's interest lay in a "more open and equal relationship" with current SACU members. But since the negotiations began, they have been dogged by conflicts over the formula for revenue sharing and a new trade regime.[17]

The most potentially destabilizing conflict was between SADC and COMESA, successor to the Preferential Trade Area (PTA), whose membership stretches from Eritrea in the north to Zimbabwe in the south. COMESA's long-term goal of free trade involving the free movement of goods and services and the removal of all nontariff barriers duplicates SADC objectives. Although the ANC had pledged to explore the possibility of affiliating with COMESA to craft an appropriate institutional basis for deepening beneficial and equitable relations, once in power, it repudiated this position.[18] In August 1994, nine SADC members proposed to split COMESA into two subregions: a southern zone comprising existing SADC members and a northern one of non-SADC members. SADC's executive secretary, Kaire Mbuende, argued that the split would solve problems of overlapping memberships and allow the two organizations to play their own roles as building blocks for an African economic community. Nonsouthern African states fiercely opposed the split, perceiving it as a plot to dampen the momentum for a more effective organization.[19]

At the formal launching of COMESA in December 1994, Botswana's vice president, Festus Mogae, indicated that despite opposition to the split, SADC would have no role in COMESA: "It's highly unlikely and improbable that SADC leaders would want to go back on their SADC commitments. . . . I don't think there will be a deadline [for quitting], and I don't think there should be one. The countries concerned will move out at their own pace."[20] In 1997, Lesotho and Mozambique quit COMESA, followed in July 1999 by Tanzania. Explaining Tanzania's move, Minister of Foreign Affairs Jakaya Kikwete observed: "We were faced with the option of either getting out of SADC or COMESA. . . . We therefore opted to pull out of COMESA because we have invested so much in SADC. We opted to stay in SADC because unlike COMESA, whose thrust is to create a common market for selling goods, SADC's emphasis is to develop the capacity building for producing goods."[21] Tanzania's president, Benjamin Mkapa, was more blunt in explaining why COMESA was unnecessary: "We have a propensity for starting and joining all kinds of organizations. The result was that we were spending more time in conferences than implementing the decisions."[22]

Although a decisive vote of confidence in SADC, Tanzania's action has not resolved the larger question of harmonization of institutions; eight of fourteen SADC states are still members of COMESA. Tanzania's withdrawal also led to corresponding attempts by Uganda to join SADC, ostensibly at South Africa's invitation. In August 2000, during a visit to Uganda, South Africa's deputy minister of trade and industry, Lindiwe Hendriks, announced that South Africa would not oppose Uganda's application for membership in SADC.[23] But in a sign of internal dissension, the acting executive secretary of SADC opposed the hasty expansion of the bloc: "I strongly believe that before we can think of expansion, we should first try to deepen co-operation. With the 14 member states, we think we need annual growth of 6.8 per cent to make a dent in poverty and unemployment. If we were to admit other countries the situation would have to change, because there would be an increase in the population numbers and other needs."[24]

The initial enthusiasm that greeted South African entry into SADC began to dissipate toward the end of the 1990s, as there was little progress on the ratification of SADC's trade protocol and on dealing with South Africa's obduracy in negotiations with SACU members.[25] Moreover, despite the emphasis on trade and investment promotion, by the end of July 1998, the bulk of SADC's Programs of Action was concentrated primarily in the transportation and communications sectors. This meant, in effect, that rather than deepening integration, SADC was merely reinforcing the sectoral orientation of SADCC.[26] Reflecting its declining interest in the region, South Africa has been looking to the entire African continent and the world at large to advance its economic interests. Reaching into virtually all corners of the continent, South Africa has become Africa's biggest investor in areas ranging from mining, agriculture, manufacturing, and petrochemicals to financial services. As it moves farther north, South Africa is doubly accused of abandoning southern Africa and becoming a new imperialist power. Thus although many African states welcome South Africa's investment and technological input, some, such as Kenya and Zimbabwe, are alarmed at the commercial and industrial intrusion without reciprocal trade advantages. As *African Business* shows: "South Africa's investment has in turn attracted charges of South Africa becoming Africa's new economic imperialist, using its money and its muscle to suborn its African family of nations. Such resentment is unlikely to ease in the early years of the 21st century, especially as African nations battle each other for trade concessions and retreat into regional economic blocs."[27]

The signing of the separate Free Trade Area Agreement between South Africa and the EU chagrined SADC and SACU states, which saw it as a clear departure from South Africa's role of economic leadership. Although South Africa has indicated that the agreement would not have a negative impact on its neighbors, there have been growing demands that SADC states explore means of fending for themselves in future.[28]

❏ *Security Dimensions*

Security issues form the gist of foreign policy making in southern Africa, since they speak to internal and external vulnerabilities of states and regimes. The decline of regional sources of insecurity elevated domestic problems such as ethnicity, inequitable distribution of resources, and constricted participation to the core of new sources of threats to elite survival. But unlike the economic issues, about which there was widespread consensus on the institutional contours for collective endeavors, questions of regime security elicited varying approaches across the regional spectrum. There was recognition that domestic insecurities needed to be preempted through national institutions supplemented by regional ones, yet deep disagreements abounded on the nature of national institutions and their relations to regional institutions. As a result, regional states have faced more challenges as they have moved into the uncharted territory of forging a consensus on modes of security collaboration.

Article 5 of SADC's charter emphasizes peace and security issues: "War and insecurity are the enemy of economic progress and social welfare. Good and strengthened political relations among the countries of the region, and peace and mutual security, are critical components of the total environment for regional cooperation and integration. The region needs, therefore, to establish a framework and mechanism to strengthen regional solidarity and provide for mutual peace and security."[29] In this regard, major regional actors explicitly related the enhancement of security to fostering democracy, transparency, and respect for human rights. SADC's executive secretary, Kaire Mbuende, noted that the new postapartheid era would be one of forging a "common value system in politics and economics."[30]

Putting democracy and human rights at the center of security coincided with the global concerns for pluralism and the Africa-wide shift in conceptions of security to embrace peoples and governments. As part of this conceptual shift, African policymakers spoke of the intimate links between national and regional security and prescribed mechanisms for common security and good neighborliness.[31] Southern Africa embraced these views of security, as demonstrated in the SADC Ministerial Workshop on Democracy, Peace, and Security in July 1994, which Nathan and Honwana describe as a "watershed event" in the growing debate on the nonmilitary dimensions of security. In August 1994, an SADC summit of heads of state approved the creation of a sector within SADC that would deal with politics, diplomacy, international relations, defense, and security.[32]

A civil conflict in Lesotho starting in January 1994 helped define the parameters of the emerging norm on peace and security. The first phase of the crisis began when the government of elected prime minister Ntsu Mokhehle, faced with a mutiny from a faction of the Lesotho military, requested South African military help to neutralize the army. Instead of intervening militarily, however, South Africa, Botswana, and Zimbabwe created an informal regional task force to reconcile the warring factions.[33] Zimbabwe's foreign minister, Nathan Shamuyarira, described the task force as the "beginning of regional security cooperation to ensure peace and stability in the region. It was an arrangement to defend democratic trends in our region and to ward off the dictatorship and militarism present in other parts of the world."[34] In the same vein, SADC's executive secretary, Kaire Mbuende, noted that there was a need for new structures to deal with political crises in member states, since "political instability in Lesotho poses a serious threat to peace and democracy in the region."[35]

In August 1994, the collapse of civilian authority was exacerbated by the decision of King Letsie III to depose the prime minister. This action, supported by the army and civilian opposition, led to more clashes in Maseru between antimonarchists and security forces. Responding to this phase of the crisis, Presidents Mandela, Masire, and Mugabe launched another round of high-level diplomatic efforts to convince the king to reverse the royal coup. Mugabe reiterated that the region would not settle for anything less than reinstatement of Mokhehle: "What we want is for the people of Lesotho to find a solution to this problem of unconstitutionality. If they are not able to find that solution, then we will find it for them and that might mean imposing sanctions."[36] In coordinated action on the beleaguered state, the three states interspersed negotiations with military pressure and threats of economic sanctions. As result, the king reversed the unconstitutional decree by restoring democratic order in September 1994.[37]

The collective intervention in the restoration of democracy in Lesotho featured significantly in subsequent efforts to define the principles and strategies of what became the SADC Organ for Politics, Defense, and Security, approved in June 1996. As the security arm of SADC, the Organ's objectives are safeguarding the region against instability from within and without; promoting political cooperation and common political values (including the promotion of democracy and human rights); developing a common foreign policy; establishing security and defense cooperation through conflict prevention, management, and resolution; developing preventive diplomacy mechanisms with punitive measures as a last resort; establishing sustainable peace and security through peacemaking and peacekeeping; developing a collective security capacity and mutual defense pact; developing a regional peacekeeping capacity; coordinating the participation of members in international and regional peacekeeping operations; and addressing extraregional conflicts that affect peace and security in southern Africa.[38]

From its inception, the SADC Organ had tenuous relations with SADC's economic sectors, a consequence of a long-standing dispute between Zimbabwe and South Africa over its mandate and legal framework. Whereas Zimbabwe preferred a more autonomous security mechanism on the lines of the previous FLS, South Africa and most of the SADC members insisted that the Organ must operate fully within the overall institutional framework of the SADC. Moreover, a majority of SADC members were wary of allocating responsibility for regional security to a single state in the contemporary context of shared roles and collective duties. To reconcile these positions, SADC agreed on rotating the chairmanship of the Organ among the heads of state on an annual basis and placed the oversight responsibilities in the ministerial Interstate Defense and Security Committee. Despite these provisions, Mugabe appropriated the position as initial chair of the Organ (remaining unchallenged until 2000) in order to control its operation. Steeped in two competing visions of regional leadership, the conflicts between Zimbabwe and South Africa on the Organ's institutional autonomy could be held in abeyance as long as SADC faced no serious regional crisis.

Although the implementation of most of the provisions of the SADC Organ has proceeded piecemeal because of uneven resource and political commitments and different magnitudes of security threats, there was significant progress in joint military exercises and training for peacekeeping. This progress was exemplified by two SADC multinational military peacekeeping exercises, one in Zimbabwe in September 1997 and one in South Africa in April 1999.[39] Even though SADC has not formally created a peacekeeping force, observers have hailed these exercises as precursors to the region's indigenous capacity for peacekeeping. In 1999, SADC's Interstate Defense and Security Committee proposed to set up a brigade-size multilateral force that promises to broaden the support base of southern Africa's regional peacekeeping capabilities.[40] In another critical area of security coordination, SADC heads of police created the Southern African Regional Police Chiefs Cooperation Organization (SARPCCO) in August 1995 to foster strategies in combating cross-border crime. This action was followed by the 1996 SADC Protocol on Illicit Drug Trafficking.[41]

The resurgence of domestic conflict in Lesotho and the DRC in 1998 tested the sturdiness of SADC's new security institutions and exposed the limits of forging a regional foreign policy. The previous crisis in Lesotho established a diplomatic practice whereby core SADC states intervened without specific authorization from their regional allies. Lesotho was again plunged into severe instability after three opposition parties demanded the annulment of the May 1998 election results, accusing the ruling party of massive electoral fraud. Four months of election protests led to the complete collapse of the civilian order, and when sections of the Lesotho military joined the opposition protests, the government requested South African military intervention. In September 1998, 600 South African troops (later joined by 300 from Botswana) intervened in SADC's name to restore law and order in an operation that unexpectedly met intense resistance from the rebellious military. As John Seiler has argued, South African intervention lacked genuine consultation with and formal endorsement by SADC, under whose aegis the initiatives took place: "The decision to intervene involved no more than an informal consultation by acting [South African] president Mangosuthu Buthelezi with a few Southern African Development Community (SADC) presidents. Hiding the unilateral nature of that intervention with the last-minute resort to Botswana troops and then insisting it was a SADC operation was deceitful."[42]

In a major breakthrough in October 1998, the parties reached an agreement to form a transitional committee that would prepare for fresh elections in eighteen months. As the constitutionally elected government gained more control, South African and Botswana troops withdrew in April 1999.[43] The intervention by South Africa and Botswana contained the renegade elements in the Lesotho military and allowed the Lesotho civilian opposition and the government to settle their differences in a more stable environment, but it reinforced the informal nature of decisionmaking and cast doubts on multilateral coordination of security by the SADC Organ.

The absence of a genuine and broad-based national and regional consultative process was to afflict SADC's foray into the DRC beginning in August 1998. President Laurent Kabila's decision to join SADC in 1997 expanded Congo's economic and security options, but it invariably saddled southern Africa with all the baggage and insecurities of the Great Lakes region, which René Lemarchand and John F. Clark illustrate in their chapters. When his initial allies, Uganda and Rwanda, turned against him in August 1998, Angola,

Namibia, and Zimbabwe intervened militarily, invoking SADC security arrangements. The South Africans, in contrast, saw the conflict as a civil one, to be resolved by negotiation. At the Non-Aligned Summit in Durban, South Africa, in September 1998 Zimbabwe stood firm in its determination to respond with military force to the rebel threat in the DRC. Although Mugabe successfully checked South Africa's opposition to intervention by deploying an SADC force, the stalemate in the war forced Zimbabwe's acceptance of mediation in Lusaka, Zambia, led by President Chiluba.[44]

Despite the peace process, the escalation of the war widened splits within SADC, exposing the fragility of institutions for collective security. In addition, it highlighted the persistence of decision-making practices that characterized African foreign policies in most of the postcolonial period. The intervention reveals that weak regimes confronted by multiple domestic challenges are most likely to seek solace in debilitating foreign policy adventures irrespective of countervailing pressures from their domestic and international environments. Thus although Angola, Namibia, and Zimbabwe have described their intervention as a defense of the DRC's territorial sovereignty, domestic and foreign critics have cast doubt on their motives and capabilities, accusing them of frittering away resources in pursuit of questionable objectives. Mugabe interpreted the rebel insurgency in the DRC as a threat to his regional authority. In Zimbabwe, where Mugabe made the decision to intervene without consulting his cabinet or parliament, opposition parties have used the intervention to campaign against the government. As Margaret Dongo, president of the Zimbabwe Union of Democrats, asked: "Why are our children dying in the DRC? What does Zimbabwe as a country stand to benefit except that a few corrupt individuals are lining their pockets with diamonds from that country?"[45] Similarly, civic and opposition groups in Namibia have castigated the government of Sam Nujoma for devoting enormous resources to a foreign policy venture that serves more private than state interests.[46]

The DRC war has forced the intervening partners to enhance defense budgets at the expense of social and infrastructural investment, consolidating the influence of the military in regional politics and national contests over the parameters of state power. The impact of the DRC conflict on SADC institutions has been even more far-reaching. Despite Chiluba's mediation, the strains on relations within southern Africa culminated in a decision spearheaded by Mugabe in

April 1999 to create a new defense pact of SADC states embroiled in the war. With most SADC states reluctant to provide concrete support to the DRC, Mugabe used his role as chairman of the SADC Organ to formalize the pact among Angola, the DRC, Namibia, and Zimbabwe. Although the signatories invited other SADC states to join the new defense pact, the latter were unwilling to be dragged into the DRC conflict.[47] The defense pact formalized the role of SADC allied forces in the DRC, but the dilemma became whether Mugabe could persist in using the SADC Organ as a unilateral instrument for his own aggressive foreign policy.

At a SADC summit in Maputo, Mozambique, in September 1999, the leaders confronted the unresolved question of the Organ's institutional standing by dissuading Mugabe from using it without consultation. Although Mugabe retained the chairmanship of the Organ for six months, under pressure from other SADC leaders, he agreed to make future security decisions in consultation with South Africa, Namibia, and Mozambique. In the face of a majority view that any political and security arm should be clearly and firmly tied to SADC's procedures to prevent any single head of state to act alone in future, the summit authorized the SADC Council of Ministers to "review the operations of all SADC institutions, including the Organ on Defense, Politics and Security and report back within six months."[48]

The Maputo compromise preempted widening rifts in SADC over Zimbabwe's leadership of the SADC Organ. It also allowed new initiatives to break the deadlock, culminating in the Piggs Peak Draft, a set of proposals agreed upon at a ministerial meeting in Swaziland in May 2000 and ratified in Harare in November 2000.

Under these proposals, the ministers recommended that the SADC Organ should be an integral part of SADC's structures rather than an autonomous entity subject to manipulation by a single leader. Although SADC leaders will still have to study and approve these proposals, their adoption by the ministers underscored the determination to curtail Mugabe's stranglehold over a critical regional institution.[49] In the short term, SADC still confronts the problem of insulating its institutional security structures from perennial conflicts. But the lessons from the smoldering war in the DRC and what some have called the "Congo effect" on southern Africa might be to encourage renewed thinking about the kinds of institutions for collective security.

No less severe has been the specter of civil war in Angola, a symbol of continuing insecurity for peoples and states in southern

Africa. At the end of the Cold War, the UN, Western powers, and regional states renewed their efforts to find a peaceful settlement to
the conflict, but the stakes and positions of the ruling MPLA and its
opponent, the National Union for the Total Independence of Angola
(UNITA), have remained almost constant. Portugal negotiated a
peace agreement, the Bicesse Accord, in 1991 that was an attempt to
end the conflict through unification of rival armies and an elected
government of national unity. When UNITA lost in the September
1992 presidential elections, its leader, Jonas Savimbi, refused to accept the results and plunged the country back into a bloody war.[50]
Under renewed UN and regional efforts, the two parties signed another agreement, the Lusaka Protocol, in November 1994, but peace
in Angola has remained illusive, as the country has been bifurcated
between two movements with the impoverished population caught in
between. UNITA's control over diamond mines has afforded its army
the equipment and skills to occupy one-third of the country and control the borders with the DRC, Namibia, and Zambia.[51]

Since the mid-1990s, Angola's foreign policy has focused on
mobilizing international sanctions against UNITA and reinforcing its
military capability to recapture lost territory. Although SADC lent
diplomatic support to Angola, attempts to secure military support faltered repeatedly.[52] Moreover, Angola's relations with Zambia were
strained by accusations that Chiluba's government allowed the flow
of military assistance and logistical supplies to UNITA-held territory
in western Angola. On three separate occasions starting in 1997, Angola warned Zambia of possible military action if Chiluba's government continued to aid Savimbi's military machine. As the accusations mounted and Angola seemed ready to retaliate against Zambia,
SADC states appointed a mediation committee to reconcile them. In
early 1999 at the UN, there were heightened tensions when Angola
publicly condemned the Chiluba regime for continuing to supply
UNITA, naming former ministers in Chiluba's government as key
players in arms deals in exchange for UNITA diamonds.[53]

The April 1999 defense pact among Angola, the DRC, Namibia,
and Zimbabwe was in part a reflection of these countries' disap-
pointment with the muted regional response to Angola's call for
stronger regional action against UNITA. A more binding arrangement that promotes concerted action against their combined enemies
would prove more useful to the DRC and Angola, as was demonstrated in the latter half of 1999 when Angola used the DRC territory

to oust UNITA from some of its entrenched positions. As a result, the Angolan army recaptured UNITA's headquarters in the central highland towns of Bailundo and Andulo in October 1999.[54]

Similarly, Namibia reversed its long-standing neutrality in the war by inviting Angola to use the Caprivi Strip and the northern region for attacks on Savimbi. This reversal came in the wake of a growing alliance between UNITA and the Caprivi Liberation Army (CLA), which in August 1999 mounted a surprise attack on Namibian government installations in the Caprivi Strip. Subsequently, leaders of the CLA, claiming marginalization in Namibia, announced plans to secede through guerrilla warfare. Furthermore, the CLA tried to mobilize Lozi-speaking compatriots in Botswana and Zambia to agitate for separatist goals.[55] In December 1999, Angolan and Namibian troops captured UNITA's stronghold of Jamba, a victory that gave the government control of the southern border and closed UNITA's main supply lines from Namibia. In giving up its neutrality in the Angolan war, however, Namibia has invited retaliation from UNITA and its sympathizers. Since the Angolan-Namibian military collaboration began, northern Namibia has witnessed an upsurge of violence and insecurity, shaking a ten-year period of stability. With the militarization of the Angola-Namibia border, human rights organizations have accused Angolan and Namibian security forces of human rights violations in the volatile Okavango region.[56]

The shifts in regional alliances and Angola's military power balance made Zambia's security more precarious. When thousands of UNITA troops retreated into the vast and remote areas along the Angola-Zambia border, the MPLA put pressure on Zambia to grant permission for attacks against UNITA from its territory. But Zambian policymakers, wary of reversing their neutrality in the conflict, rejected this move, fearing that there were no guarantees that the MPLA would defeat UNITA militarily. Massive military mobilization by Angola and Zambia along their common border in early 2000 began an era of tensions in bilateral relations. Angola launched cross-border air and ground attacks in January and March, leaving several Zambians dead and creating a new wave of internally displaced persons.[57]

The Angolan conflict illustrates the ability of old conflicts to spawn new ones and, in turn, complicate the efforts of regional institutions to evolve predictable security mechanisms. The conflict has engulfed the DRC, Namibia, and Zambia in new levels of violence and insurgencies, and SADC's dream of regional stability remains distant. The Angolan war will continue to draw in more states and nonstate actors. Confronted with Savimbi's tenacity, SADC has vacillated between negotiations and diplomatic isolation; in September 1999 it finally decided, against South African opposition, to label him a war criminal. This action diminished the chances of a negotiated settlement without resolving the underlying military stalemate. Thus twenty-five years after it began, the Angolan conflict has essentially settled into a familiar pattern of oscillating military fortunes where one of the protagonists makes fleeting gains that are then extinguished by the revitalization of the fighting capacity of its opponent. In breaking with SADC's position on Savimbi, South African foreign minister Nkosana Dlamini-Zuma, noted: "The MPLA government has not won the war for 30 years and is not about to win it now."[58]

■ THE FUTURE OF FOREIGN POLICY MAKING
IN SOUTHERN AFRICA

South Africa's major disagreement with its neighbors over Angola and the DRC centers on the basis of its foreign policy: domestic values and priorities. First, it prefers negotiated solutions in war-torn societies because its successful transition resulted from compromises crafted through multiparty negotiations. Second, the enormous tasks of postapartheid reconstruction leave few resources for external military and political engagements.[59] Even though self-serving, this enunciation of norms and objectives that undergird foreign policy puts a clear perspective on future trajectories of decisionmaking throughout southern Africa.

If foreign policy were closely aligned with prevailing resources and capabilities, a bulk of southern African states would not have much in the way of external commitments. Realistically, beyond the traditional roles of participation in international institutions in order to derive material and symbolic goals, foreign policy already occupies a secondary position in most of these states. The many socioeconomic ills buffeting the state in the early twenty-first century are forcing state elites to choose among diminishing priorities. But for individual states, aligning domestic and foreign policy is a process predicated on nurturing a consensus about national interests and the means of attaining them. Where foreign policy is tied to inchoate national interests and where it reflects the insecurity of elites, the alignment of domestic and foreign policy objectives is bound to be a contested one, as revealed in Mugabe's behavior. Where there are no organizing domestic values that inform foreign policy decisions, erratic and ruinous actions often result.

Southern Africa's greatest strength has been the legacy of institution building, which lends meaning to foreign policy actions of otherwise poor and weak states. Regional aggregation around critical issue areas since the 1960s gave elites a set of collaborative mechanisms in which to project their voices. Over time, these institutions became the embodiment of shared responsibilities, particularly with the emergence of new collective challenges. Moreover, as Africa's marginalization in the world heightened, regional economic institutions seemed to offer the potential for marshaling collective clout to bargain with external actors. But SADC's function as the coalescence of southern African foreign policies and the organizational framework for problem solving is still hostage to unresolved national questions.

Weak states furnish fragile bases for regionalism. By the same token, regionalism might not be an antidote for the problems that engulf weak states. As southern Africa has tried to deepen economic integration and enhance security collaboration, it has found itself mired in conflicts that regional institutions are insufficiently prepared to handle. What was thus supposed to be a smooth transition from a political and security front line to a common economic house has resulted in new sources of antagonism among elites about the nature and purpose of institutions. More than ever before, effective regional institutions are dependent on strong states. This is why the debilitating conflicts in Angola, the DRC, Lesotho, and Zimbabwe nullify institution building and postpone the creation of sturdy mechanisms for both economic development and security. As a reluctant hegemon, South Africa is unwilling and unable to shoulder the escalating burdens of jump-starting weak neighbors.

SADC is incapable of meeting problems of internal implosion and civil wars, and its role in building values and norms has been equally problematic. This is understandable, however, since rule making by regional institutions is intimately tied to leadership, that is, the ability to provide overarching incentives and disincentives for the enforcement of rules. Since the 1990s, the experiments at norm building for

security have yielded ambiguous outcomes. Democracy and pluralism have been on the regional agenda, but SADC has enforced them
selectively: Its military intervention in Lesotho put subtle pressures
on Swaziland to democratize, but it has been conspicuously silent
when Zambia and Zimbabwe have infringed on human rights and
civil liberties.[60]

As a result of SADC's rhetorical commitment to these values,
most of southern Africa is replete with fragile and unconsolidated
democracies, straining under the weight of popular pressure and inadequate channels of representation. The promise of democracy has
waned as constitutional amendments, clampdowns on press free-
doms, human rights abuses, and political intolerance have reap-
peared.[61] Part of the reason is that old and new regimes assumed that
multiparty structures and elections were the end rather than the start
of democratization. Moreover, there has been a tendency to implant
democratic structures without supportive liberal and independent institutions that guarantee the circulation and competition of ideas.
Steven Chan has correctly described Zambia and Zimbabwe as cases
of "troubled pluralisms," a term that seems to have wider regional
application.[62]

Nongovernmental groups (NGOs) have emerged on the margins
of SADC as alternative purveyors of norms and policies that have a
regional reach. Sandra MacLean has examined several ways in
which NGOs have influenced policy: "Some directly advocate a regional approach to security and peace building in Southern Africa.
Others inadvertently contribute to regionness when they organize regionally for functional benefits, such as having a broader base of expertise available nearby for dealing with specific interests. Finally,
external funding agencies frequently deal with NGOs on a regional
basis because of the economies of scale provided, thereby helping to
reinforce a sense of regionness."[63]

Since the early 1990s, various national civic associations have
coalesced into regional networks and initiated conventions to guide
state and interstate behavior on human rights, gender equity, and environmental security. Regional institutions such as the African Center for the Constructive Resolution of Disputes (ACCORD) and the
Southern African Human Rights Network (SAHRNGON) reflect the
determination of NGOs to have a permanent voice on matters of regional security and stability.[64] Drawing from the experience of nonstate actors, opposition parties in eight SADC states in February

1999 launched an initiative that would create a regional alliance that would counter oppressive measures by governing parties.[65]

Alliance building across all sectors of societies in southern Africa is a significant trend in regional socialization and constituency building for foreign policy. Yet hostile domestic environments and inordinate dependence on external sources for sustenance limit NGOs. Their effectiveness in regional policymaking ultimately hinges on open and transparent national domains, where meaningful mobilization on foreign policy questions ought to begin. In the absence of successful coalition building at national levels, NGOs are likely to be consigned to the margins of foreign policy decisionmaking. Moreover, regional aggregation around concerns such as health, immigration, and environment security cannot substitute for broad-based consultative mechanisms anchored in strong independent national institutions. As southern Africa's NGOs become more dependent on donor funding for a wide range of goals, their relationships with weak governments are bound to deteriorate.[66]

The fading of the decolonization front line has exposed multiple sources of insecurity that continue to tax foreign policy makers. In between the permanent civil war of Angola and the relative stability of Botswana is a string of institutional experiments that have not yielded much regime stability. As the political and economic gains in southern Africa since the early 1990s face the threat of persisting internal conflicts, intolerant political practices, and fragile economies, there has been an equal loss in the momentum for collective foreign policy making. The economic and security interdependence fostered by previous patterns of behavior and institution building guarantees long-term prospects of collaboration, but in the medium term, southern Africa is incapable of insulating itself from the daunting problems embroiling most of its members.

Highlighting the dilemma of regional interdependence is the fate that hangs over Zimbabwe, described by one opposition critic as "a state whose leader is commonly perceived as a deranged despot."[67] Embroiled in its worst economic and political crisis since independence, Mugabe resorted to populist incitement of landless blacks to seize control of white-owned farms, in turn diminishing Zimbabwe's international and regional stature. In February 1999, almost a year before the constitutional crisis, Amnesty International urged southern African leaders to speak to their Zimbabwean counterparts "to reaffirm the importance of the rule of law, the freedom of the press and the independence of the judiciary. . . . If the rule of law is undermined in Zimbabwe, it will have an impact on other southern African countries."[68] A year later, the Mugabe government launched an organized assault on white farmers by encouraging war veterans and their supporters to occupy more than 1,000 white-owned farms across Zimbabwe. As the crisis deepened, South Africa witnessed foreign capital flows that depreciated the rand and exacerbated economic difficulties among SADC countries.[69]

Despite international and regional calls for a more forceful SADC response to arrest the deteriorating situation, a summit meeting of the leaders of Zimbabwe, South Africa, Mozambique, and Namibia praised Mugabe's actions. Although ostensibly favoring private diplomacy on Zimbabwe, the SADC approach seemed to tarnish southern Africa's efforts to build predictable institutions. In May 2000, after signing legislation that allowed him to seize white-owned farms without compensation, Mugabe took the crusade to the region by urging landless Namibians and South Africans to follow Zimbabwe's example: "It is a simple solution. If the other neighboring countries have problems similar to the ones we have encountered, why not apply the same solution as Zimbabwe. If the white commercial farmers are ready to discuss with you and give land then there is no need for a fight. But in Zimbabwe the British are not ready and we are making them ready now."[70]

Zimbabwe's political woes have led to a decline of its economy and contributed to the negative international perceptions of the economic prospects of southern Africa as a whole. Emboldened by the groundswell of internal opposition in the aftermath of the Zimbabwe elections of June 2000, President Thabo Mbeki departed from South Africa's quiet diplomacy by issuing an unprecedented condemnation of Mugabe for his disregard for the rule of law and his country's economic decline. In addition, in November 2000 Mbeki enlisted Nigeria's president, Olusegun Obasanjo, in forming a diplomatic initiative to prod Mugabe into a solution to the deteriorating land and economic issue.[71]

Less certain was how SADC and South Africa, in particular, would deal in the long run with growing opposition to the monarchy in Swaziland. In November 2000, 800 Swazi pro-democracy groups led by the Swaziland Federation of Trade Unions (SFTU) crossed the border into South Africa and issued the Nelspruit Declaration, an ultimatum to the government to lift the ban on political parties and the twenty-seven-year-old state of emergency and create a constitutional monarchy. With the tacit support of the massive Confederation of South African Trade Unions, COSATU, the SFTU has emerged as a leading voice of dissent in Swaziland, where real political debates have been absent. In a collaborative show of force, demonstrators from SFTU and COSATU blocked a major border-crossing post in late November 2000 in an effort to cripple the Swazi economy.[72]

Like the Lesotho conflict in the 1990s, internal stirrings in Swaziland will test the regional resolve to reconcile norms of participation, accountability, and responsiveness with the established but declining norms of sovereignty. Equally significant, as Swaziland degenerates into violence and unrest reminiscent of Lesotho, the pro-democracy movement will increasingly look on South Africa as the regional power to take the lead in intervening to resolve the internal conflict. With strong allies in South Africa's trade union movement, Swazi opposition might potentially force the hand of Pretoria and its allies to engage in vigorous preventive diplomacy, SADC's professed approach to the region's conflicts.

■ NOTES

1. For other recent analysis of South Africa's foreign policy see Marie Muller, "South African Diplomacy and Security Complex Theory," *Round Table*, no. 352 (1999): 585–620; Graham Evans, "South Africa's Foreign Policy After Mandela: Mbeki and His Concept of an African Renaissance," *Round Table*, no. 352 (1999): 621–628; Peter Vale and Ian Taylor, "South Africa's Postapartheid Foreign Policy Five Years On—From Pariah to 'Just Another Country,'" *Round Table*, no. 352 (1999): 629–634; Janis van der Westhuizen, "South Africa's Emergence as a Middle Power," *Third World Quarterly* 19, no. 3 (1998): 435–455; and William Gutteridge, "South Africa's Future Defense and Security: Identifying National Interest," *Conflict Studies*, no. 298 (April 1997): 1–24.

2. For analyses of the historical patterns see Kenneth Grundy, *Accommodation and Confrontation in Southern Africa: The Limits of Independence* (Berkeley: University of California Press, 1973); and Gilbert M. Khadiagala, *Allies in Adversity: The Frontline States in Southern African Security, 1975–1993* (Athens: Ohio University Press, 1994).

3. Gilbert Khadiagala, "Regional Dimensions of Sanctions," in Neta C. Crawford and Audie Klotz, *How Sanctions Work* (London: Macmillan, 1999), pp. 248–253. For some analysis of Tanzania and Zambian foreign policy making see K. Mathews, "Tanzania's Foreign Policy as a Frontline State in the Liberation of Southern Africa," *Africa Quarterly* 21, no. 2

(1981): 41–61; and Douglas Anglin, *Zambian Crisis Behavior: Confronting Rhodesia's Unilateral Declaration of Independence* (Montreal: McGill University Press, 1996).

4. Stephen Davies, "Facing Goliath: Zimbabwe's Role in Conflict Resolution in Southern Africa," *South Africa International* 21, no. 4 (1991): 244–255; and Audie Klotz, "Race and Nationalism in Zimbabwean Foreign Policy," *Round Table*, no. 327 (1993): 255–279.

5. Andrew Ngwiri, "Chiluba Should Get It Right: Kaunda Is a Citizen of the World and a Zambian," *Electronic Mail and Guardian*, April 4, 1999. See also Chisepo J. J. Mphaisha, "Retreat from Democracy in Post One-Party State Zambia," *Journal of Commonwealth and Comparative Politics* 34, no. 2 (July 1996): 65–84.

6. Stephen Chan, "Democracy in Southern Africa: The 1990 Elections in Zimbabwe and 1991 Elections in Zambia," *Round Table*, no. 332 (1992): 183–200; and Lisa Laakso, "Relationship Between the State and Civil Society in the Zimbabwean Elections 1995," *Journal of Commonwealth and Comparative Politics* 34, no. 3 (1996): 218–234.

7. Cameron Hume, *Ending Mozambique's War: The Role of Mediation and Good Offices* (Washington, DC: U.S. Institute of Peace, 1994).

8. Jonathan Mayuyuka Kaunda, "The State and Society in Malawi," *Commonwealth and Comparative Politics* 36, no. 1 (1998): 48–67; Clement Ng'ong'ola, "Managing the Transition to Pluralism in Malawi: Legal and Constitutional Arrangements," *Journal of Commonwealth and Comparative Politics* 34, no. 2 (1996): 85–110.

9. *Africa Research Bulletin: Economic, Financial, and Technical Series* (August 16–September 15, 1996): 12689; *Africa Research Bulletin: Economic, Financial, and Technical Series* (July 16–August 15, 1997): 13101; and *Africa Research Bulletin: Economic, Financial, and Technical Series* (August 16–September 15, 1999): 14017.

10. See Julius Nyerere, "Foreign—Nyerere," South African Press Association, October 18, 1994.

11. David Beresford, "Mandela Rests as South African Team Attends Regional Summit," *Guardian*, August 30, 1994; Antonia Ferreira, "South Africa Joins SADC, Will Host Next Summit," South African Press Association, August 29, 1994.

12. Brendan Boyle, "Southern Africa and Europe to Meet on Trade," South African Press Association, September 1, 1994; Debra Percival, "Development—Africa: SADC Ministers' Meeting to 'Break New Ground,'" Inter Press Service Feature, September 1, 1994; Ramesh Jaura, "Development—Africa: NGOs Say EU/SADC Berlin Declaration Lacks Bite," Inter Press Service Feature, September 7, 1994.

13. John Battersby, "Striving for Links After Decades of Hostility," *Christian Science Monitor*, September 21, 1994, p. 8; Dave Chibesa, "America Revisits SADC," *Times of Zambia* (Lusaka), April 13, 1999.

14. "SADC: Protocol with US," *Africa Research Bulletin: Economic, Financial, and Technical Series* (August 16–September 15, 1999): 14017; "SADC-US Forum Praised as Great Success," Pan African News Agency, May 12, 2000.

15. For ANC's foreign policy positions see ANC, Department of International Affairs, "Foreign Policy Perspective in a Democratic South Africa," October 1993; and Nelson Mandela, "South Africa's Future Foreign Policy," *Foreign Affairs* 27, no. 5 (November-December 1993): 86–97.

16. "SADC Customs Union," South African Press Association, January 20, 1995.

17. Richard Gibbs, "Regional Integration in Post-Apartheid Southern Africa: The Case Renegotiating the South African Customs Union," *Journal of Southern African Studies* 23, no. 1 (March 1997): 67–86; and *Africa Research Bulletin: Economic, Financial, and Technical Series* (February 16–March 15, 1998): 12477.

18. "Competition Grows Between SADC and PTA as Both Take On Trade Issues," *SouthScan,* June 17, 1994.

19. Margaret A. Novicki, "Interview with Kaire Mbuende: Strengthening Southern Africa," *Africa Report* 39, no. 4 (July-August 1994): 46; Jonathon Rees, "SADC," South African Press Association, August 29, 1994.

20. Quoted in Emelia Sithole, "Malawi—SADC," South African Press Association, January 31, 1995.

21. "Why Tanzania Chose SADC Not COMESA," *Africa Research Bulletin: Economic, Financial, and Technical Series* (July 16–August 15, 1999): 14018.

22. Roger Dean, "Tanzania Finds COMESA Irrelevant to Its Economic Needs," *Electronic Mail and Guardian,* September 4, 2000.

23. For debates surrounding Uganda's application see "Kenya Not Ready to Compete in SADC," *East African,* September 11, 2000.

24. "SADC Wary About Uganda's Entry," *East African,* September 11, 2000.

25. *Africa Research Bulletin: Economic, Financial, and Technical Series* (August 16–September 15, 1996): 12689; and *Africa Research Bulletin: Economic, Financial, and Technical Series* (July 16–August 15, 1997): 13101.

26. *Africa Research Bulletin: Economic, Financial, and Technical Series* (August 16–September 15, 1996): 12689; *Africa Research Bulletin: Economic, Financial, and Technical Series* (July 16–August 15, 1997): 13101.

27. "South Africa: Investor or Imperialist?" *Africa Research Bulletin: Economic, Financial, and Technical Series* (December 16, 1999–January 15, 2000): 14164.

28. See, for instance, "Namibia Urged to Look Beyond Customs Union," Pan African News Agency, June 9, 1999.

29. Laurie Nathan and Joao Honwana, "After the Storm: Common Security and Conflict Resolution in Southern Africa," *Arusha Papers: Working Series on Southern African Security* (Center for Foreign Relations, Dar es Salaam), no. 3 (February 1995): 14–22. See also Hussein Solomon and Jakkie Cilliers, "The Southern African Development Community and Small Arms Proliferation," in Virginia Gamba, ed., *Society Under Siege: Licit Responses to Illicit Arms,* Institute for Strategic Studies, Towards Collaborative Peace Series, vol. 2, South Africa, 1998, p. 80; and Gilbert Khadiagala, "Confidence-Building Measures in Sub-Saharan Africa," in Michael Krepon

et al., eds., *Global Confidence Building: New Tools for Troubled Regions* (New York: St. Martin's Press, 1999), pp. 140–141.

30. Novicki, "Interview with Kaire Mbuende," p. 45.

31. For discussions of the new security conceptions see Africa Leadership Forum, *The Kampala Document: Towards a Conference on Security, Stability, Development and Cooperation in Africa* (Kampala, May 1991), pp. 9–10; Thomas Ohlson and Stephen John Stedman, *The New Is Not Yet Born: Conflict Resolution in Southern Africa* (Washington, DC: Brookings Institution, 1994); Willie Breytenbach, "Conflict in Sub-Saharan Africa: From the Frontline States to Collective Security" *Arusha Papers: A Working Series on Southern African Security,* no. 2 (February 1995): 8–9; and Susan Willet, "Demilitarization, Disarmament, and Development in Southern Africa," *Review of African Political Economy,* no. 77 (1998): 413–414.

32. Nathan and Honwana, "After the Storm," pp. 10–11; Gavin Cawthra, "Subregional Security: SADC," *Security Dialogue* 28, no. 2 (1997): 207–218.

33. For a summary of this phase of the conflict see "Lesotho: Call for Peace Conference," *Africa Research Bulletin: Political, Social, and Cultural Series* (June 1–30, 1994): 11480.

34. Quoted in *Africa Research Bulletin: Political, Social, and Cultural Series* (January 1–31, 1994): 11285.

35. Quoted in Anton Ferreira, "SADC—Import," South African Press Association, August 27, 1994.

36. Quoted in "Lesotho—Mugabe," South African Press Association, September 13, 1994.

37. Keniloe Phits'ane, "Lesotho—Politics: King, Premier Agree to Resolve Differences," Inter Press Service Feature, September 3, 1994; Keniloe Phits'ane, "Lesotho—Politics: Little Light at the End of the Tunnel," Inter Press Service Feature, September 22, 1994; "King Letsie III Restores Mokhehle," South African Press Association, September 3, 1994; Lawrence Keketso, "Lesotho—Signing," South African Press Association, September 14, 1994; "Lesotho: A 'Haitian Solution,'" *Africa Confidential,* September 23, 1994, p. 8.

38. Solomon and Cilliers, "The Southern African Development Community," pp. 80–81. See also Hussein Solomon, "Southern Africa: Security in the 1990s," *Strategic Analysis* 19, no. 3 (1996): 303–391.

39. For accounts of these exercises see Khadiagala, "Confidence-Building Measures in Sub-Saharan Africa," p. 141; "SADC Armies Ready for Peace Keeping Duties," Pan African News Agency, January 14, 1999; and Tony Lamberti, "SADC Troops Learn to Keep Peace," *Business Day,* April 23, 1999.

40. John Seiler, "Is Military Peacemaking Really Possible?" *Electronic Mail and Guardian,* April 8, 1999.

41. Solomon and Cilliers, "The Southern African Development Community," pp. 86–88.

42. Seiler, "Is Military Peacemaking Really Possible?"

43. For accounts of this phase of the conflict see William Boot, "The Lesotho Crisis Deepens," *Electronic Mail and Guardian,* July 31, 1998; Boot, "Meltdown in the Kingdom," *Electronic Mail and Guardian,* August

14, 1998; Alex Duval Smith, "South Africa Botches the Invasion," *Electronic Mail and Guardian,* September 23, 1998; and "Major Breakthrough for Lesotho," *Electronic Mail and Guardian,* October 15, 1998.

44. For the evolution of the conflict see Lewis Machipisa and Jean Baptiste Kayigamba, "Congo Conflict Spreads," *Electronic Mail and Guardian,* October 22, 1998; "Zimbabwe Rejects South African Peace Proposal," *Electronic Mail and Guardian,* January 28, 1999; and Howard Barrell, "Allies Pressure Kabila into Peace Deal," *Electronic Mail and Guardian,* February 5, 1999.

45. Daniel Manyandure, "Fighting the Richest Political Party in Africa," *Zimbabwe Standard* (Harare), April 4, 1999.

46. Dickson Jere, "Nujoma Explains His Intervention in DRC," *Post of Zambia* (Lusaka), April 15, 1999.

47. Iden Wetherell, "Mugabe Crafts a New Africa Defense Pact," *Electronic Mail and Guardian,* April 16, 1999. See also "As SADC Split Deepens, Kabila's Allies Renew Commitment to War," *Zimbabwe Independent* (Harare), April 16, 1999.

48. Howard Barrell, "SADC Stops Mugabe's Abuse," *Electronic Mail and Guardian,* September 17, 1999.

49. "SADC Clips Mugabe's Wings," *Zimbabwe Independent* (Harare) December 1, 2000.

50. Carrie Manning, "The Collapse of Peace in Angola," *Current History* 98, no. 628 (May 1999): 208–212.

51. For accounts of this phase of the war see Chris Gordon and Howard Barrell, "Angola's War Could Spill over Borders," *Electronic Mail and Guardian,* July 31, 1998; Victoria Brittain, "UN Pull-out an Admission of Failure," *Electronic Mail and Guardian,* January 19, 1999; Mercedes Sayagues, "Five Years of Promises Betrayed," *Electronic Mail and Guardian,* March 1, 1999.

52. "SADC: Should It Intervene?" *Africa Research Bulletin: Political, Social, and Cultural Series* (October 1–31, 1999): 13642.

53. "SADC Sets Meeting to Sort Out Angola," *Business Day,* no. 48, April 2–8, 1999; Ivor Powell, "Increased Fears of Zambia Aid to Angolan Rebels," *Electronic Mail and Guardian,* April 9, 1999.

54. "Angola: Bailundo Falls," *Africa Research Bulletin: Political, Social, and Cultural Series* (October 1–31, 1999): 13711–13713.

55. "Namibia: Could Caprivi Attack Have Regional Significance?" *Africa Research Bulletin: Political, Social, and Cultural Series* (August 1–31, 1999): 13639–13642.

56. "Namibia Sucked In," *Sunday Times,* January 9, 2000; "New Concerns as Angolan War Spills into Namibia," *Electronic Mail and Guardian,* December 27, 1999; "Namibia and Angola Accused of Human Rights Abuses," *Electronic Mail and Guardian,* January 27, 2000.

57. *Africa Research Bulletin: Political, Social, and Cultural Series* (January 1–31, 2000): 138820–138821.

58. Quoted in *Economist,* January 15, 2000.

59. For a summary of this position see *Financial Mail,* October 8, 1999. See also Evans, "South Africa's Foreign Policy After Mandela," pp.

624–628; and Muller, "South African Diplomacy and Security Complex Theory," pp. 585–612.

60. For an interesting critique of SADC's double standards see Rodger Chongwe, "Do We Still Need the SADC?" *Electronic Mail and Guardian,* September 28, 1998. See also Khabele Matlosa, "Democracy and Conflict in Post-Apartheid Southern Africa: Dilemmas of Social Change in Small States," *International Affairs* 74, no. 2 (1998): 319–337.

61. For perspectives on democratic change see John Saul, "Liberal Democracy vs. Popular Democracy in Southern Africa," *Review of African Political Economy,* no. 72 (1997): 219–236; Saul, "'For Fear of Being Condemned as Old Fashioned': Liberal Democracy vs. Popular Democracy in Sub-Saharan Africa," *Review of African Political Economy,* no. 73 (1997): 339–353; and Kenneth Good, "Accountable to Themselves: Predominance in Southern Africa," *Journal of Modern African Studies* 35, no. 4 (1997): 547–573.

62. Stephen Chan, "Troubled Pluralisms: Pondering an Indonesian Moment for Zimbabwe and Zambia," *Round Table,* no. 349 (1999): 61–76.

63. Sandra J. MacLean, "Peace Building and the New Regionalism in Southern Africa," *Third World Quarterly* 20, no. 5 (1999): 948.

64. Tabby Moyo, "SADC Challenged on Human Rights," *Electronic Mail and Guardian,* September 8, 1997.

65. Douglas Hampande, "SADC Opposition Seeks Alliance," *Times of Zambia,* February 17, 1999; and Kondwani Chirambo and Pamela Chinaka, "SADC Parliaments Want Accelerated Regional Integration," *Southern African Research and Documentation Center (SARDC),* May 31, 2000.

66. For analysis of limits of NGOs on foreign policy see Khadiagala, "Confidence-Building Measures in Sub-Saharan Africa," pp. 124, 153–156.

67. "Opposition Lashes Mugabe," British Broadcasting Corporation, *Summary of World News,* April 9, 2000.

68. "Apparitions in Zimbabwe," *Economist,* April 3, 1999, p. 38.

69. For analyses of the land-invasion crisis see Chris Erasmus, "Why South Africa Is 'Supporting' Mugabe," *Electronic Mail and Guardian,* May 1, 2000; Mercedes Sayagues, "A Leader out of Touch with the Modern World," *Electronic Mail and Guardian,* May 5, 2000; "U.S. Official Condemns Zimbabwe," Associated Press, May 9, 2000.

70. "Mugabe Urges Regional Land Grab," British Broadcasting Corporation, May 26, 2000.

71. "Pressure Mounts on Mugabe," *Zimbabwe Independent* (Harare), December 1, 2000.

72. "Swazi Army, Police Gear Up for Pro-Democracy Protests," African Eye News Service (South Africa), November 29, 2000.

8

South African Foreign Policy Decisionmaking in the African Context

Denis Venter

Postapartheid South Africa came into being amid expectations that its domestic transition would be accompanied by equally significant change in foreign policy. But many analysts argue that South Africa's new foreign policy lacks both vision and direction. In a sense, however, there has been a clear change in foreign policy orientation: an attempt to position South Africa within the international community and Africa.[1] The groundwork for this change was laid in the early 1990s when the reformist National Party government began to move away from old-style apartheid, dismantled the country's clandestinely developed nuclear weapons program, acceded to the Nuclear Non-Proliferation Treaty (NPT), and set out to win friends and influence abroad.

Since May 1994, the quest to become a respected world citizen has been accompanied by the concern to alleviate the material deprivation of the majority of South Africans, primarily by securing foreign investment and trade. To many critics, this concern and the country's broader-stated foreign policy goals are in tension. They complain that the new government has abandoned international principles in the search for economic advancement at any price.[2] Until very recently, there seems to have been no systematic and strategic analysis, either inside or outside the Department of Foreign Affairs (DFA), of how South Africa should conduct its foreign policy. Discussion of the government's conduct of international relations is seldom systematically linked to its stated goals, making it almost impossible to establish whether it is consistent in pursuing them.

■ DEFINING FOREIGN POLICY

Foreign policy is directed at, and implemented in, the environment external to the state; it is, therefore, that "area of governmental activity that is concerned with the relationship between the state and other actors, particularly other states in the international system."[3] Put differently, it is "the system of activities evolved by communities for changing the behavior of other states, and for adjusting their own activities to the international environment."[4] However, these definitions tell us little about foreign policy as a means of pursuing domestic goals. Taken a step further, foreign policy can denote actions articulated by the decisionmakers of a state vis-à-vis other states and international actors that are aimed to achieve goals defined as national interests. Thus foreign policy involves a dynamic application of relatively fixed interests to the international environment to develop a course of action, followed by the diplomatic implementation of guidelines and principles.[5]

Foreign policy seldom, if ever, proceeds logically and chronologically; its major procedures include translating interpretations of national interest into concrete goals, determining domestic and international factors related to these goals, analyzing and assessing the state's capabilities to pursue these goals, developing a plan of action to deal with these variables, and periodically evaluating progress toward the desired end. More often, it is difficult to assess the effects of foreign policy actions because short-term advantages must be weighed against long-term consequences, and some policy outcomes may contain a mixture of success and failure.[6]

■ NATIONAL INTEREST, NATIONAL IDENTITY, AND THE ROLE OF CIVIL SOCIETY

The debate on national interest and identity in South Africa has just started, and it goes to the heart of the process of internal democratization and reintegration into the international system and Africa. Most of the criticism leveled against South African foreign policy has tended to highlight the need for it to reflect the national interest.[7] Attempting to define the national interest, however, seems an elusive task because of the conflicting interests of civil society. Historically, governments have advanced the notion of the national interest as a common rallying point for conflicting internal interests and as a vehicle to conduct external relations. Although this approach may have had negative consequences for different groups in society, it also had at its core the positive aspect of coherence, encapsulated in the equation "national interest equals one nation and one vision." There are always tensions within groups and between them and the government on the definition of national interest.

A September 1996 Department of Foreign Affairs (DFA) and civil society workshop on South African foreign policy debated a suitable definition of national interest. Unsurprisingly, given the different groups present, there was no consensus that would provide clear-cut guidelines to foreign policy decisionmakers. What emerged from the meeting was a broad and vague statement that it is "the duty of government to promote the security and welfare of South Africa's citizens within the means at its disposal." Leaving the definition of national interest deliberately vague potentially gave the government wide latitude to justify any policy.

This debate missed the essential point that national interest is a multifaceted concept with conflicting hues and economic overtones that reflect the interests of different groups in civil society; there is no single national interest. Moreover, definitions of national interest depend primarily on the socioeconomic positions of both those entrusted with foreign policy making and those trying to influence the policymaking process.

Similarly, national identity is related to the social fabric of society, its politicoeconomic history, and the development challenges it faces.[8] These challenges involve consolidating a fledgling democracy and addressing its vast inequities. The prioritization of issues relating to South Africa's foreign policy at the political and economic levels should, therefore, be anchored in its national identity. This means that policymakers would have to make trade-offs, through the mediation of government institutions and representative forums of civil society in attempts to meet the security and welfare of the citizenry.

Although it is now generally accepted that civil society groups should become actively involved in foreign policy making—through

regular hearings before the Parliamentary Portfolio Committee on
Foreign Affairs (PPCFA) and the drafting of reports on key foreign
policy issues—these groups are still largely excluded from the foreign policy making process. [9] But there has been a conscious effort
by government departments involved in foreign affairs to solicit the
ideas and advice of academics and some nongovernmental organizations (NGOs) in the formulation of policies. Similarly, the press and
the electronic media have also played an important role in increasing
public awareness on foreign policy issues.

The involvement and participation of nonstate actors in foreign
policy making is, however, fraught with many dangers. First, there is
the danger that the co-optation of civil society structures in a consultative government mechanism might render them ineffective. The problem is that popular participation in foreign policy making can undermine the role of the state. This multiplicity of actors involved in policy
formulation encourages accusations of incoherence, inconsistency, and
opaqueness. Second, because a large number of South Africans are still
illiterate and uneducated, they do not have the intellectual resources to
enter into a public debate on foreign policy. Finally, there is a lack of
financial, organizational, and conceptual capacity in many organs of
civil society to educate the broader public, to facilitate dialogue between foreign policy makers and civil society generally, and to publish
information on and analyses of foreign policy issues.

■   SOUTH AFRICAN FOREIGN
     POLICY MAKERS AND STRATEGIES

As early as 1993, Nelson Mandela outlined the following underpinnings of South Africa's postapartheid foreign policy: the centrality
of human rights in international relations; embracing the economic,
social, and environmental spheres; the promotion of democracy
worldwide; justice, and respect for international law; peace as a goal
toward which all nations should strive through agreed upon nonvio-
lent mechanisms, including effective arms control regimes; the reflection of African concerns and interests in policy choices; and
growing economic cooperation in an interdependent world.[10] These
visionary and enlightened principles in foreign policy form a more
or less coherent belief system.[11]

An objective review of events since May 1994 suggests that these principles have, however, with few exceptions, been honored more in the breach than in the observance. Instead of stressing human rights, South Africa has sought to establish cordial relations with some of those who abuse human rights; instead of a concern for peacekeeping, there has been an insular attempt to avoid concrete engagements—except for the ill-advised military intervention in Lesotho in September 1998 and a promised military contingent (as part of a multinational peacekeeping force) to be sent to the Democratic Republic of Congo (DRC); instead of a clear commitment to Africa, there has been a perceived attempt to align the country with the developed nations of the world; and despite the advent of democracy, foreign policy making remains opaque to South African citizens (as, admittedly, it does in many other countries, whether democratic or authoritarian).[12] The claim that South African foreign policy has been "de-ideologized" only seems to confirm the quick flight from principle in international relations.[13]

The postapartheid government has insisted that it remains committed to human rights; in fact, it has used this issue as a reason for not selling arms to countries such as Turkey. Yet it retained good relations with Sani Abacha's Nigeria and Hassan al-Bashir's Sudan, both acknowledged human rights violators. Critics also insist that foreign policy is geared toward Western Europe and the United States, turning Africa into a concern, not a priority.[14] On the multilateral front, South Africa was welcomed into a host of intergovernmental organizations—such as the UN, the Commonwealth of Nations, the Non-Aligned Movement (NAM), the Organization of African Unity (OAU), and the Southern African Development Community (SADC)—but joined without much critical reflection on the implications of membership. Neither was much thought given to the problems within, for example, the OAU and NAM and South Africa's precise contribution to strengthen their capacity. South Africa's foreign policy is professed to be one of nonalignment, but nonalignment in the present context of international relations has lost much of its raison d'être. South Africa has joined these organizations to identify with Africa and to participate fully in international efforts toward disarmament, peacekeeping, and the creation of a more just world order, but there has been little activity in these areas besides intervention to secure an indefinite extension to the NPT.

The problem partly stems from the lack of consensus among key decisionmaking elites about the substance, process, and goals of foreign policy. Significantly, during the Mandela presidency, there were conflicting views as to the relative influence of President Nelson Mandela, Deputy President Thabo Mbeki, or Foreign Minister Alfred Nzo and their respective advisers—including Defense Minister Joe Modise and Safety and Security Minister Sydney Mufamadi. Evidence under the Mbeki presidency suggests that foreign policy making is an elite-driven, bureaucratic process in which decisions are concentrated in the hands of a strong president and an inner loop of senior ministers, notably Nkosazana Dlamini-Zuma, foreign affairs; Alec Irwin, trade and industry; Trevor Manuel, finance; and Mosioua Lekota, defense.

At times, prior to May 1999, President Mandela determined the foreign policy agenda without much criticism (or sanction) from other ministers or opposition leaders. The decision to write off Namibia's debt of some R 800 million was made during the president's state visit to that country without any cabinet deliberations or consultation with the African National Congress (ANC), let alone opposition parties. Highly personalized styles of policymaking and decisionmaking were common then and are even more common today under the Mbeki presidency.[15] Mandela's towering personality, international prestige, and stature made him an important figure in South Africa's foreign relations. His command and seeming domination of every major foreign policy decision almost overshadowed the role of the cabinet, parliament, and the DFA.[16] As a result, policy "often followed [the president's] public statements, rather than the other way around."[17] Nevertheless, ideally the cabinet—and, to a lesser extent, parliament—should maintain checks and balances on presidential authority. Procedurally, the president has to consult with and get the approval of the cabinet on every major foreign policy decision.[18]

President Mbeki is a very skilled statesman: While in exile, he was the ANC's chief diplomat, and his outlook is distinctly internationalist. Like Mandela, he has had a hand in fashioning the contours of South Africa's foreign relations; he has been the prime architect of reconfiguring South Africa's relations with Africa by articulating a visionary policy framework around the concept of an African renaissance, which advocates a renewal of the African continent by seeking African solutions to African problems.[19] In addition, the Co-ordination and Implementation Unit (CIU) in the office of

the president facilitates coordination across all government departments.[20] However, Mbeki's drive to centralize control (he is variously
regarded as a control freak) and run a backroom presidency—which
can be seen, for example, in the creation of a president's office in excess of 330 personnel and his control over key appointments—as
well as the circumvention of parliament in policymaking is, in itself,
an illustration of the fine balance between legitimate structuring to
ensure effective performance and an authoritarian government.[21]

Yet there is a need to imbue the professionals in the foreign
service with a sense of purpose and direction—they should know
where they are heading and what role they can play in contributing
constructively to stated goals. In spite of the positive image generated as a result of the energy Foreign Minister Dlamini-Zuma displayed in trying to secure a peace settlement in the DRC, early in
her term there were reports of great unhappiness in the ranks over
the role she played. Her management style and attitude allegedly led
to her falling out with her director-general, Jackie Selebi.[22] At the
core of these allegations rested the fear that foreign policy was being
run out of the president's office rather than the ministry and that, in
the words of more than one official, the department was "operating
as little more than the Foreign Minister's travel agency." The inherent danger in foreign policy being run out of the presidency is that it
becomes an executive, top-down practice rather than an output of the
integrated machinery of government.[23]

Usually, the foreign minister is a specialist with a technical
grasp of the complexities of day-to-day decisions and an apprecia-
tion of the larger internal and external operational environments. In
addition, he or she is the administrative head of the foreign ministry
and plays a decisionmaking and advisory role.[24] However, former
foreign minister Nzo was widely regarded as lacking authority, and
the DFA has been characterized as a "bureaucratic labyrinth."[25] Of
all government departments, its role as the custodian of foreign policy has been mired in controversy and subjected to contestation. The
DFA inherited a highly fragmented and ideologically polarized staff,
and the integration of old-style bureaucrats ("neo-mercantilists")
with a new corps of government officials ("internationalists") has
not been a smooth process.[26] Many critics, therefore, place the
blame for the current lack of policy on the DFA, noting that old-
order officials continued to predominate until recently, particularly
in missions abroad. Then there are internal departmental confusion

and incoherence: Budget cuts have left many key positions vacant, and affirmative action measures have decimated the middle and top strata of experienced officials. Consequently, foreign policy has been beset with tensions between continuity and change, pragmatism and principle.

In many cases, the DFA has also received contradictory cues from government. This department is also not the only arm of government responsible for foreign policy. The DFA is today more than ever competing with other institutions in performing its functions. One important competitor under the new regime is parliament, the PPCFA in particular. Others are the Department of Defense, the intelligence community, the Department of Trade and Industry, and civil society and public opinion in general.[27] Even provincial governments have increasingly become involved in foreign affairs.

Parliament has a distinct constitutional duty in government, since it is "the pre-eminent institution through which the public expresses its views concerning foreign policy."[28] In this context it is important to note that the PPCFA is a specialist, activist, multiparty body of representatives trying to ensure that parliament's oversight and review function is properly executed and that democratic procedures and principles are observed.[29] But a key feature of foreign policy making is the growing hostility between the DFA and the PPCFA. The executive ministry prefers that the parliamentary committee ignore the electorate generally when formulating policy. Although tension between government departments and parliamentary portfolio committees is an inevitable and healthy feature of the new constitutional order, the conflict between the DFA and the PPCFA seems particularly intense. It should be remembered that the primary function of parliamentarians is to legislate, ratify treaties, and approve budgets for government departments. Although the ratification of treaties and the approval of budgets have enhanced the position of the PPCFA, there is little or no foreign affairs legislation per se. The committee's role is largely reactive, and its very generalized input is often impaired by the fact that a foreign policy decision may be made before it has the opportunity to meet with government decisionmakers. Moreover, it does not work with the DFA in framing legislation, and its formal role is limited to applying sanctions on the department through, for example, obstructing the budget. This role makes an adversarial relationship more likely.[30] Interestingly, however, there seems to be little tension between the PPCFA and Mbeki (and before him, Mandela), who is widely seen as the real power in foreign policy making. Moreover, the ANC, through its National Executive Committee's Subcommittee on International Relations, is making regular, behind-the-scenes input on foreign policy.

The military, as well as the Department of Defense, has simply become one of several important actors in the foreign policy decisionmaking process. In southern African regional security matters, the South African National Defense Force (SANDF) is playing a key role in the operational planning of the SADC Organ on Politics, Defense, and Security through its involvement in the Inter-State Defense and Security Committee (ISDSC). Furthermore, although extremely contentious, an increasing role for the SANDF is contemplated in peacekeeping, peacebuilding, and conflict prevention on the African continent.[31] The National Intelligence Coordinating Committee (NICO) centrally evaluates the work of the intelligence community—the National Intelligence Agency (NIA), the South African Secret Service (SASS), and the Military Intelligence Agency (MIA)—in the foreign policy arena. These agencies jointly provide information on external security and related matters; consequently, they are in a position to substantially influence how a particular foreign policy problem is understood, conceptualized, and, eventually, resolved.[32]

Some have contended that in the post-1994 era, civilians have replaced the military and intelligence in foreign policy decisionmaking as the locus of decisionmaking has shifted from a highly centralized circle of militarists to an open relationship between key individual decisionmakers.[33] However, the resurgence of the dominating influence of "securocrats" in subregional affairs—almost rising like the proverbial Phoenix from the ashes of yesteryear's destabilization strategy—manifesting itself in the pivotal role played by former safety and security minister Sydney Mufamadi (and, to a lesser extent, former defense minister Joe Modise) in the ill-advised military intervention in Lesotho in September 1998, seems to contradict this viewpoint.[34] In the southern African subregion, the ANC government has sharply veered from its previous policy of preventive diplomacy to an approach of aggressive interventionism despite rather feeble attempts at ex post facto rationalization. Operation Boleas—executed in the name, and hidden by the fig leaf, of a flimsy SADC mandate—must rank as postapartheid South Africa's most serious foreign policy blunder. In stark contrast, South Africa's first foreign policy success under a new ANC government, its diplomatic intervention in the Lesotho crisis of

September 1994, was brokered by a senior DFA official, former director-general Rusty Evans. This example has shown at least a capacity to deal with a potentially explosive situation by using a judi-
cious mix of traditional diplomatic instruments, albeit executed
under a clear multilateral mandate.[35]

The role of the Department of Trade and Industry (DTI) is crucial because its trade policies affect foreign policy decisionmaking.
It has been instrumental in the crafting and promotion of a free-trade
protocol within the SADC. South Africa's objective is a progressive
reduction of tariff and nontariff barriers to boost intraregional trade
by 2006. However, the relationship between the DFA and DTI needs
to be reexamined, particularly with regard to rationalizing their areas
of activity and drawing fully on their respective expertise. There
should be careful consideration about their possible merger.

Given the multiplicity of actors and interests around foreign policy, the government at times appears unclear about its objectives:
Which aspects of its "pragmatic internationalism" should it prioritize? Can the principles of safeguarding human rights and promoting
democracy coexist with the imperatives of the free market?[36] Many
observers argue that South Africa does not have a foreign policy—
only accidental foreign interactions. They contend that policymaking
has been characterized more by short-range, ad hoc reaction than by
long-term strategic and visionary planning.[37] Clearly, South Africa is
still in the process of devising new foreign policy institutions and
finding new roles for existing ones. That is, perhaps, why the foreign policy making process is typically marked by inconsistencies
and incongruities, by stops and starts, by continuities and shifts, and
by reaction instead of anticipation.

South Africa shares this problem with other countries: The anarchic order of the world and its uncertainties elude a clear grasp of
events. Nevertheless, a number of issues illustrate the confusion in the
foreign policy decisionmaking process: the initial blind-eye attitude
toward human rights abuses and repression in Abacha's Nigeria and
al-Bashir's Sudan; the reticence to play a leading role in the Angolan
peace process; and an earlier reluctance to fully commit to Africa's
peacekeeping challenges—although former president Mandela has
played a pivotal role in the Burundian peace process since his retire-
ment, and Foreign Minister Dlamini-Zuma has worked tirelessly to
bring about peace between the warring factions in the DRC. These
policy deficiencies seem to reflect a serious lack of understanding of

the issues involved.[38] Ironically, this perceived ineptitude coincides with a period in which the country's standing in the world is higher than at any other time in its history. Paradoxically, this reputation merely serves to conceal the ineffectiveness of a foreign policy that has not fully taken advantage of the international dividends accruing from South Africa's negotiated political settlement.[39]

There is a pressing need in South Africa for capacity building in the foreign policy field, both public and private. Foreign policy decisionmakers must have greater access to information and advice, benefiting from the integration and coordination of the many strands of political, defense, trade, and economic policies in the foreign policy domain. If the country wishes to achieve a more purposeful foreign policy, it will have to reorganize, coordinate, and better manage its foreign policy institutions. There is a need, for example, to bring government functionaries and civil society leaders together in an independent foreign policy forum and to make the foreign policy decisionmaking process as representative and open as possible.

■ THE AFRICAN RENAISSANCE AND FOREIGN POLICY

A February 1999 policy document by the DFA argued for a higher profile and more assertive action by the foreign ministry in both wealth creation and security.[40] It envisages wealth creation through globalization, the enhancement of South Africa's image abroad, and the vigorous pursuit of trade and investment; compliance with international law and active engagement in conflict prevention, management, and resolution would be the key to security. As Jackie Selebi, former director-general of foreign affairs, noted, the idea was to make South Africa's foreign policy "predictable" and "not one that suggests [the country] collide[s] with events."[41] An additional concern of promoting democratization and a culture of human rights has recently emerged to supplement the aims of creating wealth and security. These objectives reflect President Mbeki's vision of a South African foreign policy anchored in both the developing and developed worlds. Mbeki expects South Africa to lead a renewal of the continent and project the cause of the developing world in international institutions. He believes that South Africa will achieve its foreign policy objective of contributing to Africa's rebirth if it can lead global reforms. Hence, as the most powerful African actor, South

Africa seeks a major role in economic development issues. Since these goals cannot be attained unilaterally, South Africa has tried to obtain the cooperation of key international players to reshape the debates about changes in the multilateral system.[42]

Since May 1999, President Mbeki has advanced the notion of an African renaissance; as a foreign policy goal, this idea includes securing the establishment of genuine and stable democracies in Africa, mobilizing efforts against corruption, and implementing economic reforms to attract foreign direct investment.[43] These views dovetail with the ANC's own foreign policy document, which has put the concept of an African renaissance as "the main pillar of our international policy not only relating to Africa, but in all our international relations globally."[44] But these foreign policy proclamations need to be evaluated on the basis of whether the idea of the African renaissance can be translated into a coherent foreign policy. The notion of an African renaissance lacks conceptual clarity and operational significance, problems that are compounded by its obscure linkage with "African identity" and "African-ness." Moreover, it is being articulated at a time when the African continent is best known by conflict and discord rather than harmony.

There have been wide-ranging debates in South Africa about the African renaissance.[45] Reuel Khoza, for instance, has noted that whereas a renaissance denotes a "process of rebirth, renewal, revival, revitalization, re-awakening, and self-reinvention," Africa is far from such renewal, since it is "a pathologically diseased, drug addicted, malnourished patient. No amount or quantity of institutional forms or structures will be sufficient to rehabilitate Africa unless [the continent] unconditionally acknowledges and admits its problems, develops a sufficient understanding of the problem, expresses a desire and exhibits an unwavering will to solve the problems."[46] Recognizing the myriad obstacles confronting Africa's renewal, John Stremlau nevertheless suggests several avenues for the rejuvenation of Africa's international relations, such as limiting the abuse of power; encouraging political pluralism and civic nationalism; promoting development, human rights, and conflict prevention; establishing "African coalitions of the willing" for the purpose of conflict prevention; and seeking international partnerships that share the same interests and values.[47]

What should be the substantive expression of the African renaissance in South African foreign policy? The foreign ministry's mission statement speaks of enhancing South Africa's international capability by furthering the African renaissance, the creation of wealth, and the improvement of the quality of life of its citizens. President Mbeki has underscored the importance of the revival of foreign investment in Africa and the need to establish conditions enabling such investment. From this approach, the African renaissance is about making African economies competitive in the global context and making the continent safe for business. Despite South Africa's growing business links with the rest of Africa, its continental foreign policy cannot be focused exclusively on export promotion. It has to take a broader view of its African role, linking it with efforts to improve democracy and human rights, safeguard the environment, and curb cross-border crimes. The continued instability in Africa has highlighted the need for fresh thinking in South African foreign policy on issues that highlight the importance of civil institutions in continental governance.[48]

The transition of African states to democratic and free-market governance also necessitates a shift in focus from personalities to national institutions. The African renaissance paradoxically proposes the devolution of power away from leadership to prevent the personalizing of interests yet stresses the need for visionary, selfless leaders. Devolving the responsibility of governance to pragmatic, informed officials is arguably a precondition for the success of the African renaissance. The difficulties of negotiation serve to illustrate that South Africa, intent as it is on the promotion of an African renaissance, will have to select its conflict-resolution efforts wisely—focusing its diplomatic energies on those closer to home, where clearly identifiable national interests are at stake. These interests will have to be discerned against the backdrop of South Africa's own developmental needs, most notably those of economic growth and job creation.[49]

President Mbeki has said that the African renaissance will not occur in the absence of a philosophical search for Africa's rightful place in the world.[50] For this vision to be realized, however, it will have to match expediency with principle and united action with moral authority. How can this goal be achieved in the face of immense development and security challenges in Africa? To bridge the gap between the rhetoric of the African renaissance and achievable goals, South Africa will have to establish an exemplary record of dealing with national issues that the rest of the continent can emulate. The renaissance will be realized at the interstate level if it entails operational engagement to address the insecurities that exist within and between states.[51] As Thabo Mbeki has argued: "The peoples of Africa entertain the legitimate expectation that the new South Africa, which they helped to bring into being, will not only be an expression of the African renaissance by the manner in which it conducts its affairs, but will also be an active participant with other Africans in the struggle for the victory of that renaissance throughout the continent."[52]

There are also expectations that South Africa will play a leading role as representative of the developing world in its relations with the developed countries. In southern Africa, South Africa is the pivotal power within the SADC; with India and Australia it forms the foundational triangle of the Indian Ocean Rim Association for Regional Cooperation (IOR-ARC); in a global context, its leadership role has extended to NAM, the Commonwealth, the UN Conference on Trade and Development (UNCTAD), and also the disarmament community—in contributing to an indefinite, conditional extension to the NPT, in establishing the terms and conditions for a global land-mine ban, and in chairing the preparatory committee for the Comprehensive Test Ban Treaty (CTBT). Elsewhere, South Africa has played an important role on behalf of the developing world in the World Trade Organization (WTO) millennium round and in the Okinawa summit of the G-8 group of countries (especially on the issues of debt relief and poverty alleviation), as well as in the Cairns group of unsubsidized agricultural exporting countries.

■ THE ECONOMIC IMPERATIVES OF FOREIGN POLICY

One major outcome of the end of the Cold War is that politics and economics have become more closely intertwined than ever before. South Africa's domestic realities—severe inequities, growing unemployment, and depressing poverty—necessitate an emphasis on the economic dimension of policy. However, South Africa lacks the resources to address its socioeconomic challenges without significant foreign direct investment and trade. The quest for foreign markets and investments has been heightened by the need to reconstruct an economy devastated by economic and financial sanctions and by the recognition of the limits of foreign aid. By and large, foreign investors have not been entirely keen to invest in the South African economy. Although prospective investors are impressed with the country's sophisticated environment, competent management skills, advanced physical infrastructure, and mineral wealth, they also harbor concerns about escalating crime, low productivity, and rising labor costs.[53]

An increasingly common feature of South African foreign policy is the tendency to let economic interests hold sway over political principle in policy formulation. Some observers have criticized the inordinate emphasis on trade and investment as the principal themes of South African foreign policy. However, the pursuit of economic goals is a fundamental concern of modern diplomacy and has become the major rationale of interstate relations. South Africa has reentered the world economy at a time of increased globalization propelled by free-market ideas. Since the country perceives itself as a developing nation, the government has been pursuing what could be called managed trade: negotiating on behalf of the business sector for access to international markets and urging South African manufacturers to become internationally competitive.[54]

In international economic relations, South Africa has projected itself as a developing country. It pursued this strategy assiduously in its initial attempt to gain preferential access to the European Union (EU) market under the Lomé Convention. This strategy has as much to do with maximizing South Africa's position in an important market as with seeking solidarity with other African or third world countries. However, the EU has been prepared to offer South Africa only an asymmetrical trade agreement, which was finally concluded in October 1999.[55] Another component of international economic relations has been South Africa's membership in regional economic organizations such as the newly created IOR-ARC. Currently focusing on trade and investment promotion, IOR-ARC members hope to broaden the organization into the proposed Zone of Peace and Cooperation in the South Atlantic (ZPCSA).[56]

South Africa's membership in IOR-ARC and ZPCSA has profound implications for its commitment to the regional institutions in southern Africa, especially the Southern Africa Customs Union (SACU) and the SADC. Some analysts have argued that South Africa's membership in the IOR-ARC and ZPCSA might offer SADC countries little tangible benefits and might compound the problem of institutional overlap.[57] Others, however, counter that benefits accruing to South Africa through these arrangements could revitalize the SADC region. These observers also note that South Africa's membership in

IOR-ARC could counter its economic dominance in southern Africa, help to diversify markets and trade patterns, and attract foreign investment.[58]

Despite the dangers of institutional overlaps, South Africa's gradual reintegration into the world economy will be influenced to a large degree by the kind of economic relationship it develops with its SADC partners. It is for this reason that South Africa has been at pains to stress that it does not intend to shirk from its responsibility to the region. Southern Africa, in particular, and Africa, in general, is already the market for a third of South Africa's exports, surpassing the EU as the country's largest export region. In addition, South Africa sees the SADC as a vehicle for economic stability in a region with daunting economic challenges.[59]

■ AFRICAN PEACEKEEPING AND FOREIGN POLICY

In the area of peacekeeping, South Africa seems to prefer a multilateral approach. It has achieved some moderate successes, including its contribution to peace efforts in Lesotho and Mozambique (in August-September and October 1994), its belated reaction to the breakdown of peace in Angola, its humanitarian response to the Rwandan crisis, and its commitment to play a role in the potentially explosive Burundian situation—through the mediation efforts of former president Mandela. Each of these actions has been in concert with other countries and under the auspices of SADC and the OAU. But beyond these success stories, the country's foreign policy remains opaque. The government has been careful not to become directly and, especially, militarily involved in regional peacekeeping (with the exception of the September 1998 Lesotho debacle and a promised military contingent for a multinational UN force in the DRC). Instead, Pretoria seems to prefer utilizing the tools of preventive diplomacy and offering logistical support for peacekeeping. To play a constructive mediating role, South Africa insists that it will not side with any party to an interstate or intrastate armed conflict. Nevertheless, South Africa's insistence on neutrality has in some instances been construed as a reluctance to intervene; and this perception has added fuel to the charge that it is tolerant of human rights abuses and genocide in Africa.

South Africa's neutrality is evident in the government's call for respect for human rights and its willingness to provide humanitarian assistance and logistical support to peacekeeping efforts on the continent. But the country seems to be hampered by two telling factors. First, South Africa's history of destabilization in the southern African region makes some SADC countries less inclined to trust its intentions. Second, it has (with the exception of the September 1998 intervention in Lesotho) no experience in African peacekeeping exercises. There are also other players trying to establish peace in the region: In Angola, the UN and Portugal are involved; in Rwanda, France and the UN; and in Burundi, Belgium and the UN. South Africa's involvement in these conflict-resolution exercises is limited to humanitarian assistance and logistical support and, more specifically, as a member of OAU task teams, to peacemaking efforts in Rwanda, Burundi, and, more recently, the DRC and the Comoros Islands.[60]

Although not directly involved in conflict-resolution exercises, the South African government has played the important role of endorsing agreements reached by conflicting parties, preferring preventive diplomacy and peacemaking (as in Lesotho and Mozambique in 1994).[61] Despite regional pressures to more actively involve itself in the Angolan crisis, South Africa has been reluctant to take a leadership role, preferring to work with SADC and the OAU on efforts to deal with the deteriorating civil war between the MPLA government and the UNITA rebel movement.

South Africa has used quiet diplomacy to boost peace prospects in Africa and the region. For instance, Archbishop Desmond Tutu, Deputy President Mbeki, and Foreign Minister Nzo led missions to General Sani Abacha in Nigeria; President Mandela prodded King Mswati III of Swaziland and President Frederick Chiluba of Zambia to promote the principles of democracy in those countries; and President Mbeki and Olusegun Obasanjo of Nigeria led a mission to Zimbabwe to persuade President Robert Mugabe to rethink the policy of expropriation of white-owned farms. Although there are limits to moral diplomacy (particularly when African states invoke solidarity to gloss over abuses in their midst), this diplomatic approach reflects the conviction that a meaningful South African democratic transition must be linked to the external promotion of democratic principles and human rights.[62]

Given the limitations of armed interventions to secure peace, it is unlikely that South Africa will play a vigorous peacekeeping role. This stance reflects more prudence than indifference. A recent Department of Defense report concedes that South Africa is "unable to maintain its army, navy or air force at anything near operational readiness"; special forces no longer have "any covert tactical mobility," have equipment equivalent only to light infantry, and are experiencing "an ineffective rapid-reaction capability"; and "future communication security and interoperability" is "at risk of failure."[63] Furthermore, given the catch-22 situation facing possible South African intervention anywhere—the danger that South Africa will be denounced as a hegemon if it does step in and dismissed as callous if it does not—an emphasis on preventive diplomacy may well be its only option.

As southern Africa pursues its socioeconomic and development agenda, there are bound to be misunderstandings and tensions over issues such as trade policies, environmental policies and the utilization of scarce resources such as water, cross-border health problems affecting both humans and livestock, and migration and immigration policies.[64] The institutional mechanism SADC has created to deal with these problems is the Organ on Politics, Defense and Security, formed in January 1996. But as some of the discussion in Chapter 7 showed, the operation of the Organ was stymied from the outset by conflicts between Presidents Mandela and Mugabe, who had diametrically opposed views on the conceptual and institutional framework for the Organ. These conflicts have yet to be resolved and might become a potential source of conflict in the region.

SADC's reluctance to exercise regional leadership in preventive diplomacy and conflict management stems from the fact that certain heads of state have faced severe criticism for authoritarianism and intolerance in their own countries. This reluctance is related to the problem that many SADC countries do not share a common consensus around the political values that are reflected in the SADC treaty. Moreover, the admission of the DRC to SADC might well prove to have been a monumental blunder, committed collectively by all SADC member states. Politically the DRC is a collapsed state—an ungovernable pseudo-entity—that has become a liability for the rest of southern Africa. The admission of the DRC has transformed SADC into a grouping of subequatorial states (whose northern boundary now extends north of the Equator). It would have been much more prudent for SADC to have consolidated its functional roles before inviting new members. Given its amorphous geographical reach, it will become difficult in future for SADC to deny admission to countries such as Congo-Brazzaville, Gabon, Uganda, Kenya, Rwanda, and Burundi.

■ CONCLUSION

South Africa is clearly suffering an identity crisis in its external relations, captured aptly in its depiction of itself as "an industrialized state of the South which can communicate with the North." The country, it is claimed, can carry on this communication "on equal terms to articulate the needs, the concerns and the fears of the developing world" and, conversely, "interpret the concerns and the fears of the developed world."[65] Whereas cynics might see this elegant formulation as a rationale for being all things to all countries, the current policymakers face the challenge of framing a coherent, defensible foreign policy. A principled foreign policy does not suggest a dogmatic obsession with morality at the expense of enlightened self-interest; instead, it suggests an attempt to harmonize the two.

Safeguarding human rights and promoting democracy as foreign policy goals, for instance, does not imply a tilt toward ethical considerations. Rather, it suggests that in South Africa's peculiar circumstances, only a principled approach can be a pragmatic approach.[66] In relations with Zimbabwe, for example, there needs to be a balance between quiet and public diplomacy; between recognizing the legitimacy of the land issue in that country and the real grievances of those in Zimbabwe's opposition; between engagement and critical, punitive distance.[67] As Zimbabwe slid into chaos in advance of its June 2000 elections, the world looked to Pretoria to take a leading role in defense of democratic values. By adopting the preferred quiet-diplomacy approach toward President Mugabe, the Mbeki administration underscored the limitations of South Africa's willingness and ability to overtly challenge the norm of nonintervention in the internal affairs of member states in the SADC and, by implication, Africa as a whole.

The dilemma of abjuring the issues of human rights and democracy in South Africa's foreign policy is that this stance amounts to a denial of the core elements of its national character. Yet when the country pursues an ethical foreign policy, its moral posture comes across as unbearably preachy, particularly by most insecure and unstable African leaders. South Africa lacks the will and the capacity to deploy economic or military instruments to induce states to conform to the strictures of the African renaissance, making Pretoria look like a well-intentioned but irrelevant missionary instead of a regional power. Besides, South Africa has been unable to prompt other powers—the United States, France, Britain—to follow its lead and support its policies, particularly when faced with wars and situations apparently as intractable and complex as those in the DRC, Angola, and, more recently, Zimbabwe.[68]

As a middle-ranking power, South Africa has devoted its limited energies to issues that are of national importance and to places where it can make a difference. Whereas the Mandela presidency was characterized by the need for reconciliation, transformation, and policy development and by the blanket policy response of "universality," Mbeki's tenure will have to display less prevarication and more policy implementation. This approach will inevitably mean making hard choices. In an era of increasing demands, leadership must prioritize and pursue those goals that best serve the national interest and that can be realized with the available time and human and financial resources. Clearly, South Africa's challenges necessitate the definition of its foreign policy in terms primarily of domestic needs—an increase in economic growth and a reduction in unemployment; arguably, along with racial and political conciliation, these are the key contemporary challenges facing the country. Regional interests hinge on the potential economic value to South Africa of the continent. Conversely, instability and economic decline on the continent affect South Africa—hence the need to encourage conditions of good governance and, if necessary, peacekeeping. To capitalize on its strengths as a regional economic and military power, South Africa will have to provide leadership in Africa, leadership that will inevitably be accompanied by responsibilities along with political challenges and costs.

South Africa's development will shape the character of external relations in southern Africa and Africa for the foreseeable future. However, as yet no real consensus has emerged within its decision-making community and its attentive public, either on the ranking of priorities or on the conceptual basis of what needs to be formulated. The present debate about the focus and direction of foreign policy reflects a tension or interplay between the pragmatists, who wish to anchor South Africa's ambitions to nationally defined objectives within the constraints imposed by internal socioeconomic conditions, and the idealists, who seek an avowedly normative stance where considerations of justice and concern for human rights and democracy lie at the very center of foreign policy deliberations.[69] These ends need not be mutually exclusive; they can be merged in the foreign policy of the new South Africa.

■ NOTES

1. See Alfred Nzo, "Statement by the Minister of Foreign Affairs, Mr. Alfred Nzo, Before the Portfolio Committee on Foreign Affairs, March 14, 1995," in *Policy Guidelines by the Minister and Deputy Minister of Foreign Affairs* (compiled by the Department of Foreign Affairs, Pretoria: Government Printer, 1995), p. 5. See also Denis Venter, "South Africa and Africa: Relations in a Time of Change," in Walter Carlsnaes and Marie Muller, eds., *Change and South African External Relations* (Johannesburg: International Thomson, 1997), pp. 73–101.

2. Chris Landsberg and Zondi Masiza, *Strategic Ambiguity or Ambiguous Strategy? Foreign Policy Since the 1994 Election* (Johannesburg: Centre for Policy Studies Policy Review Series, October 1995), p. 7.

3. Brian White, "Analysing Foreign Policy: Problems and Approaches," in Michael Clark and Brian White, eds., *Understanding Foreign Policy: The Foreign Policy Systems Approach* (London: Edward Elgar, 1989), p. 5. See also Joseph Frankel, *The Making of Foreign Policy* (London: Oxford University Press, 1963), p. 1.

4. George Modelski, *A Theory of Foreign Policy* (London: Pall Mall Press, 1962), pp. 6–7. See also Graham Evans and Jeffrey Newnham, *The Dictionary of World Politics: A Reference Guide to Concepts, Ideas and Institutions* (London: Harvester Press, 1990), p. 123.

5. Jack Plano and Roy Olton, *The International Relations Dictionary* (Oxford: Oxford University Press, 1988), p. 5.

6. Ibid.

7. See Lisa Thompson and Anthony Leysens, "The Elusive Quest for the National Interest," *Global Dialogue* 2, no. 1 (February 1997): 29–30.

8. Ibid., p. 30.

9. See Phindile Dyani, "The Role of Civil Society in South Africa's Foreign Policy-Making," *Global Dialogue* 2, no.1 (February 1997): 28–29.

10. Nelson Mandela, "South Africa's Future Foreign Policy," *Foreign Affairs* 72, no. 5 (1993): 87.

11. Garth le Pere and Anthoni van Nieuwkerk, "Making Foreign Policy in South Africa," in Patrick McGowan and Philip Nel, eds., *Power, Wealth and Global Order—International Relations for Southern African Students* (Cape Town: University of Cape Town Press, 1999), p. 4.

12. Landsberg and Masiza, *Strategic Ambiguity or Ambiguous Strategy?* p. 10.

13. Nzo, "Statement," p. 10.

14. See Foreign Minister Nzo's assurance that "Africa is clearly . . . a priority in the years ahead," in Nzo, "Statement," p. 8.

15. See Chris Landsberg, "South Africa's Foreign Policy Style Is Out of Step with Its New Image," *Transact* (Johannesburg Centre for Policy Studies) 2, no. 6 (June 1995): 10.

16. Le Pere and van Nieuwkerk, "Making Foreign Policy in South Africa," p. 11.

17. Greg Mills, "Leaning All Over the Place? The Not-So-New South Africa's Foreign Policy," in Hussein Solomon, ed., *Fairy Godmother, Hegemon or Partner: In Search of a South African Foreign Policy,* Monograph

Series no. 13 (Midrand: Institute for Security Studies, 1997), p. 24.

18. Le Pere and van Nieuwkerk, "Making Foreign Policy in South Africa," p. 11.

19. See Peter Vale and Sipho Maseko, "South Africa and the African Renaissance," Chris Landsberg and Francis Kornegay, "The African Renaissance: A Quest for Pax Africana and Pan-Africanism," and Vusi Mavimbela, "The African Renaissance: A Workable Dream," in Garth le Pere, Anthoni van Nieuwkerk, and Kato Lambrechts, eds., *South Africa and Africa: Reflections on the African Renaissance,* occasional paper no. 17, Foundation for Global Dialogue, Johannesburg, October 1998, pp. 2–15, 16–28, and 29–34.

20. Le Pere and van Nieuwkerk, "Making Foreign Policy in South Africa," p. 11.

21. Greg Mills, *The Wired Model: South Africa, Foreign Policy and Globalization* (Cape Town: Tafelberg, 2000), p. 327.

22. See Howard Barrell, "Zuma's Department of Foreign Despairs," *Daily Mail and Guardian,* November 26, 1999.

23. Mills, *The Wired Model,* p. 335.

24. Abdul A. Said et al., *Concepts of International Politics in Global Perspective* (Englewood Cliffs, NJ: Prentice-Hall, 1995), p. 40.

25. Landsberg, "South Africa's Foreign Policy Style," p. 10.

26. Le Pere and van Nieuwkerk, "Making Foreign Policy in South Africa," p. 9.

27. Marie Muller, "The Institutional Dimension: The Department of Foreign Affairs and Overseas Missions," in Walter Carlsnaes and Marie Muller, eds., *Change and South African External Relations* (Johannesburg: International Thomson, 1997), p. 70.

28. Raymond Suttner, "Parliament and the Foreign Policy Process," in Greg Mills, ed., *South African Yearbook of International Affairs, 1996* (Johannesburg: South African Institute of International Affairs, 1996), p. 136.

29. Vale and Maseko, "South Africa and the African Renaissance," p. 12.

30. Landsberg and Masiza, *Strategic Ambiguity or Ambiguous Strategy?* p. 14.

31. See Hussein Solomon and Maxi van Aardt, eds., *"Caring" Security in Africa,* Monograph Series no. 20 (Midrand: Institute for Security Studies, 1998).

32. Vale and Maseko, "South Africa and the African Renaissance," p. 14.

33. Ibid., p. 14.

34. Landsberg, "South Africa's Foreign Policy Style," p. 10.

35. Rusty Evans, "Preventive Diplomacy in Lesotho and Mozambique," paper presented at the SAIIA/IDP conference South Africa and Peacekeeping in Africa, Johannesburg, July 13–14, 1995.

36. See Roger Southall, "A Critical Reflection on the GNU's Foreign Policy Initiatives and Responses," in Chris Landsberg, Garth le Pere, and Anthoni van Nieuwkerk, eds., *Mission Imperfect: Redirecting South Africa's Foreign Policy* (Johannesburg: Foundation for Global Dialogue and Center for Policy Studies, 1995), pp. 39–44.

37. Landsberg and Masiza, *Strategic Ambiguity or Ambiguous Strategy?* pp. 13–14.

38. Landsberg, "South Africa's Foreign Policy Style," p. 10.

39. Landsberg and Masiza, *Strategic Ambiguity or Ambiguous Strategy?* p. 14.

40. See Department of Foreign Affairs, *Thematic Reviews/Strategic Planning* (Pretoria: Department of Foreign Affairs, February 1999).

41. See address by Jackie Selebi to the South African Institute of International Affairs, Johannesburg, May 18, 1999.

42. Mills, *The Wired Model,* pp. 303–308.

43. See address by Deputy President Thabo Mbeki at the congress of the Corporate Council on Africa, Chantilly, Virginia, April 19–22, 1997. See also Chris Alden and Garth le Pere, "From Pariah to Global Player: The Transformation of South African Foreign Policy," paper prepared for publication in *Les Temps Modernes* (Paris), November-December 2000, p. 12.

44. See the discussion document of the African National Congress, "Developing a Strategic Perspective on South African Foreign Policy."

45. See Vusi Mavimbela, "An African Renaissance Could Be Far More Than a Dream," *Sunday Independent* (Johannesburg), June 15, 1997. See also Moeletsi Mbeki, "The African Renaissance," in Greg Mills, ed., *South African Yearbook of International Affairs, 1998/99* (Johannesburg: South African Institute of International Affairs, 1999).

46. See Reuel Khoza, "The Institutional Forms or Structures That Should Underpin the African Renaissance," paper presented at the African Renaissance Conference, Midrand, September 28, 1998.

47. See John Stremlau, "African Renaissance: Beyond Nationalism and Internationalism," paper presented at the African Renaissance Conference, Midrand, September 28, 1998.

48. Mills, *The Wired Model,* pp. 318–319.

49. Ibid., pp. 319–320.

50. See Thabo Mbeki, "The African Renaissance," *Getaway* (April 2000).

51. Mills, *The Wired Model,* pp. 322–324.

52. Mbeki, "The African Renaissance," p. 45.

53. See Tim Read, "The 'New' South Africa," paper presented at the Wilton Park conference South Africa: One Year Later, Wilton Park, Sussex, March 27–31, 1995. See also ABSA Bank, *Quarterly South African Economic Monitor,* 4th quarter, 2000.

54. Landsberg and Masiza, *Strategic Ambiguity or Ambiguous Strategy?* pp. 16–17.

55. Ibid., pp. 17–18.

56. See Denis Venter, "The Indian Ocean Rim Initiative: A Vehicle for South-South Co-operation," *Indian Journal of African Studies* 7, no. 1–2 (1996): 15–35; Denis Venter, "South Africa, Brazil and South Atlantic Security: Towards a Zone of Peace and Co-operation in the South Atlantic," in S. Pinheiro Guimarães, ed., *South Africa and Brazil: Risks and Opportunities in the Turmoil of Globalization* (Brasília: National Council for Scientific and Technological Development and the International Relations Research Institute, 1996), pp. 17–48; and Robert Davies, Dot Keet, and Mfundo Nkuhlu, "Reconstructing Economic Relations Within the Southern African Region: Issues and Options for a Democratic South Africa," working paper

no. 1, Macro-Economic Research Group, Johannesburg, 1993. The current members of the IOR-ARC are Australia, India, Indonesia, Kenya, Madagascar, Malaysia, *Mauritius, *Mozambique, Oman, Singapore, *South Africa, Sri Lanka, *Tanzania, and Yemen (countries with an asterisk are SADC members). The twenty-one countries that are members of the ZPCSA are those along Africa's western seaboard, from Senegal in the north to South Africa in the south, including the offshore island states, and the three South American countries of Argentina, Uruguay, and Brazil on that continent's eastern shores.

57. For some of these debates see Marina Mayer, "The Feasibility of Including the Southern Africa Customs Union (SACU) and the Southern African Development Community (SADC) in an Indian Ocean Rim Association for Economic Co-operation," paper presented at the conference France, Southern Africa and the Indian Ocean: Past and Present Economic and Cultural Relations, organized by the Africa and Indian Ocean Project, University of the Witwatersrand, Johannesburg, and the French Institute for Scientific Research on Development in Co-operation, held at the French Institute of South Africa, Johannesburg, September 5–8, 1995, p. 3; Agence France Presse (Port Louis), May 16, 1996; Davies, Keet, and Nkuhlu, *Reconstructing Economic Relations Within the Southern African Region*; Johan Marx, "South African Foreign Policy in the New Era: Priorities in Africa and the Indian Ocean Islands," *South African Journal of International Affairs* 2, no. 2 (Winter 1995): 7. Also see Gwyn R. Campbell and Mario Scerri, "The Prospects for an Indian Ocean Rim (IOR) Economic Association," *South African Journal of International Affairs* 2, no. 2 (Winter 1995): 12; and Paul-Henri Bischoff, "Democratic South Africa and the World One Year After: Towards a New Foreign Policy Script," Southern African Perspectives Working Paper Series no. 46, Centre for Southern African Studies, University of the Western Cape, Bellville, July 1995, p. 8.

58. Venter, "The Indian Ocean Rim Initiative," p. 23; Erich Leistner, "Prospects for Increasing Regional Co-operation: A South African Perspective," *Africa Insight* 25, no. 1 (1995): 55–60; Gavin Maasdorp, *A Vision for Economic Integration and Co-operation in Southern Africa* (Pretoria: Department of Trade and Industry, March 1994).

59. See Denis Venter, "South African Foreign Policy in a Time of Change: The African Dimension," *Journal of the Third World Spectrum* 5, no. 2 (Fall 1998): 14. South Africa now has a trade balance in excess of R20 billion with the rest of the African continent. See also Graham Evans, "South Africa in Remission: The Foreign Policy of an Altered State," *Journal of Modern African Studies* 34, no. 2 (1996): 260. Evans suggests that the focus of South African foreign policy "should relate to the area within which it has the competitive edge: namely, the southern African region, where it maintains a 5:1 trade surplus based on the export of manufactured goods."

60. Venter, "Angola: Back from the Brink?" p. 112; Roger Kibasomba, "Understanding the Great Lakes Crisis: Whither the DRC?" paper presented at the Africa Institute, Pretoria, February 24, 2000; Alden and le Pere, "From Pariah to Global Player," p. 11.

61. See Rusty Evans, "Preventive Diplomacy in Lesotho and Mozam-

bique," paper presented at the SAIIA/IDP conference South Africa and Peacekeeping in Africa, Johannesburg, July 13–14, 1995.

62. Venter, "South African Foreign Policy in a Time of Change," pp. 23–24.

63. See "Big Gaps in South Africa's Defense Capability," *Pretoria News* (Pretoria), October 6, 2000.

64. Ami Mpungwe, "Policy Considerations for the Evolution of Sustainable Peace and Stability in Southern Africa," in Mark Malan, ed., *Resolute Partners: Building Peacekeeping Capacity in Southern Africa,* Monograph Series no. 21 (Midrand: Institute for Security Studies, February 1998), p. 80; and Denis Venter, "Regional Security in Sub-Saharan Africa," *Africa Insight,* 26, no. 2 (1996): 173.

65. Nzo, "Statement," p. 12.

66. See Mervyn Frost, "Pitfalls on the Moral High Ground: Ethics and South African Foreign Policy," in Walter Carlsnaes and Marie Muller, eds., *Change and South African External Relations* (Johannesburg: International Thomson, 1997), pp. 231–251.

67. See Greg Mills, *Creative Diplomacy or Creating Confusion?* (Johannesburg: South African Institute of International Affairs, May 26, 2000).

68. Mills, *The Wired Model,* pp. 338–361.

69. Evans, "South Africa in Remission," pp. 262–263; Southall, "A Critical Reflection," pp. 39–40.

9

External Relations of Weak States and Stateless Regions in Africa

William Reno

Some analysts see the collapse of state institutions as a result of misguided policies.[1] Others regard state collapse as an outcome of a conscious policy choice: A regime plans the dissolution of conventional state institutions and exploits aspects of the process of collapse, integrating them into its political strategies.[2] In this chapter I build on the latter perspective in examining how regimes that preside over the disintegration of formal state institutions use private actors both to conduct interstate diplomacy and to garner external resources to ensure regime survival.

The privatization of internal violence and diplomacy is the point of departure for exploring this process of regime survival amid state collapse. This analysis focuses in part on mercenary companies that some regimes use to manage internal security threats.[3] Related to this practice is state officials' voluntary relinquishing of control over resources to private mining companies. Some regimes recruit mining companies to control access to resources, occasionally in tandem with mercenaries or with industrial security guards, who play a role in the host state regime's security strategies. Mining companies often play a key role in bringing this military expertise and in denying resources to rivals. In this chapter I also examine how mining firms function as tools for some regimes to exercise influence abroad through "private diplomacy" and to relieve these regimes of

the necessity of exercising territorial control within the globally recognized borders of the state.[4]

These strategies of regimes that preside over collapsing formal
state institutions shed light on the changing role of sovereignty in
very weak states and on the nature of interstate relations among
states of radically differing power. Some foresee the eventual extinc-
tion of states that do not abide by certain principles of state sovereignty, namely that a state controls a territory, presides over an administrative hierarchy, and maintains the capacity to conduct formal
diplomatic relations. These principles barely apply in the states stud-
ied in this chapter.[5] The model developed further on of regime politics in the context of state collapse does not include formal state ex-
tinction, even in places such as the Democratic Republic of Congo
(DRC). Instead, this model shows that global recognition of even
very weak states' sovereignty, and the role such recognition plays in
the privatization of diplomacy and internal security for these regimes, serve not only regime interests but also the interests of officials and investors in powerful states. The failure of insurgencies
that do not gain external recognition highlights that rulers who do
gain it are empowered by it.

Paradoxically, the further relaxation of conventions of internal
(de facto) sovereignty—uniform control over territory, state-to-state
diplomacy, and an internal monopoly on the exercise of violence—
gives a wider range of global actors an interest in maintaining external recognition of the sovereignty of seemingly defunct states such
as the DRC and Somalia. Private global actors are indeed central to
the survival of Africa's system of states and the regimes that rule
these states. This chapter presents evidence that this "globalization,"
in the sense of intensified interstate commercial transactions, bol-
sters not only Africa's states and regimes but the very weakest states
everywhere; the involvement of global actors does not, however,
strengthen these states' internal institutional capacities.

I conclude by comparing contemporary privatization of external
relations of weak states to external relations of African authorities in
the nineteenth century, prior to the extension of formal imperial control. This change in the conduct of external relations, caused by
shifts in the domestic political economy of weak states, points to the
reassertion of a global society that accepts the conduct of private external relations on the part of authorities in economically marginal
areas.

■ THE ENHANCED ROLE OF
PRIVATE ACTORS IN WEAK-STATE POLITICS

Why would foreign firms do business in very weak states where regimes cannot guarantee the security of property or provide even minimal public order? Reports of investor interest filtered out of Zaire even late in Mobutu's (mis)rule, including plans in 1995 to invest $600 million to mine copper.[6] This and other investments, examined further on, suggest that internal disorder need not impede commerce, especially if compact, valuable natural resources are present. A few entrepreneurs may even prefer minimal government control. A European businessman, for example, observed in Zaire: "The absence of a banking system is far more of an opportunity than a hindrance. You set up your own network and make your own rules. I find it quite inspirational."[7]

In fact, political risk-analysis services rate all of the five top recipients of foreign investment in Africa as "most risky" (Table 9.1). Each of these five countries is also highly dependent on a single commodity export to generate foreign exchange (Table 9.2). Internal anarchy and dependence on a single resource may be related. That is, extreme dependence on enclave economies (which the figures in Tables 9.1 and 9.2 represent) can reflect not so much a comparative advantage in mineral resources as the dearth of taxable economic activity as the state institutional regulation of markets and public order collapses.

Political instability and institutional decline are not necessarily an insurmountable concern for enclave investors. Political instability emerges as a dilemma of variable proportions depending on the organization and resources of the firm. High but tolerable levels of

Table 9.1 Investment Patterns in Mineral-Producing Sub-Saharan Countries

Country	Percent Investment (1994–1996 average)	Risk (1996)
Angola	15.8	6 (highest)
Congo (Zaire)	n/a	6
Equatorial Guinea	10.1	6
Zambia	4.3	6
Nigeria	37.1	6

Source: OECD, *Geographical Distribution of Financial Flows to Developing Countries* (Washington, DC: OECD, 1998).

Table 9.2   The Structure of Mineral Exports Among Sub-Saharan Countries

	Single Commodity Export	
Country	1982–1986 (%)	1992–1996 (%)
Angola	83 (oil)	96 (oil)
Congo (Zaire)	58 (copper)	n/a
Equatorial Guinea	54 (cocoa)	87 (oil)
Zambia	98 (copper)	98 (copper)
Nigeria	90 (oil)	96 (oil)

Source: OECD, *Geographical Distribution of Financial Flows to Developing Countries*
(Washington, DC: OECD, 1998).

uncertainty for one firm, for example, might deter competitors from
investing. More flexible firms that can manage their own local economic environments through employing private security forces or
arming politically well-connected paramilitaries may use this comparative advantage to gain greater market shares and extract higher
profits from a risky operation.[8] At the very least, some firms prove
remarkably impervious to internal anarchy near investment sites. In
Nigeria, for example, despite a military coup in 1993 that ousted an
elected civilian regime and subsequent sanctions from abroad, oil
sector investment rose from $450 million in 1993 to about $600 million in 1996.[9] As we will see, some of these investors became closely
involved with the Nigerian regime's strategies for controlling internal opponents and for dealing with critics abroad. Developments in
Nigeria also point to pitfalls that investors face in unstable states if
their involvement in political affairs causes local populations to assume that these firms play a major role in generating and distributing valuable political resources.

   A broader look at the political context of private foreign investment in Africa's weakest states will reveal how foreign investors and
rulers of weak states with resources cooperate with each other to
generate and protect material benefits. Consolidating these gains requires a fair measure of negotiation with actors outside of Africa to
mediate between chaotic domestic economies and global markets.
Firms and rulers manipulate market opportunities to recruit additional external actors to this coalition. Thus the survival of rulers of
very weak states need not require wholesale economic reform, at
least in terms of building formal state institutions and regulations directed at economic activities. Without reform as conventionally

understood in the context of state institutions, survival in states
bereft of bureaucratic administration is likely to require a major reconfiguration of the conduct of external relations to sustain a new
rent-seeking alliance based on a more globalized and often more violent local economy.

Enclave economies and the foreign firms they attract provide a
variety of political resources to rulers of institutionally weak states.
This observation contradicts analyses of democratization in Africa that
regard public opinion as ultimately forcing patronage-based regimes
to build capable state institutions to provide public services.[10] The
analysis here supports Terry Lynn Karl's study of enclave oil economies around the world. Karl highlights a shared pattern of intensified
rent-seeking among elites, even in the midst of seemingly significant
reforms, and explains how the informal politics of ruling elites works:
Elites manipulate access to resources from enclave economies to preserve private-group privileges. This manipulation can occur alongside
institutional reform, usually feeble or faked, which impresses outsiders enough to provide additional benefits and access to markets. It
may also provide political cover for other outsiders who need diplomatic and financial help from non-African state officials to exploit
economic opportunities in supposedly reforming states.[11]

Further examination of the internal politics of very weak states
shows that this external strategy can improve the security of regimes
in these states. Their rulers likely prefer a smaller government administration, an inclination outsiders may interpret as support for bureaucratic efficiency and less state interference in markets. This preference for scaled-down administration is especially true where rulers
do not have absolute control over the distribution of benefits from
state offices and are compelled to share the rents with subordinates
as a condition for retaining power. Historically, this sharing of resources has made ruling sub-Saharan African states a risky job. Actu-
arial figures indicate that incumbent African rulers have a 60 percent
chance of either being killed on the job, usually by close associates,
or suffering imprisonment or exile. Postcolonial regime transitions in
the five countries in Tables 9.1 and 9.2, transitions that have included
considerable violence in three states and a civil war in one, should
give incumbent rulers concern for their personal safety.[12]

Some analysts for multilateral creditors take a more instrumental
approach to limiting reform in weak states. Two International Monetary Fund researchers, for example, express concern that too much

creditor pressure on regimes to dismantle patronage-based bureaucracies "could lead to anarchy rather than efficiency, since it destabilizes predatory dictatorships and hastens the path towards internal revolt."[13] The threat of the loss of central control, which translates into civil violence and state collapse, emerges as a political concern for creditors. Likewise, Susan Rose-Ackerman warns: "Reform is risky if it releases opposition forces that undermine current regimes."[14]

Rulers may invite foreign firms to exploit local mineral resources in order to reduce these internal security threats. The enclave nature of these operations, along with the private security forces firms often employ, helps to deny resources to rival elites. Foreign firms can also help rulers recentralize the distribution of resources without the burden of building indigenous state revenue-collecting and security administrations. Creating such institutions diverts scarce resources needed in the short run to defend a regime's patronage network, and they could themselves become bases from which rivals could launch their own bids for power.

Thus hard-pressed rulers may ignore the rhetoric of economic reformers who stress efficiency and who are critical of widespread patronage. In Sierra Leone, for example, multilateral creditors since the 1980s have stressed the importance of bringing in large foreign operators to occupy key sites and "regularize" natural resource extraction, that is, halt untaxed, clandestine operations. Successive Sierra Leone presidents have recognized that clandestine mining operations have financed groups that threatened their hold on power.[15] In the early 1990s, for example, concession negotiations with foreign firms were accompanied by military campaigns that targeted the mining operations of rival politicians and local strongmen.[16]

This internal strategy helps rulers to weather reductions in state-to-state aid and harsher conditions for loans, since "reforms" of this sort can be presented to possible trading partners as increasing a ruler's centrality as a patron. The recent shift to a "trade, not aid" approach by some U.S. agencies highlights the conflict between starkly different visions of political change. U.S. officials stress that policy should support not only aid to but investment in African states. Investment, they argue, will create incentives for African rulers to implement market-oriented reforms and adopt more effective, rule-based administrative styles to attract investors, indigenous and foreign alike. "We want to work with them as partners," remarked Assistant Secretary of State for African Affairs Susan Rice, "in promoting our mutual interest in building democracy, safeguarding human rights, and generating the economic prosperity that will benefit Africans and Americans alike."[17]

In 1996, the U.S. Congress cut overall direct assistance to African governments by $130 million, or 20 percent, compared to the average yearly appropriations from 1992 to 1995.[18] However, Congress has approved the creation of new, privately managed equity financing funds associated with the quasi-official Overseas Private Insurance Corporation (OPIC) and oriented toward promoting private investment in Africa.[19] Congressional passage of the Africa Growth and Opportunity Act in 2000 made available $830 million in government-backed private equity financing for private U.S. business ventures in Africa. The OPIC initiative and earlier U.S. government initiatives of this sort generate financing that carries with it statutory requirements that it be directed toward bolstering private investment in Africa. In addition, OPIC provided insurance for $745 million in private investments in Africa by the end of 1997. Other U.S. government agencies add to this total. The Export-Import Bank (Eximbank) in 1997 held $1.3 billion in escrow to indemnify large infrastructure investments in Africa. Department of Transportation support included a $67 million loan guarantee to Ghana's government to purchase two power generators from a U.S. firm.[20] Similar shifts in priorities characterize aid to Africa from other states.[21] Officially backed U.S. private investment in Angola's oil industry, explored further on, takes place amid an ongoing civil war. These investments, accounting for a combined $.5 billion in Eximbank and OPIC insurance and loan guarantees as of 1999, play a major strategic role in the Angolan government's efforts to generate revenues it can use to conduct its war against insurgents.

This international promotion of private investment in very weak states has a strategic dimension for non-African officials. The deaths of over fifty UN soldiers in Somalia by October 1993 and the $3.5 billion price tag of the intervention helped spur a growing reluctance by non-African states to intervene in civil wars outside of strategically central areas. Following the U.S. withdrawal from Somalia, the Clinton administration issued Presidential Decision Directive 25 of May 1994, which institutionalized U.S. wariness to become directly involved in internal wars in regions peripheral to the country's security. Yet Angola, the sixth largest supplier of oil to the United States in 1998, is not completely absent from officials' concerns. The oil output of this non-OPEC member is projected to double between 1998 and 2005, mostly through the efforts of U.S. firms that have been awarded the bulk of new offshore production agreements.[22] As a result, there has emerged a competitive scramble among oil companies from other Western countries to gain stakes in Angola's oil industry. A newsletter remarked that the dominant view of policymakers is, "Let Dos Santos win the war, then we can deal with the grand corruption and human rights issues afterwards."[23]

Decreasing state-to-state aid encourages rulers to seek private help to gain access to these external resources, provided this help does not impinge on their own rents and their control over patronage to others. This shift from bilateral aid to promotion of commerce enhances the role of foreign firms as the key to tapping into and controlling internal resources. In addition, rulers desiring access to overseas aid earmarked to assist foreign investment require such firms to act as interlocutors to request assistance for a particular project. Subsidized equity financing and insurance can help foreign firms protect their investors and their own profit margins from the risks of business in very weak states, perhaps making these firms more likely to invest. Some firms will invest in enclave operations in even the most tumultuous places if compact, valuable resources can be easily extracted. But larger firms with more fixed investments, and with the ear of officials in a foreign capital, may perform a political role out of proportion to the size of their investment. Thus rulers who preside over enclave economies find incentives to base their rule more exclusively on partnerships with foreigners to extract resources, in part because they (and more important, other investors and the ruler's enemies) believe that these partnerships signal external political support. Investors whose activities deprive rivals of access to resources also enable rulers to more safely jettison costly and politically threatening associates and clients in areas they control.

Presented with these incentives and resources, rulers of already weak states—provided they exercise juridical sovereignty over sufficiently attractive resources—logically prefer a smaller government administration as a way of ridding patronage networks of subordinate officials. If a ruler has done little in the past to provide government services relevant to citizens' needs and fears being overthrown, then he will likely calculate that new spending on health workers, teachers, and agricultural extension services simply wastes resources that could be distributed to security forces or loyal clients. Spending on social services also weakens a ruler's direct control over rents, since administrators who deal directly with the public are in a position to extract bribes from citizens seeking special treatment. In contrast, a ruler who intentionally destroys state institutions presides over citizens who face far greater obstacles to organizing than do small groups of strongmen affected by unplanned and precipitous cuts in patronage.

Institutional destruction is not a new strategy for rulers of heavily patrimonialized states. For example, state spending in former Zaire in 1990 to support agriculture, the occupation of 80 percent of the country's people, accounted for about 4 percent of the official budget. By 1992 (the last year Zaire's government produced an official budget), spending for social services in urban areas had fallen to zero.[24] In that same year in Gabon and Congo-Brazzaville, state expenditures on agriculture fell to less than 1 percent of official budgets.[25] The difference between these and more recent cases lies in the greater role of officials outside of Africa. These officials actively promote and help underwrite private investment in risky areas in Africa, making investment more likely there (provided the state has sufficiently attractive natural resources), at the same time that non-African governments and multilateral creditors push regimes in weak states to jettison expensive and inefficient patronage networks.

Enclave investment within this political calculus is compatible with no improvement in, and even subsequent declines in, the wealth of ordinary citizens. Per capita income figures from the highly concentrated enclave economy countries featured in Tables 9.1 and 9.2 indicate that this is so.[26] Free (or more free) of threatening rivals, a rent-seeking ruler's preference for economically efficient exploitation of the source of rents rises. Insofar as outside donors and creditors wish to further integrate Africa into global markets, they will at least tolerate this internal political shift provided foreign investors can reap some advantage. As Rose-Ackerman's previous statement suggests, outsiders may also conclude that there is little else that can be done to avoid the turmoil of state collapse short of bolstering the centrality and capabilities of the predatory ruler who created these negative conditions in the first place. Foreign firms thus become critical intermediaries in weak-state rulers' management of relations with outsiders and also become increasingly integral to these rulers' internal political strategies.

■   WEAK STATES AND PRIVATE DIPLOMACY

The intersecting interests of firms, overseas governments, and regimes presiding over very weak states become more evident as we look at specific examples of foreign investment in Africa's weakest states. One U.S. investor, for example, recognized the joint commercial and political advantages of using strong-state backing to launch his investment in Angola with its risky economy and a long-running civil war. Maurice Templesman, long active in risky but mineralogically well-endowed African states, sought Eximbank financial backing for a three-way diamond-marketing consortium. The consortium was to include Templesman's firm, the Angolan diamond-marketing parastatal, and a diamond-marketing arm of União Nacional para a Independencia Total (UNITA) rebels. Templesman billed the deal as a way to settle violent conflicts over diamond resources between the Angolan government and UNITA.[27] A former U.S. national security adviser reportedly instructed an aide to inform OPIC and Eximbank about the proposal. The aide told Angolan president dos Santos that the deal "will take on greater meaning if the U.S. is involved through such mechanisms as Eximbank or OPIC." A State Department official also reported that "Templesman wanted us to tell Ex-Im 'this is a foreign policy imperative. We would like you to do it even if it is risky.'"[28]

Ultimately the deal fell through. Nonetheless, it appears that the non-African state officials thought about investment promotion in strategic rather than solely commercial terms and in ways compatible with investor concerns about profit and host-state regime concerns about security. Elsewhere, too, one finds investors with U.S. official backing helping to enhance weak-state regime relations with powerful states. For example, the oil field service firm Halliburton (which counted a former U.S. defense secretary and vice presidential candidate as its general manager) received a $150 million low-interest loan to do business in Algeria; the U.S. government reassessed its previously distant relationship with that regime, which has battled insurgents since a civil war broke out in 1992. Eximbank also helped Halliburton with an $88.5 million loan guarantee for a joint venture with Angola's state-run oil company, part of a wider $316 million Eximbank commitment to the Angolan hydrocarbon sector.[29] Possessing the world's fifth largest deposits of oil, Angola, as well as its regime's internal security problems, is of strategic as well as commercial interest to U.S. officials. These interests are even more difficult to separate because Angola's regime does not possess very strong state institutions and would find it difficult to build them given the tendency for its own officials to make deals with rebel miners for private profit. Foreign investment in and export from Angola's enclave oil economy at least gives the Angolan regime access to more foreign exchange with which to buy weapons to bolster internal security and battle rebels. Higher production figures also give the regime greater creditworthiness so that it can mortgage future production for cash to buy arms now.

Direct foreign investor provision of military services is another way around the problem of weak-state institutions, both for host-country regimes and for concerned officials in strong states. These firms use private security services—derogatorily referred to as mercenaries, although the contractors prefer "military trainers" or "industrial security guards" to create their own local environment of stability. The Florida-based firm Airscan, for example, protects the Cabinda Gulf Oil Company (Chevron) from attack from a Cabindan separatist group, the Frente de Liberação do Enclave do Cabinda (FLEC).[30] Strictly speaking, this group is an industrial security guard firm and does not engage in combat. Nonetheless, it contributes to regime security through training local employees in militarily useful skills and in collecting intelligence on rebel activities. Likewise, a U.S.-Canadian firm protects its Angolan diamond-mining operations from UNITA attacks with the services of its business partner, International Defense and Security.[31] Another firm with mining operations in Angola's war zone, and in areas of Sierra Leone threatened by attack from the Revolutionary United Front (RUF), took over a South African–run security firm, ArmSec, to oversee mine site security.[32] Yet another Canadian firm, this one with previous associations with a South African–Angolan security firm is seen, along with those previously mentioned, as part of an Angolan regime strategy to strengthen government positions in militarily vulnerable, resource-rich areas by granting licenses to companies that combine mining and security.[33]

Mining operations in Sierra Leone reveal a similar interplay of commercial opportunity, regime security, and the strategic interests of officials from powerful states. Two mining operations in Sierra Leone use private security to defend mine sites in areas vulnerable to rebel attack. Golden Prospects Mining contracted security to U.K.-run Cape

International.[34] Another Canadian firm, Diamondworks, employed Lifeguard, the head of which was formerly associated with the firm Executive Outcomes.[35] Executive Outcomes earlier, from 1995 to 1997, had a contract directly with the Sierra Leone government to provide security and anti-insurgency training for paramilitary forces.[36] It is significant, in light of weak-state regime wariness of formal state institutions, that Executive Outcomes trained forces directly loyal to the president and separate from the formal military, parts of which had collaborated in rebel attacks. This military service firm's anti-insurgency tactics were sufficiently effective to convince even a critical UN observer that the firm kept the elected civilian government in power against its rebel enemies.[37]

The private assistance rendered to Sierra Leone and Angola is not an isolated incident. In Nigeria, for example, Shell Oil's local subsidiary imported weapons and armed a paramilitary dedicated to protecting oil installations against regime opponents.[38] The local military government of Nigeria's oil-producing areas has used these paramilitaries and the Rivers State Task Force as reliable coercive agents to cow regime opponents while avoiding reliance on politically more suspect regular army units.

The question of direct strong-state support for commercial proxies arises in other aspects of Sierra Leone's insurgency. The armed restoration in February 1998 of an elected civilian government that was ousted in May 1997 by a combined RUF–Sierra Leone military force highlighted the diplomatically dramatic (if not militarily decisive) role of private security forces as a proxy for British official policy. Sandline, a British firm, produced documents to bolster its claims that it helped arm the (now restored) civilian government with official British help and U.S. complicity.[39] Ensuing debates in parliament underscored the advantages to strong-state officials of deploying foreign investors in strategic locations and then leaving them to contract out security to private firms, rather than using private security firms directly. This strategy provides officials with a better political buffer and ties security directly to the revenue-generating activities of the foreign firms that pay for it.

Other African states with vulnerable regimes have merged mining and security operations. Members of the family of Zimbabwe's President Mugabe, for example, use their positions in state-run firms to participate in joint mining ventures in Congo. These commercial activities—from the beginning relatively immune to popular criticism or qualms about mixing state institutional and presidential family interests—are attached to a military effort to bolster Congo's former president Kabila against Rassemblement Congolais pour la Démocratie (RCD) rebels.[40] Akin to state-to-state alliances of Cold War Africa, this arrangement adds a commercial component to military assistance wherein profits from mining schemes defray the costs of military support.

This private channel of relations between weak and strong states offers weak-state rulers, some of whom lack the resources to even field conventional diplomatic staffs, new ways to exercise influence over officials outside of Africa. Military success and revived commercial prospects in Sierra Leone addressed creditors' main concerns about that country. One report even alleges that at a critical point in Sierra Leone's discussions with creditors in late 1995, Executive Outcomes advanced money to the Sierra Leone government to make a token payment of arrears.[41] In any case, Sierra Leone was relatively well treated at Paris Club debt negotiations in early 1996, which reduced Sierra Leone's debt by 20.1 percent to $969 million.[42] Improved relations with creditors cleared the way for bilateral aid projects and budget support that totaled $204 million in 1995, compared to $62 million three years earlier.[43] The tight relationship between mining companies and private security firms also has the advantage of fitting well with creditors' preference that corrupt, inefficient bureaucracies in weak states privatize as much of their operations as possible.

Foreign embassies and officials in other states apparently appreciated the role of Executive Outcomes—and, later, of Lifeguard—in pacifying the countryside and supporting a central government that could function as a diplomatic interlocutor.[44] Foreign private aid and charitable organizations also benefited from the foreign firm's provision of security to large areas of the countryside. Said a worker for Save the Children of the South African security company: "They bang heads very efficiently, the fighting stops—and that's when babies get fed."[45] Bilateral aid programs share in this approval to the extent that these programs rely on private contractors to distribute goods and provide services.

■   WHY WEAK STATES ARE BETTER AT
     PRIVATE DIPLOMACY THAN INSURGENTS

One might expect that local strongmen who actually control natural resources would attract their own commercial operators to perform the same internal security, economic, and diplomatic tasks that some firms perform for rulers of weak states. Charles Taylor, leader of the National Patriotic Front of Liberia (NPFL) from 1990 to 1997, for example, controlled about 95 percent of the territory of Liberia at the height of the NPFL's powers.[46] Taylor's organization concluded an agreement with Firestone Tire and Rubber, and the firm agreed to pay "taxes" to Taylor's organization.[47] Likewise, American Mineral Fields provided financial assistance to Laurent Kabila's forces before his organization seized power in Kinshasa and was recognized globally as the successor to the exiled President Mobutu.[48] Nonetheless, it is unlikely that either firm supposed that it would do business for any long period with an authority that lacked global sovereign recognition. Firestone abandoned its arrangement with Taylor after the NPFL failed to capture Monrovia in its Operation Octopus assault of October 1992. (It was not clear that Firestone's home office managers were fully aware of the lengths to which their local agents went to placate Taylor's rebel group.) American Mineral Fields, however, calculated correctly that its partner would become the globally recognized head of Congo (Zaire) and therefore be in a position to justify these business dealings to outsiders.

It is this global recognition of a weak state's sovereignty, and the sovereign state's status as an anchor for international commercial jurisprudence, that bind firms to rulers of weak states to the great detriment of insurgencies. In the regulation of commercial disputes, firms (and so far, judges and arbiters) can find no credible alternative to a global society made up of sovereign states. Thus firms seek agreements with authorities deemed sovereign. U.S. courts and other forums guided by U.S. litigation style, such as the Paris-based International Chamber of Commerce, reinforce this global commercial norm.[49] For example, Firestone faced claims for damages in U.S. district courts from the externally recognized sovereign government of the Republic of Liberia even though that sovereign authority controlled only a small enclave centered on the capital city at the time of Firestone's agreement with Taylor.[50]

Several other commercial disputes in U.S. courts related to the Liberian civil war reinforced the inability of insurgencies to acquire judicial standing in order to assert their own commercial claims. The New York District Court, for example, ruled that the Monrovia enclave authority had standing in U.S. courts irrespective of the fact that the regime did not enjoy explicit diplomatic recognition (due to its supposed temporary status pending a final peace agreement). This judicial determination of sovereignty was based on the principle that whoever occupied the capital of the already recognized state was entitled to present claims and defenses in U.S. courts on behalf of the Republic of Liberia.[51]

This ruling also opened the way for firms to sue the globally recognized Liberian government.[52] But even this potential liability translated into an important political resource for the Monrovia regime. Though Charles Taylor and his NPFL may have had more access to resources and controlled more territory, his immunity from suit in foreign courts rendered any dealings with his organization hazardous—as several logging companies that did business in areas under his control and then suffered expropriation of assets were to discover.[53] Doing business with a globally recognized regime, in contrast, has the practical advantage of enabling firms to indemnify operations, as any underwriter would insist that the local authority have standing in foreign courts sufficient for the underwriter's clients (and the underwriter) to press claims in the event of a dispute. Insofar as the "trade, not aid" policies of the United States are reserved for firms that do business with regimes in very weak, but still sovereign, states, similar benefits will be denied to firms that do business with insurgents. Although firms in both circumstances usually have to provide their own security, firms doing business with insurgents lack the external risk-management tools of private insurance and recognized courts and arbiters. Also, globally recognized states doing business with firms that enjoy U.S. (or other strong state) backing are more likely to respect contracts, since doing otherwise triggers statutory sanctions against them in commercial and financial markets.

The head of the military service firm that intervened in Sierra Leone's conflict made clear that "Executive Outcomes concluded contracts only with lawfully constituted and lawfully established Governments, not with armed opposition movements or groups of rebels or insurgents."[54] This policy offered that and other military service firms several positive commercial advantages. First, mining firms with which any military service or industrial security firms are associated (and which ultimately generate the foreign exchange with which they are paid) need the externally supplied legal security to conclude contracts with the government receiving "aid" and to make insurance claims abroad should insurgents interfere with operations. Second, in the case of Executive Outcomes, managers were anxious to secure contracts from other states, and aiding insurgents would make other potential client regimes wary. Third, legal innovations such as the U.S. Alien Tort Claims Act, designed to allow private actors to be liable for war crimes and other damages, leaves firms that do business in sovereign states relatively protected. Those who operate on behalf of nonrecognized authorities do not enjoy similar protection, clearly a matter of concern for firms that critics often label as mercenary.[55]

The legal standing in commercial jurisprudence of very weak states helps marshal further external private support for rulers who team up with foreign firms. That is, firms and investors prefer a global society in which each state has a single, unambiguous authoritative interlocutor. Official investment insurance schemes will indemnify operations and, in some instances, provide preferential access to credit, and capital markets will rate the firm's level of risk as tolerable. These firms are thus free riders, benefiting from the advantages of sovereignty that other organizations provide to weak states.

■ ARE PRIVATE INTERSTATE RELATIONS IN AFRICA NEW?

On the face of it, the relationship between very weak state rulers, foreign firms, powerful states, and institutions that organize the terms of transnational commerce revives aspects of the "imperialism by invitation" that Michael Doyle describes in nineteenth-century Africa. That is, rulers during Africa's late precolonial period, especially those who were close to the coast, commonly took advantage of access to and control over commerce with Europeans to increase their personal power. These commercial contacts often helped shift the local balance of power. But from the point of view of nineteenth-century business partners, local collaborators who exercised precarious control could not be relied on to provide order. Thus European traders tended to prefer a missionary presence too and called for (or themselves provided) armed troops to boost the favored ruler's local political control and restrain the ruler's neighbors or local rivals, who often reacted violently toward what they understood to be agents of a decisive political shift.[56] The activities of mining companies, military trainers, and industrial security guards and the diminishing role of local adjudication appear to revive much of the substance of nineteenth-century practice.

There is a major difference today, however. Changes in the international environment make it virtually impossible to extinguish the sovereignty of even the very weakest states. Somalia does not exist as a de facto state in any conventionally recognized sense. The northern region, Somaliland, does possess a public authority organized along more conventional administrative lines. Yet even in Somaliland, authorities base their claims for recognition on respect for former colonial boundaries (the territory was once a British colony, amalgamated with Italian Somalia in 1960) and argue that their claim of sovereignty completes Africa's process of self-determination within the confines of inherited colonial boundaries. None of the various rebel groups in Congo's ongoing civil war publicly discusses breaking up the country as a reasonable goal. Likewise, in Liberia, some observers picked up on Charles Taylor's early claims to build a new greater Liberia. Yet he also focused his discussions with outsiders on asserting his right to become the globally recognized head of the Republic of Liberia, which he did in an election in 1997.[57] Any control he does exercise beyond Liberia's borders (in Sierra Leone and Guinea) he pursues through proxies rather than expanding his regime's formal administrative reach or claiming additional territory. Nor do insurgents in Africa's dozen or so other states facing internal warfare, such as Sudan, Guinea-Bissau, Burundi, Congo-Brazzaville, Sierra Leone, or Angola, assert a consistent claim for separate sovereignty.

Unlike in the nineteenth century, commercial agents usually seek advantages that an alliance with a de jure sovereign provides rather than a partnership with whoever happens to control a particular piece of territory at a given moment. Paradoxically, globalization of the late twentieth century in this fashion buttresses the state system in marginal areas of the global economy, in contrast to the late-nineteenth-century period of global economic expansion that undermined both de facto and de jure independence of political units (to the extent that the latter was recognized in the first place). Private security firms have, in serving these interests, become agents sustaining states in the absence of Cold War–era superpower support. These and other private actors pursuing private gain do so in important ways that are compatible with the needs and strictures of the post–Cold War state-based international system beyond Africa.

■ NOTES

1. I. William Zartman, "Posing the Problem of State Collapse," in I. William Zartman, ed., *Collapsed States: The Disintegration and Restoration of Legitimate Authority* (Boulder: Lynne Rienner, 1995), pp. 1–11; Robert Kaplan, "The Coming Anarchy," *Atlantic Monthly* 273, no. 2 (February 1994): 44–76.

2. Béatrice Hibou, *Afrique Est-Elle Protectionniste? Les Chemins Buissonniers de la Libéralisation Extérieure* (Paris: Kathala, 1996); Jean François Bayart, Stephen Ellis, and Béatrice Hibou, *Criminalization of the State in Africa* (Portsmouth, NH: Heinemann, 1998); William Reno, *Warlord Politics and African States* (Boulder: Lynne Rienner, 1998).

3. Herbert Howe, "Private Security Forces and African Stability: The Case of Executive Outcomes," *Journal of Modern African Studies* 36, no. 2 (June 1998): 307–331; David Shearer, "Outsourcing War," *Foreign Policy* (Fall 1998): 68–81; Al J. Venter, "Market Forces: How Hired Guns Succeeded Where the United Nations Failed," *Jane's International Defense Review* (March 1998): 23–26.

4. See Christopher Clapham, *Africa and the International System* (New York: Cambridge University Press, 1996), pp. 244–266.

5. For example, see Jeffrey Herbst, "Responding to State Failure in Africa," *International Security* 21, no. 3 (Winter 1996–1997): 120–144; Donald McNeil Jr., "A War Turned Free-for-All Tears at Africa's Center," *New York Times,* December 6, 1998, Week in Review, p. 5.

6. "Zaire: SWIPCO Pact a Major Boon," *Africa Energy & Mining,* May 24, 1995.

7. Michela Wrong, "Banking Thrives in Chaotic Zaire," *Financial Times,* March 7, 1995, p. 7.

8. Jedrzej George Frynas, "Political Instability and Business Focus on Shell in Nigeria," *Third World Quarterly* 19, no. 3 (September 1998): 457–478.

9. David Knott, "Interest Grows in African Oil and Gas Opportunities," *Oil & Gas Journal* (May 12, 1997): 41.

10. Michael Bratton and Nicolas van de Walle, *Democratic Experiments in Africa* (New York: Cambridge University Press, 1997).

11. Terry Lynn Karl, *The Paradox of Plenty* (Berkeley: University of California Press, 1997). See also Douglas Yates, *The Rentier State in Africa* (Trenton, NJ: Africa World Press, 1996).

12. John Wiseman, "Leadership and Personal Danger in African Politics," *Journal of Modern African Studies* 31, no. 4 (December 1993): 657–660. The five countries in Tables 9.1 and 9.2 experienced fifteen regime transitions between 1960 and 2000. Three were peaceful changes. In six, rulers lost power in coups; three were in exile for varying periods. Five were killed by opponents while in office.

13. J. Charap and C. Harm, "Institutionalized Corruption and the Kleptocratic State," IMF working paper 99/91, Washington, D.C., July 1999, p. 20.

14. Susan Rose-Ackerman, *Corruption and Government: Causes, Consequences, and Reform* (New York: Cambridge University Press, 1999), p. 200.

15. Fred Hayward, "The Development of a Radical Political Organization in the Bush: A Case Study in Sierra Leone," *Canadian Journal of African Studies* 6, no. 1 (1972): 1–28; Alfred Zack-Williams, *Tributors, Supporters and Merchant Capital: Mining and Underdevelopment in Sierra Leone* (Aldershot: Avebury Press, 1995).

16. "Fighting for Diamonds," *West Africa,* June 24, 1991, p. 1034.

17. Susan Rice, remarks at the U.S. Conference of Mayors, Washington, D.C., January 28, 1998.

18. U.S. House of Representatives, "Foreign Operations, Export Financing, and Related Programs Appropriations Bill," September 15, 1998, p. 6.

19. U.S. International Trade Commission, *U.S.-Africa Trade Flows and the Effects of the Uruguay Round Agreement and U.S. Trade and Development Policy* (Washington, DC: USITC, 1997).

20. James Bennet, "Throngs Greet Call by Clinton for New Africa," *New York Times,* March 24, 1998, p. 1.

21. Peter Schraeder, Steven Hook, and Bruce Taylor, "Clarifying the Foreign Aid Puzzle: A Comparison of American, Japanese, French, and Swedish Aid Flows," *World Politics* 50, no. 2 (January 1998): 294–323.

22. Economist Intelligence Unit, *Angola,* 1st quarter, 2000, pp. 21, 30.

23. "Angola: Not Yet Endgame," *Africa Confidential,* January 21, 2000, p. 2.

24. Banque du Zaire, *Rapport Annuel* (Kinshasa: Banque du Zaire, 1992), p. 28; Economist Intelligence Unit, *Zaire,* 3rd quarter, 1992, p. 13.

25. Economist Intelligence Unit, *Gabon, Equatorial Guinea,* 4th quarter, 1997, pp. 12, 14.

26. The World Bank's *African Development Indicators* (Washington, DC: World Bank, 1997), p. 35, shows the following figures.

	1990	1996
Angola	$780	$340
Congo (Zaire)	230	110
Equatorial Guinea	360	380
Zambia	420	430
Nigeria	460	280

27. "Diamond Dealer Turns Peacemaker," *Electronic Mail & Guardian* (Johannesburg), August 15, 1997.

28. Susan Schmidt, "DNC Donor with an Eye on Diamonds," *Washington Post,* August 2, 1997, p. 1.

29. Patrick Smith, "Cursed for Their Mineral Wealth: Business in War Zones," *Financial Mail* (Johannesburg), August 14, 1998, p. 30.

30. Al J. Venter, "Winds of War Set to Blow Across Angola," *Jane's Intelligence Review* 10, no. 10 (October 1998): 37–39.

31. "The Crackdown Begins," *Africa Energy & Mining,* January 28, 1998.

32. Economist Intelligence Unit, *Guinea, Sierra Leone, Liberia,* 2nd quarter, 1997, pp. 32–33.

33. Economist Intelligence Unit, *Angola,* 3rd quarter, 1997, p. 18.

34. Economist Intelligence Unit, *Guinea, Sierra Leone, Liberia,* 2nd quarter, 1997, p. 33.

35. Ibid.

36. Al J. Venter, "Sierra Leone's Mercenary War Battle for the Diamond Fields," *International Defense Review* 28, no. 11 (November 1995): 61–66.

37. UN High Commission for Refugees, "The Rights of People to Self-Determination and Its Application to Peoples Under Colonial or Alien Domination or Foreign Occupation," E/CN.4/1998/4, para. 34.

38. Correspondence from the oil company to the inspector general of police, Lagos, Nigeria, December 1, 1993; details of arming of the contingent, April 18, 1994; arms purchase invoice, August 18, 1994.

39. Letter from S. J. Berwin & Co., Council for Sandline International, to the foreign secretary (of UK), April 24, 1998; Raymond Bonner, "US Reportedly Backed British Mercenary Group in Africa," *New York Times,* May 13, 1998.

40. "War Winnings," *Africa Confidential,* October 23, 1998, p. 8; "Strange Ridgepointe Contract," *Africa Energy & Mining,* November 4, 1998; "Rhodies to the Rescue," *Africa Confidential,* November 5, 1999, p. 5.

41. *Lettre du Continent,* December 21, 1995.

42. John Swaray, governor of the Bank of Sierra Leone, "Debt Reduction Programme," April 4, 1996 (mimeo); Bank of Sierra Leone, "Paris Club Debt Relief Negotiation," *BSL Bulletin* 2, no. 2 (April 1996): 42.

43. Economist Intelligence Unit, *Sierra Leone Country Survey, 1995–96* (London: EIU, 1996).

44. U.S. government officials met with the South African military firm on U.S. soil in June 1997 to discuss (among other matters) its potential role as a stabilizing force in other weak states.

45. Brian James, "The New Dogs of War," *Mail on Sunday,* December 7, 1997, p. 18.

46. François Prkic, "Privatisation du Pouvoir et Guerre Civile: l'Émergence de l'État-phénix au Liberia dans les Années 1990," unpublished paper.

47. National Patriotic Reconstruction Assembly Government (the rebels' political organization), "Memorandum of Understanding," and "Restart Timetable," January 16, 1992.

48. "Business at War," *Africa Confidential,* April 25, 1997, pp. 1–2.

49. Yves Dezalay and Bryant Garth, *Dealing in Virtue: International Commercial Arbitration and the Construction of a Transnational Legal Order* (Chicago: University of Chicago Press, 1996).

50. Firestone's agreement with Taylor appears in National Patriotic Reconstruction Assembly Government "Memorandum of Understanding," and "Restart Timetable." The recognized government's legal claims appear in Republic of Liberia, Ministry of Finance, "Memorandum on Behavior of Firestone During the Liberian Civil War," May 6, 1993.

51. Marian Nash, "Contemporary Practice of the United States Relating to International Law," *American Journal of International Law* 90 (April

1996): 263–265. This principle was upheld in *Liberia v. Bickford,* 787 F. Supp. 397 (SDNY 1992). Comments on the NPFL's lack of standing are in *National Patriotic Reconstruction Assembly Government of Liberia v. Liberian Services, Inc.* (92 Civ. 145, EDVa. 1992).

52. *Meridien International Bank Ltd. v. Government of the Republic of Liberia* (92 Civ. 7039 SDNY 1996).

53. *Yona International and Others v. La Reunion Francaise and Others, Queen's Bench Division Commercial Court.*

54. UN, "Rights of Peoples," para. 50.

55. Ariadne Sacharoff, "Multinationals in Host Countries: Can They Be Held Liable Under the Alien Tort Claim Act for Human Rights Violations?" *Brooklyn Journal of International Law* 23 (1998): 927–946. See also *Kadic v. Karadzic* 70 (2nd Cir., 1995).

56. Michael Doyle, *Empires* (Ithaca: Cornell University Press, 1986), pp. 162–197.

57. National Patriotic Reconstruction Assembly Government, *The Legal Status of the National Patriotic Reconstruction Government as the Defacto Government of the Republic of Liberia,* Gbarnga (Liberia), 1991; William Swidler and Mark Berlin (Taylor's Washington lobbyist), "Notes on Liberian Fact-Finding Visit," September 1, 1991.

10

Conclusion: African Foreign Policy Making at the Millennium

Terrence Lyons & Gilbert M. Khadiagala

Posing the question of African foreign policy making in the conceptually comfortable ways of thinking about change and continuity scarcely illuminates the confusing processes characterizing the late twentieth and early twenty-first centuries. Change needs to be understood on various levels: First, it denotes progress and capacity building as actors acquire new modes of confronting old (and new) battles. Second, it is preemptive; that is, we learn from previous institutional and behavioral flaws. More significant, for African states long encumbered by diverse challenges, change in the foreign policy environment ideally accompanies some marked improvement in organizational freedom at home and in opportunities abroad. The preceding contributors sought to address foreign policy concerns in Africa's major regions in order to discern patterns and practices in recent decades. We all are interested in whether changes in actors, issues, and roles constitute significant procedural and substantive shifts in foreign policies.

What most of the authors found is a consistent web of constraints on state action with ever-diminishing domestic and international opportunities. There have been changes within the structure of constraints rather than profound alterations in the policymaking environment or in outcomes. Instead of offering vistas to policymakers, past and present constraints have limited their abilities to be authoritative participants in the international system. This is more evident in the external environment, the primary arena and focus of African foreign policies. Much has changed externally; in particular, the Cold War has ended and has been followed by burgeoning economic globalization. But these changes have not improved the lot of individual or collective African state actors. In examining the differentiated impact of global transformations on African foreign policies, the contributors to this volume have highlighted contrasting trends such as the interplay between the diminished authority of formal state actors and the engagement of international nongovernmental organizations (NGOs), the demise of stultifying Cold War alliances and the reality of economic marginalization, and the growing interventionary power of international financial institutions (IFIs) and their decreasing aid commitments to African economies. Globalization has circumscribed Africa's role in the international system while engendering new actors that are making additional demands on already vulnerable actors. In the face of a less benign and charitable international environment, African decisionmakers are nevertheless forced to pay attention to multiple external constituencies—NGOs, IFIs, and MNCs (multinational corporations) as well as Cable News Network (CNN)—invariably raising the costs of foreign policy.

The central question about globalization will remain what poor and small states can do to sustain the interest of external actors preoccupied with what they perceive as more worthwhile concerns. Similarly, since marginality breeds its own sources of vulnerability, African states will continually struggle to control unwanted external interference. These themes constitute a promising avenue of future research. It would, for instance, be enlightening to examine the specific challenges that globalization poses to African foreign policies that transcend the sterile end-of-Cold-War models. If, as Reno and Adibe have suggested, NGOs, militias, and transnational economic business organizations are now more influential in African foreign policy, how do we measure their influence? Are these actors transitional or permanent elements on the foreign policy landscape? How do these actors alter the conception of national interest? In addition, since interminable wars seem to propel humanitarian organizations to the forefront of African foreign policy, from what institutions do these organizations derive their authority and how do they establish mechanisms of accountability and probity? Equally, since major external state actors are more willing to subcontract their foreign and security policies to private actors, how do they overcome questions of policy coordination within an untidy arena of competing states and private actors? In establishing better conceptual links between state and nonstate actors, we need to understand whether the latter's interests are independent or mediated by state institutions.

As in the 1960s and 1970s, some African states and leaders have been successful in seizing opportunities and avoiding some of the most restrictive constraints; others have made the worst of a bad environment. A few leaders have recognized emerging trends and garnered the benefits of being ahead of the curve. Ghana won significant international resources by serving as an early model for structural adjustment, Benin won favor (particularly in Washington) for its initial moves toward democracy, and Namibia and Mozambique benefited from the international community's desperate need for examples of successful peacebuilding. Similarly, as Lemarchand and Iyob note, leaders in Ethiopia, Eritrea, Uganda, and Rwanda seemed to represent a "new generation of leaders," thereby earning international assistance and visits by U.S. officials that bestowed legitimacy to their regimes. Nelson Mandela's inspiring life from prison to the presidency ensured South Africa's place at the top of the continent's hierarchy in world opinion, as discussed by Venter. Other leaders have exploited the darker side of international concerns, as when Zaire's Mobutu manipulated refugees to gain international assistance or when leaders in the Horn forged the frontline states' alliance against Sudan and won the support of the United States in response.

At the same time that some leaders found new ways to demonstrate their value to external patrons and resources, some old mechanisms had lost their effectiveness. Clark shows that without the ability to play a role in the anticommunist and Cold War agendas of the broader world, most states and leaders lost their relevance to decisionmakers outside of Africa. As the importance of access to foreign military facilities declined, states such as Somalia and the Central African Republic (CAR) lost leverage while Mombasa retained its importance as a port for humanitarian assistance to central Africa and the Horn.

Forces of globalization are not alone in reducing the leverage of state actors tasked with formulating and articulating foreign policy. In regional and continental contexts where African states traditionally had more latitude, there has been no appreciable improvement in the circumstances for major actors singly or collectively to build institutions for development and security. Africa's phase of sturdy

regionalism centered on economic integration schemes was interrupted in the mid-1970s by heady nationalism and by ideological
and personality conflicts. In the new phase prompted by globalization, African states seek more ambitious institutional forms of regionalism but against the backdrop of accelerating strains of civil wars
and border conflicts. Regionalism in Africa has not found a formula
that reconciles trade expansion, harmonization of currencies, and
open borders with the centrifugal challenges of unviable states.

There has been a reinvigoration of African regional organizations—such as the Economic Community of West African States
(ECOWAS), the Southern Africa Development Community (SADC),
the Intergovernmental Authority on Development (IGAD), and the
East African Community (EAC)—to boost economic integration, but
their attempts to expand into new roles have met with insurmountable obstacles. Adibe and Khadiagala suggest that the innovations in
security building shown in ECOMOG's experience in Liberia and
Sierra Leone and SADC's interventions in Lesotho are improvised
works in progress rather than profound breakthroughs in the norms
and practices of African collective security. Besides, for the core regional states, intervention to check the implosion of weak neighbors
expands the burdens and distracts from the primary objectives of
economic integration, a theme reiterated in the chapters by Adibe,
Lemarchand, and Venter. Whether Nigeria's energies are better ex-
pended in fostering regional trade and investment (in addition to putting its own political house in order) than in deploying forces to battle the Revolutionary United Front (RUF) rebels in Sierra Leone is a
question that now confronts foreign policy makers who are increasingly facing domestic pressures for regional disengagement.

ECOMOG and SADC regional interventions have helped pave
the way for the erosion of the principles of sovereignty. Although
this erosion can be justified in the concept of sovereignty as responsibility, African states have ventured into the untested area of military intervention with thus far uncertain outcomes. The conflict over
the future of the Democratic Republic of Congo (DRC), analyzed by
Lemarchand, exemplifies this trend. Sustained for most of the postcolonial period by the security umbrella of the Cold War, the DRC
persists as the sick man of central Africa, weakened by a widening
domestic power vacuum. That this power vacuum has attracted the
competitive intervention of a Rwanda-led central African alliance pitted

against a Zimbabwe-led southern Africa seems, at the surface, to portend a radical alteration in the norm of territorial integrity. It is, however, more accurate to examine these alliances as a variation on the theme of weak states exporting their domestic vulnerabilities, a practice reminiscent of the foreign policies of Kwame Nkrumah and Idi Amin. Weak states on shoestring budgets that exploit power vacuums are unlikely to build long-term regional institutions for order; instead they might foster the very debilitating alliances that the Organization of African Unity (OAU) has worked for many years to preempt. It is for this reason that the intervention in the DRC needs to be seen more appropriately as a decline in norms of interstate civility and mechanisms for conflict resolution rather than a meaningful redefinition of borders and the idea of territorial integrity.

The effects of the transformations in central Africa on African interstate practices should not be understated. As Clark and Lemarchand have shown, the regional security formation centered on Uganda, Rwanda, and Burundi has, within a very short time, made a major impact on the texture of regional relationships. These "revisionist" states, imbued with both ethnic and regime security, have legitimized military intervention as a means to resolve conflicts. But, as with the temptation to embrace the concepts of "new African leaders" and "African renaissance," we should not mistake fleeting for long-run processes. This cautionary note is especially relevant in contemporary Africa, where the economic costs of leadership and rule making are higher than before.

Regional leadership in African international relations remains an intricate balance between tangible economic and military resources and a broad-based domestic consensus to employ these resources. In the context where South Africa, as Venter suggests, has shown considerable reluctance to provide continental and regional leadership and where Nigeria contemplates reducing its regional military commitments, the leadership credentials of precarious states in central Africa seem to be ephemeral. In the Horn of Africa, Iyob shows that the hope that Ethiopia and Eritrea could play constructive roles in managing conflict in Sudan and Somalia collapsed as a destructive war broke out on their border. Scholarly attempts to relate military and political intervention in neighboring countries in Africa to European processes of state making fail to appreciate the power limits of Africa's would-be hegemons. In the absence of genuine African hegemons, the norms and rules of interstate relationships established since the 1960s are likely to endure into the new century.

The region as an arena of conflict and cooperation will still constitute the densest network for African foreign policies, furnishing a fruitful avenue of research. Although there has been an attempt to define regions through institutions, most regions remain fluid with membership overlapping along geographical and functional lines. A question interesting to ponder is the array of economic and political circumstances that contribute to the triumph of regional institutions over their competitors. Why, despite initial skepticism, does the Common Market for Eastern and Southern African States (COMESA) persist in its quest for trade and integration? Will ECOWAS succeed in the long run as the institutional anchor of West Africa? Also significant in foreign policy calculus is the African propensity for joining regional organizations. Does coalescence in organizations reflect long-term economic needs or short-term strategic and political imperatives? What compels Eritrea and Sudan to join the Libyan-led Community of Sahelian and Saharan States (COMESSA), an organization that mirrors the objectives of IGAD? Future students of African regionalism will also be interested in the relationships between economic regionalism and conflict reduction. Will the accession of Burundi and Rwanda to membership in the EAC resolve their existing problems of institutional homelessness and help submerge Tutsi-Hutu conflicts in the civility of East African regionalism? Similarly, will the DRC be more stable anchored in SADC than in institutionless central Africa, or will its continued SADC membership exacerbate tensions between central and southern Africa? Will SADC admit new northerly states such as Uganda in its fold given the experience of the DRC's membership?

In the late 1990s, regions became the laboratories for external efforts to strengthen African peacekeeping capacity, notably the U.S. African Crisis Response Initiative (ACRI) and the French Reinforcement of Capabilities of African Missions of Peacekeeping (RECAMP). These initiatives are efforts to bridge the gap between facile "African solutions to African problems" and international disinterestedness, but there are questions that remain about their institutional locus. In particular, there is little clarity as to whether these initiatives are geared to boost the peacekeeping abilities of SADC and ECOWAS or those of individual states such as Uganda and Senegal. The fact that ACRI-trained soldiers have been deployed in internal conflicts, as in Senegal, and regional wars, as with Uganda's intervention in the DRC, demonstrates that the new military capacities may be used in ways not anticipated by foreign trainers. Increasing local and foreign military exercises throughout Africa are bound to focus attention on diverse efforts to fashion alternative security arrangements. An interesting area of analysis is whether joint military training and exercises for peacekeeping socialize African militaries into new positions as protectors of civilian institutions or perpetuate their previous roles as sources of instability.

Most of the chapters have pointed to institutional and leadership incoherence as one of the continuing obstacles to effective decision-making in African foreign policies, which reflect the endurance of state- and nation-building imperatives. In recent years, internal fragmentation of sovereignty and authority has stymied predictable patterns in foreign policy roles, a phenomenon that has assumed two extreme trajectories (with considerable variations in between). At the first level are states such as the DRC and Liberia where civil wars spawn multiple power centers that stake competing claims and positions in international and regional arenas. Second are states such as Kenya, Togo, and Zambia, where fragmented pluralism puts ruling groups and their domestic challengers at opposite ends of the foreign policy spectrum. In both cases, the outcomes are multiple foreign policy actors inviting assorted outsiders to be on their side and lending a remarkable degree of confusion to decisionmaking. This is the broader context in which Clark treats democratization as a source of regime vulnerability.

As Adibe, Clark, and Reno have emphasized, the process of the deinstitutionalization of the state and the related privatization of diplomacy has placed African foreign policies in a profound crisis of consistency and direction. Realist assumptions of state-centeredness are shamed by the specter of the African state weighed down by various internal actors and increasingly unable to compete with internal challengers in the foreign policy arena. It is no longer a question of whether foreign policy is the preserve of the president or the foreign minister but of whether any organized body is in charge. The implosion of the African state since the early 1990s highlights themes of foreign policy incoherence but also the contested nature of national interests. States that are rapidly weakening are bound to have inchoate national interests, and for those suffering from anarchy and inertia, foreign policy loses relevance.

Analysts will not cease to prescribe liberalization and democratization as the solution to Africa's problems, but their impact on foreign policy decisionmaking is not certain, particularly when the state has virtually been hollowed out and IFIs and NGOs are at the forefront of determining the parameters of African external and internal policies. Democratic procedures understandably increase demand-makers that jostle for positions in a variety of policy realms, an aspect of liberalization underscored by Schraeder. But as Clark, Khadiagala, and Venter suggest, liberalization in most of Africa has not enhanced the power of opposition groups and civil society regarding foreign policy. Criticisms from parliamentary opposition or the vibrant media have not deterred Museveni and Mugabe from intervening in the DRC; neither have they dissuaded Frederick Chiluba of Zambia and Daniel arap Moi of Kenya from devoting a disproportionate amount of their energies to regional diplomacy. Emerging parliaments in some parts of Africa might have tamed the presidencies, but they have crowded decisionmaking without substantially altering policy outcomes.

A more enduring legacy of democratization on foreign policy processes in Africa is, perhaps, the increase in the density of cross-regional functional and professional organizations seeking a voice on a variety of issues. The much-touted role of civil society in contemporary Africa is often exaggerated, but the fact that more groups with diverse interests are able to forge common positions along salient issues such as human rights, gender equity, regional security, and the environment demonstrates the potential for collaborative coalescence. Although these groups alone might not have that much influence on foreign policies in their individual countries, the flourishing alliances across issues bolster their collective latitude. As the pattern of NGOs in southern Africa reveals, a climate of openness in core states contributes to the emergence of new pressure groups and strengthens the organizational ability of existing ones. But the influence of these groups on state behavior hinges on their ability to organize and mobilize resources along existing institutional lines. Thus the upsurge of academic, labor, parliamentary, and civic associations organized under the SADC rubric broadens regional institutions, propelling them in new directions of mutual constraints and reciprocity. When these groups become institutional watchdogs routinely scrutinizing SADC states, they might deepen the ties that southern Africa has been assiduously constructing.

The growing literature on the links between globalization and the weakening of the African state forms a rich conceptual base for more research on actors behind these processes. Of note is how the multitude of domestic actors such as NGOs and opposition groups fosters strategic links with international networks to subvert the policy roles of formal state actors. Which local actors are empowered by specific globalization processes? Does supplanting foreign ministries with transnational networks (such as human rights organizations and aid agencies) and their local allies augur well for domestic institution building? What are the long-run consequences of the domestic fragmentation of decisionmaking on the articulation of national interests?

Since taking office, UN Secretary-General Kofi Annan has perennially harangued African states to settle current conflicts and restore internal and external peace lest history judge them as architects of the continent's self-inflicted destruction. This admonition underscores the intractability of unsettled scores and the monumental challenges that have characterized African foreign policies since the 1960s. In institutional and behavioral terms, foreign policies in Africa have mediated internal and external demands and expectations. Although structures have always mattered as sources of constraints and opportunities, leadership remains central to foreign policy making. Leadership reflects attempts by actors to work internally with diverse constituencies to improve socioeconomic conditions of citizenries and to engage other states in developing common institutions to organize Africa's place in the international order.

Throughout the 1960s and 1970s, scholars grappled with the influence of momentous concerns such as decolonization, nationalism, Pan-Africanism, and apartheid on African foreign policies. Despite variations in policies, these issues gave African decisionmakers a shared view of foreign policy as an enterprise for managing the novelty of independence. This period also marked a phase of relative stability in which Africa devoted foreign policy energies to the creation of regional and continental institutions against the backdrop of a generous international environment. The era that began in the 1980s with profound economic collapse in Africa continues into the new millennium with globalization severely constricting the ability of actors to use foreign policy for old and new goals. At national and regional levels, this phase is characterized by an ideological vacuum and a paucity of grand visions.

In the past, the actors, targets, and outcomes of African foreign policy were less ambiguous. Even the more elusive national interests could be gleaned from policy proclamations at the annual OAU summits. As few African leaders have bothered to attend these summits, it has become more difficult to discern interests and gauge positions. There was also precision in the previous models of African foreign policy as scholars sought explanations that best tied domestic contexts to the external realm. With the multiplicity of actors, amorphous targets, and uncertain outcomes, African foreign policy has entered uncharted territory. When there were coherent states and when Africa exuded the ability and faith to make a difference in an asymmetrical world, there was a pattern to foreign policy, but in the absence of these variables, foreign policy has become an untidy process of improvisation.

Bibliography

Abdullah, Ibrahim (1998). "Bush Path to Destruction: The Origin and Character of the Revolutionary United Front/Sierra Leone," *Journal of Modern African Studies* 36(2).

Abdullah, Ibrahim, and Patrick Muana (1998). "The Revolutionary United Front of Sierra Leone," in Christopher Clapham, ed., *African Guerrillas*. Oxford: James Currey.

Adibe, Clement (1994). "ECOWAS in Comparative Perspective," in Timothy M. Shaw and Julius E. Okolo, eds., *The Political Economy of Foreign Policy in ECOWAS*. New York: St. Martin's Press.

———— (1996). *Managing Arms in Peace Processes: Liberia*. Geneva: UN.

———— (1997). "The Liberian Conflict and the ECOWAS-UN Partnership," *Third World Quarterly* 18(3): 471–488.

Africa Leadership Forum (1991). *The Kampala Document: Towards a Conference on Security Stability, Development and Cooperation in Africa*. Kampala, May.

Afrifa, A. A. (1967). *The Ghana Coup*. London: Frank Cass.

Agbese, Pita O. (1996). "The Military as an Obstacle to the Democratization Enterprise: Towards an Agenda for Permanent Military Disengagement from Politics in Nigeria," *Journal of Asian and African Studies* 31: 82–98.

Ajayi, J. F. Ade, and Michael Crowder, eds. (1972). *History of West Africa*. New York: Columbia University Press.

Allison, Graham T. (1969). "Conceptual Models of the Cuban Missile Crisis," *American Political Science Review* 63(3): 689–718.

Aluko, Olajide (1976). *Ghana and Nigeria, 1957–1970: A Study in Inter-African Discord*. London: Rex Collings.

Anderson, Benedict (1991). *Imagined Communities*. Rev. ed. New York: Verso.

Anglin, Douglas (1996). *Zambian Crisis Behavior: Confronting Rhodesia's Unilateral Declaration of Independence*. Montreal: McGill University Press.

Asante, S.K.B. (1977). *Pan-African Protest: West Africa and the Italo-Ethiopian Crisis, 1934–1941*. London: Longman.

Ayele, Negussay (1977). "The Foreign Policy of Ethiopia," in Olajide Aluko, ed., *The Foreign Policies of African States*. London: Hodder and Stoughton.

Ayoob, Mohammed (1998). "Subaltern Realism: International Relations Theory Meets the Third World," in Stephanie Neumann, ed., *International Relations Theory and the Third World*. New York: St. Martin's Press.

Bach, Daniel C. (1983). "The Politics of West African Economic Cooperation: CEAO and ECOWAS," *Journal of Modern African Studies* 21(4): 605–623.

——— (1993). "Régionalismes Francophones ou Régionalisme Franco-Africain," in Daniel C. Bach and Anthony A. Kirk-Greene, *États et Sociétés en Afrique Francophone*. Paris: Économica.

Baniafouna, Calixte (1995). *Congo Démocratie: Les Déboires de l'Apprentissage*. Paris: l'Harmattan.

Bascom, Jonathan (1998). *Losing Place: Refugee Populations and Rural Transformations in East Africa*. New York: Berghahn Books.

Bayart, Jean Francois, Stephen Ellis, and Béatrice Hibou (1998). *Criminalization of the State in Africa*. Portsmouth, NH: Heinemann.

Becker, Charles, Saliou Mbaye, and Ibrahima Thioub, eds. (1997). *AOF: Réalités et Héritages: Sociétés Ouest-Africaines et Ordre Colonial, 1895–1960*. 2 vols. Dakar: Direction des Archives du Sénégal.

Beshir, Mohamed Omer (1975). *The Southern Sudan: From Conflict to Peace*. London: C. Hurst.

Besteman, Catherine (1999). *Unraveling Somalia: Race, Violence and the Legacy of Slavery*. Philadelphia: University of Pennsylvania Press.

Braeckman, Colette (1992). *Le Dinosaure: Le Zaire de Mobutu*. Paris: Fayard.

Bratton, Michael (1989). "Beyond the State: Civil Society and Associational Life in Africa," *World Politics* 41 (April).

Bratton, Michael, and Nicolas van de Walle (1997). *Democratic Experiments in Africa: Regime Transitions in Comparative Perspective*. New York: Cambridge University Press.

Breytenbach, Willie (1995). "Conflict in Sub-Saharan Africa: From the Frontline States to Collective Security," *Arusha Papers* (Center for Foreign Relations, Dar es Salaam) 2: 8–9.

Burstein, Stanley (1998). *Ancient African Civilizations: Kush and Axum*. Princeton, NJ: Markus Wiener.

Buzan, Barry (1991). *People, States and Fear: An Agenda for International Security Studies in the Post–Cold War Era*. Boulder: Lynne Rienner.

Callaghy, Thomas M. (1984). *The State-Society Struggle: Zaïre in Comparative Perspective*. New York: Columbia University Press.

——— (1994). "Africa: Back to the Future," *Journal of Democracy* 5(4): 133–145.

——— (2000). "Africa and the World Political Economy: More Caught Between a Rock and a Hard Place," in John W. Harbeson and Donald Rothchild, eds., *Africa in World Politics: The African State System in Flux*. Boulder: Westview Press.

Callaghy, Thomas M., and John Ravenhill, eds. (1993). *Hemmed In: Responses to Africa's Economic Decline*. New York: Columbia University Press.

Campbell, Gwyn R., and Mario Scerri (1995). "The Prospects for an Indian Ocean Rim (IOR) Economic Association," *South African Journal of International Affairs* 2(2).

Cawthra, Gavin (1997). "Subregional Security: SADC," *Security Dialogue* 28(2): 207–218.

Chirambo, Kondwani, and Pamela Chinaka (2000). "SADC Parliaments Want Accelerated Regional Integration," Southern African Research and Documentation Center (SARDC), Harare.

Clapham, Christopher (1996). *Africa and the International System: The Politics of Survival*. New York: Cambridge University Press.

——— (1998). "Being Peacekept," in Oliver Furley and Roy May, eds., *Peacekeeping in Africa*. Aldershot, England: Ashgate.

Clapham, Christopher, ed. (1977). *Foreign Policy Making in Developing States: A Comparative Approach*. New York: Praeger.

——— (1998). *African Guerrillas*. Oxford: James Currey.

Clark, John F. (1997). "The Extractive State in Zaire," in Leonardo Villalon, ed., *Critical Juncture: The African State Between Disintegration and Reconfiguration*. Boulder: Lynne Rienner.

——— (1997). "Petro-Politics in Congo," *Journal of Democracy* 8(3): 62–76.

——— (1998). "Democracy Dismantled in the Congo Republic," *Current History* 97(619): 234–237.

Clark, John F., and David E. Gardinier, eds. (1997). *Political Reform in Francophone West Africa*. Boulder: Westview Press.

Clough, Michael (1992). *Free at Last: U.S. Policy Toward Africa and the End of the Cold War*. New York: Council on Foreign Relations.

Collins, Robert O. (1971). *Land Beyond the Rivers: The Southern Sudan, 1898–1918*. New Haven: Yale University Press.

——— (1996). *The Waters of the Nile: Hydro-Politics and the Jonglei Canal, 1900–1988*. Princeton, NJ: Markus Wiener.

——— (1999). "Africans, Arabs, and Islamists: From the Conference Tables to the Battlefields in the Sudan," *African Studies Review* 42(2): 105–123.

Connell, Dan, and Frank Smyth (1998). "Africa's New Block," *Foreign Affairs* 77(2): 80.

Control Risk Group (1998). *Outlook 98: The World in 1998*. London: Control Risk Group.

Cox, Ronald W., ed. (1996). *Business and the State in International Relations*. Boulder: Westview Press.

Croft, Stuart (1998). "International Relations and Africa," *African Affairs* 96(385): 607–611.

Daddieh, Cyril K. (1997). "South Africa and Francophone African Relations," in Larry A. Swatuk and David R. Black, eds., *Bridging the Rift: The New South Africa in Africa*. Boulder: Westview Press.

Davies, Robert, Dot Keet, and Mfundo Nkuhlu (1993). *Reconstructing Economic Relations Within the Southern African Region: Issues and Options for a Democratic South Africa*. Macro-Economic Research Group Working Paper no. 1.

Davies, Stephen (1991). "Facing Goliath: Zimbabwe's Role in Conflict Resolution in Southern Africa," *South African International* 21(4): 244–255.

de Benoist, Joseph Roger (1982). *L'Afrique Occidentale Française de la Conference de Brazzaville (1994) à l'Independence (1960)*. Dakar: Les Nouvelles Éditions Africaines.

Decalo, Samuel (1998). *The Stable Minority: Civilian Rule in Africa*. Gainesville: Florida Academic Press.

Decalo, Samuel, Virginia Thompson, and Richard Adloff (1996). *Historical Dictionary of Congo*. Lanham, MD: Scarecrow Press.

Deng, Francis M. (1995). *War of Visions: Conflict of Identities in the Sudan*. Washington, DC: Brookings Institution.

Deng, Francis M., Sadikiel Kimaro, Terrence Lyons, Donald Rothchild, and I. William Zartman (1996). *Sovereignty as Responsibility: Conflict Management in Africa*. Washington, DC: Brookings Institution.

Deng, Francis M., and Terrence Lyons, eds. (1998). *African Reckoning: A Quest for Good Governance*. Washington, DC: Brookings Institution.

De Wall, Alex (1997). "Democratizing the Aid Encounter in Africa," *International Affairs* 73(4): 623–640.

Dezalay, Yves, and Bryant Garth (1996). *Dealing in Virtue: International Commercial Arbitration and the Construction of a Transnational Legal Order*. Chicago: University of Chicago Press.

Diamond, Larry, ed. (1997). *Transition Without End*. Boulder: Lynne Rienner.

Diop, Momar-Coumba, ed. (1994). *Le Sénégal et Ses Voisins*. Dakar: Sociétés-Espaces-Temps.

Donham, Donald, and Wendy James, eds. (1986). *The Southern Marches of Imperial Ethiopia: Essays in History and Social Anthropology*. Cambridge: Cambridge University Press.

Doyle, Michael (1986). *Empires*. Ithaca: Cornell University Press.

Dunn, D. Elmwood, and Byron S. Tarr (1988). *Liberia: A National Polity in Transition*. Methuen, NJ: Scarecrow Press.

East, Maurice A. (1973). "Foreign Policy-Making in Small States: Some Theoretical Observations Based on a Study of the Uganda Ministry of Foreign Affairs," *Policy Sciences* 4(4): 491–508.

Eduard, Bustin (1987). "The Foreign Policy of the Republic of Zaire," *Annals* 489 (January): 63–75.

Ellis, Stephen (1998). "Liberia's Warlord Insurgency," in Christopher Clapham, ed., *African Guerrillas*. Oxford: James Currey.

Evans, Graham (1996). "South Africa in Remission: The Foreign Policy of an Altered State," *Journal of Modern African Studies* 34(2): 260.

—— (1999). "South Africa's Foreign Policy after Mandela: Mbeki and his Concept of an African Renaissance," *Round Table* 352: 621–628.

Evans, Graham, and Jeffrey Newnham (1990). *The Dictionary of World Politics: A Reference Guide to Concepts, Ideas and Institutions.* London: Harvester.

Fafowora, O. O. (1983–1984). "The Role of the Ministry of External Affairs in the Formulation of Nigerian Foreign Policy: Personal Reminiscences," *Quarterly Journal of Administration* 18(3-4): 92–110.

Fage, J. D. (1969). *A History of West Africa: An Introductory Survey.* Cambridge: Cambridge University Press.

Farrell, R. Barry, ed. (1966). *Approaches to Comparative and International Politics.* Evanston, IL: Northwestern University Press.

Fauré, Yves (1993). "Democracy and Realism: Reflections on the Case of Côte d'Ivoire," *Africa: Journal of the International African Institute* 63(3): 313–329.

Faye, Ousseynou (1994). "La crise casamançaise et les relations du Sénégal avec la Gambie et Guinea-Bissau (1980–1992)," in Momar-Coumba Diop, ed., *Le Sénégal et ses voisins.* Dakar: Societes-Es-paces-Temps.

Foltz, William, and Henry Bienen, eds. (1985). *Arms and the African: Military Influences on Africa's International Relations.* New Haven: Yale University Press.

Frankel, Joseph (1963). *The Making of Foreign Policy.* London: Oxford University Press.

Frost, Mervyn (1997). "Pitfalls on the Moral High Ground: Ethics and South African Foreign Policy," in Walter Carlsnaes and Marie Muller, eds., *Change and South African External Relations.* Johannesburg: International Thomson.

Frynas, Jedrzej George (1998). "Political Instability and Business Focus on Shell in Nigeria," *Third World Quarterly* 19(3): 457–478.

Furley, Oliver, ed. (1995). *Conflict in Africa.* London: Tauris Academic Studies.

Garba, Jospeh N. (1991). *Diplomatic Soldiering: The Conduct of Nigerian Foreign Policy, 1975–1979.* Rev. 2nd ed. Ibadan: Spectrum Books.

Gardinier, David E. (1997). "Gabon: Limited Reform and Regime Survival," in John F. Clark and David E. Gardinier, eds., *Political Reform in Francophone Africa.* Boulder: Westview Press.

Garten, Jeffrey E. (1993). *A Cold Peace: America, Japan, Germany, and the Struggle for Supremacy.* New York: Twentieth Century Fund.

Geiss, Immanuel (1974). *The Pan-African Movement.* London: Methuen.

Gibbs, Richard (1997). "Regional Integration in Post-Apartheid Southern Africa: The Case Renegotiating the South African Customs Union," *Journal of Southern African Studies* 23(1): 67–86.

Glaser, Antoine, and Stephen Smith (1994). *L'Afrique sans Africains: Le Rêve Blanc du Continent Noir.* Paris: Éditions Stock.

Global Witness (1999). *A Crude Awakening: The Role of the Oil and Banking Industries in Angola's Civil War and the Plunder of State Assets.* London: Global Witness.

Good, Kenneth (1997). "Accountable to Themselves: Predominance in Southern Africa," *Journal of Modern African Studies* 35(4): 547–573.

Gordon, Colin, ed. (1980). *Power/Knowledge: Selected Interviews and Other Writings 1972–1977, Michel Foucault.* New York: Pantheon Books.

Griffiths, L. I. (1995). *The African Inheritance.* London: Routledge.

Grundy, Kenneth (1973). *Accommodation and Confrontation in Southern Africa: The Limits of Independence.* Berkeley: University of California Press.

——— (1985). "The Impact of Region on Contemporary African Politics," in Gwendolen M. Carter and Patrick O'Meara, eds., *African Independence: The First Twenty-Five Years.* Bloomington: Indiana University Press.

Gutteridge, William (1997). "South Africa's Future Defense and Security: Identifying National Interest," *Conflict Studies* 298: 1–24.

Harris, Joseph E. (1969–1970). "Soliaman Bin Haftoo: Ethiopian Imposter in India?" *Journal of Ethiopian Studies* 7–8: 15–18.

Harris, P. B. (1970). *Studies in African Politics.* London: Hutchinson University Library.

Hayward, Fred (1972). "The Development of a Radical Political Organization in the Bush: A Case Study in Sierra Leone," *Canadian Journal of African Studies* 6(1): 1–28.

Hazelwood, Arthur, ed. (1967). *African Integration and Disintegration: Case Studies in Economic and Political Union.* London: Oxford University Press.

Herbst, Jeffrey (1996–1997). "Responding to State Failure in Africa," *International Security* 21(3): 120–144.

Hibou, Beatrice (1996). *Afrique, Est-Elle Protectionniste? Les Chemins Buissonniers de la Liberalization Extérieure.* Paris: Kathala.

Himwork, John, Michel Le Gall, and James L. Watson, eds. (1980). *Asian and African Systems of Slavery.* Berkeley: University of California Press.

Hobsbawm, E. J. (1990). *Nations and Nationalism Since 1780: Program, Myth, Reality.* Cambridge: Cambridge University Press.

Hoogvelt, Ankie (1997). *Globalization and the Postcolonial World: The New Political Economy of Development.* Baltimore, MD: Johns Hopkins University Press.

Horton, James Africanus (1868/1969). *West African Countries and Peoples.* Edinburgh: Edinburgh University Press.

Howe, Herbert (1998). "Private Security Forces and African Stability: The Case of Executive Outcomes," *Journal of Modern African Studies* 36(2): 307–331.

Huliaras, C. Asteris (1998). "The 'Anglo-Saxon Conspiracy': French Perceptions of the Great Lake Crisis," *Journal of Modern African Studies* 36(4): 593–609.

Hume, Cameron (1994). *Ending Mozambique's War: The Role of Mediation and Good Offices.* Washington, DC: U.S. Institute of Peace.

Hutchful, Eboe (1995–1996). "The Civil Society Debate in Africa," *International Journal* 51(1): 54–77.

Ihonvbere, Julius (1995). "Where Is the Third Wave? A Critical Evaluation of Africa's Non-Transition to Democracy," *Africa Today* 43(4): 343–368.

Iyob, Ruth (1995). *The Eritrean Struggle for Independence: Domination, Resistance, Liberation, 1941–1991.* Cambridge: Cambridge University Press.

Jackson, Robert H. (1990). *Quasi-States: Sovereignty, International Relations and the Third World.* Cambridge: Cambridge University Press.

Jackson, Robert H., and Carl Rosberg (1982). *Personal Rule in Black Africa: Prince, Autocrat, Prophet, Tyrant.* Berkeley: University of California Press.

Joseph, Richard, ed. (1999). *State, Conflict, and Democracy in Africa.* Boulder: Lynne Rienner.

Kane, Moustapha (1994). "Le Sénégal et la Guinée (1958–1978)," in Momar-Coumba Diop, ed., *Le Sénégal et ses voisins.* Dakar: Societes-Es-paces-Temps.

Kaplan, Robert (1994). "The Coming Anarchy," *Atlantic Monthly* 273(2): 44–76.

Karl, Terry Lynn (1997). *The Paradox of Plenty.* Berkeley: University of California Press.

Kaunda, Jonathan Mayuyuka (1998). "The State and Society in Malawi," *Commonwealth and Comparative Politics* 36(1): 48–67.

Keller, Edmond (1987). "The Politics of State Survival: Continuity and Change in Ethiopian Foreign Policy," *Annals* 489 (January): 76–87.

Khadiagala, Gilbert M. (1994). *Allies in Adversity: The Frontline States in Southern African Security, 1975–1993.* Athens: Ohio University Press.

——— (1999). "Confidence-Building Measures in Sub-Saharan Africa," in Michael Krepon et al., eds., *Global Confidence Building: New Tools for Troubled Regions.* New York: St. Martin's Press.

——— (1999). "Regional Dimensions of Sanctions," in Neta C. Crawford and Audie Klotz, *How Sanctions Work.* London: Macmillan.

Khalid, Mansour, ed. (1987). *John Garang Speaks.* London: KPI.

Krafona, Kwesi (1986). *The Pan-African Movement: Ghana's Contribution.* London: Afroworld.

Laakso, Lisa (1996). "Relationship Between the State and Civil Society in the Zimbabwean Elections 1995," *Journal of Commonwealth and Comparative Politics* 34(3): 218–234.

Laitin, David, and Said Samatar (1987). *Somalia: Nation in Search of a State.* Boulder: Westview Press.

Landsberg, Chris (1995). "South Africa's Foreign Policy Style Is Out of Step with Its New Image," *Transact* 2(6): 10.

Landsberg, Chris, and Zondi Masiza (1995). *Strategic Ambiguity or Ambiguous Strategy: Foreign Policy Since the 1994 Election.* Policy Review Series, Centre for Policy Studies, Johannesburg, October.

Lefebvre, Jeffrey (1996). "Middle East Conflicts and Middle-Level Power Intervention in the Horn of Africa," *Middle East Journal* 50(3): 387.

Leistner, Erich (1995). "Prospects for Increasing Regional Co-operation: A South African Perspective," *Africa Insight* 25(1): 55–60.

Lemarchand, René (1997). "Patterns of State Collapse and Reconstruction in Central Africa: Reflections on the Crisis in the Great Lakes Region," *Afrika Spectrum* (Hamburg) 32(22): 173–193.

Le Pere, Garth, and Anthoni van Nieuwkerk (2000). "Making Foreign Policy in South Africa," in Patrick McGowan and Philip Nel, eds., *Power, Wealth and Global Order: International Relations for Southern African Students.* Cape Town: University of Cape Town Press.

Le Vine, Victor T. (1979). "Parliaments in Francophone Africa: Some Lessons from the Decolonization Process," in Joel Smith and Lloyd D. Musolf, eds., *Legislatures in Development: Dynamics of Change in New and Old States.* Durham: Duke University Press.

Lewis, Bernard (1990). *Race and Slavery in the Middle East.* New York: Oxford University Press.

Lewis, I. M. (1988). *A Modern History of Somalia: Nation and State in the Horn of Africa.* 3rd ed. Boulder: Westview Press.

Lugard, Lord (1922). *The Dual Mandate in British Tropical Africa.* London: n.p.

Lynch, Hollis R. (1967). *Edward Wilmot Blyden: Pan-Negro Patriot.* London: Oxford University Press.

Lyons, Terrence (1994). "Crisis on Multiple Levels: Somalia and the Horn of Africa," in Ahmed I. Samatar, ed., *The Somali Challenge: From Catastrophy to Renewal?* Boulder: Lynne Rienner.

——— (1998). "Can Neighbors Help? Regional Actors and African Conflict Management," in Francis M. Deng and Terrence Lyons, eds., *African Reckoning: A Quest for Good Governance.* Washington, DC: Brookings Institution.

Maasdorp, Gavin (1994). *A Vision for Economic Integration and Co-operation in Southern Africa.* Pretoria: Department of Trade and Industry.

Mackinder, Sir Halford J. ([1919] 1944). *Democratic Ideals and Reality: A Study in the Politics of Reconstruction.* Suffolk: Penguin Books.

MacLean, Sandra J. (1999). "Peace Building and the New Regionalism in Southern Africa," *Third World Quarterly* 20(5): 948.

Mandela, Nelson (1993). "South Africa's Future Foreign Policy," *Foreign Affairs* 72(5): 87.

Manning, Carrie (1999). "The Collapse of Peace in Angola," *Current History* 98(628): 208–212.

Manning, Patrick (1990). *Slavery and African Life: Occidental, Oriental, and African Slave Trades.* Cambridge: Cambridge University Press.

Marcus, Harold (1983). *Ethiopia, Great Britain, and the United States, 1941–1974: The Politics of Empire.* Berkeley: University of California Press.

Markakis, John (1994). "Ethnic Conflict and the State in the Horn in Africa," in John Markakis and Katsuyoshi Fukui, eds., *Ethnicity and Conflict in the Horn of Africa.* London: James Currey.

——— (1998). *Resource Conflict in the Horn of Africa.* London: Sage.

Markowitz, Irving Leonard, ed. (1987). *Studies in Power and Class in Africa.* New York: Oxford University Press.

Marmon, Shawn E., ed. (1999). *Slavery in the Islamic Middle East.* Princeton, NJ: Markus Wiener.

Martin, Guy (1995). "Francophone Africa in the Context of Franco-African Relations," in John W. Harbeson and Donald Rothchild, eds., *Africa in World Politics: Post–Cold War Challenges.* Boulder: Westview Press.

Marx, Johan (1995). "South African Foreign Policy in the New Era: Priorities in Africa and the Indian Ocean Islands," *South African Journal of International Affairs* 2(2).

Mathews, K. (1981). "Tanzania's Foreign Policy as a Frontline State in the Liberation of Southern Africa," *Africa Quarterly* 21(2): 41–61.

Matlosa, Khabele (1998). "Democracy and Conflict in Post-Apartheid Southern Africa: Dilemmas of Social Change in Small States," *International Affairs* 74(2): 319–337.

Mavimbela, Vusi (1998). "The African Renaissance: A Workable Dream," in Garth le Pere, Anthoni van Nieuwkerk, and Kato Lambrechts, eds., *South Africa and Africa: Reflections on the African Renaissance.* Occasional Paper 17, Foundation for Global Dialogue, Johannesburg.

Mayall, James (1983). "Self-Determination in the OAU," in I. M. Lewis, ed., *Nationalism and Self-Determination in the Horn of Africa.* London: Ithaca Press.

Mazrui, Ali (1979). *Africa's International Relations: The Diplomacy of Dependency and Change.* Boulder: Westview Press.

——— (1995). "The African State as a Political Refugee," in David R. Smock and Chester A. Crocker, eds., *African Conflict Resolution.* Washington, DC: U.S. Institute of Peace Press.

Mbeki, Moeletsi (1998–1999). "The African Renaissance," in Greg Mills, ed., *South African Yearbook of International Affairs, 1998/99.* Johannesburg: South African Institute of International Affairs.

McEwen, A. C. (1971). *International Boundaries of East Africa.* Oxford: Oxford University Press.

McGowan, Patrick, and Klaus-Peter Gottwald (1975). "Small State Foreign Policies: A Comparative Study of Participation, Conflict, and Political and Economic Dependence in Black Africa," *International Studies Quarterly* 19(4): 469–500.

Menkhaus, Ken (2000). "Traditional Conflict Management in Contemporary Somalia," in I. William Zartman, ed., *Traditional Cures for Modern Conflict.* Boulder: Lynne Rienner.

Millman, Joel (1997). *The Other Americans: How Immigrants Renew Our Country, Our Economy, Our Values.* New York: Viking Penguin.

Mills, Greg (1997). "Leaning All Over the Place? The Not-So-New South Africa's Foreign Policy," in Hussein Solomon, ed., *Fairy Godmother, Hegemon or Partner: In Search of a South African Foreign Policy,* Monograph Series 13. Midrand: Institute for Security Studies.

——— (2000). *The Wired Model: South Africa, Foreign Policy and Globalization.* Cape Town: Tafelberg.

Modelski, George (1962). *A Theory of Foreign Policy.* London: Pall Mall Press.

Morikawa, Jun (1997). *Japan and Africa: Big Business and Diplomacy.* Trenton, NJ: Africa World Press.

Mortimer, Robert A. (1996). "Senegal's Role in Ecomog: The Francophone Dimension in the Liberian Crisis," *Journal of Modern African Studies* 34(2): 293–306.

Mphaisha, Chisepo J. J. (1996). "Retreat from Democracy in Post One-Party State Zambia," *Journal of Commonwealth and Comparative Politics* 34(2): 65–84.

Mpungwe, Ami (1998). "Policy Considerations for the Evolution of Sustainable Peace and Stability in Southern Africa," in Mark Malan, ed., *Resolute Partners: Building Peacekeeping Capacity in Southern Africa,* Monograph Series 21. Midrand: Institute for Security Studies.

Muller, Marie (1997). "The Institutional Dimension: The Department of Foreign Affairs and Overseas Missions," in Walter Carlsnaes and Marie Muller, eds., *Change and South African External Relations.* Johannesburg: International Thomson.

——— (1999). "South African Diplomacy and Security Complex Theory," *Round Table* 352: 585–620.

Munro-Hay, Stuart (1991). *Aksum: An African Civilization of Late Antiquity.* Edinburgh: Edinburgh University Press.

Nash, Marian (1996). "Contemporary Practice of the United States Relating to International Law," *American Journal of International Law* 90: 263–265.

Nathan, Laurie, and Joao Honwana (1995). "After the Storm: Common Security and Conflict Resolution in Southern Africa." *Arusha Papers* (Center for Foreign Relations, Dar es Salaam) 3: 14–22.

Ndiaye, Abdoulaye (1998). "Genereaux Civils," *Jeune Afrique* 1934: 44–45.

Newbury, Colin W., ed. (1971). *British Policy Towards West Africa: Select Documents, Volume II.* Oxford: Oxford University Press.

Newbury, David (1997). "Irredentist Rwanda: Ethnic and Territorial Frontiers in Central Africa," *Africa Today* 44(2): 211–222.

Ng'ong'ola, Clement (1996). "Managing the Transition to Pluralism in Malawi: Legal and Constitutional Arrangements," *Journal of Commonwealth and Comparative Politics* 34(2): 85–110.

Niblock, Tim (1987). *Class and Power in Sudan: The Dynamics of Sudanese Politics.* Albany: State University of New York Press.

Nicol, Davidson (1969). *Black Nationalism in Africa.* New York: Africana Publishing Corporation.

Nkrumah, Kwame (1965). *Africa Must Unite.* London: Mercury Books.

Novicki, Margaret A. (1994). "Interview with Kaire Mbuende: Strengthening Southern Africa," *Africa Report* 39(4): 45–48.

Nweke, G. Aforka (1976). *External Intervention in African Conflicts: France and French-Speaking West Africa in the Nigerian Civil War, 1967–1970.* Boston: African Studies Center, Boston University.

Nwokedi, Emeka (1985). "Strands and Strains of 'Good Neighbourliness': The Case of Nigeria and its Francophone Neighbors," *Génève-Afrique* 23(1): 39–60.

Nzo, Alfred (1995). "Statement by the Minister of Foreign Affairs, Mr. Alfred Nzo, Before the Portfolio Committee on Foreign Affairs (14 March)," in

Policy Guidelines by the Minister and Deputy Minister of Foreign Affairs. Pretoria: Department of Foreign Affairs, Government Printer.

Obasanjo, Olusegun (1996). "A Balance Sheet of the African Region and the Cold War," in Edmond J. Keller and Donald Rothchild, eds., *Africa in the New International Order: Rethinking State Sovereignty and Regional Security.* Boulder: Lynne Rienner.

Oded, Arye (1987). *Africa and the Middle East Conflict.* Boulder: Lynne Rienner.

Ofuatey-Kodjoe, W. (1994). "Regional Organizations and the Resolution of Internal Conflict: The ECOWAS Intervention in Liberia," *International Peacekeeping* 1(3): 261–302.

Ohlson, Thomas, and Stephen John Stedman (1994). *The New Is Not Yet Born: Conflict Resolution in Southern Africa.* Washington, DC: Brookings Institution.

Ojo, Olatunde (1980). "Nigeria and the Formation of ECOWAS," *International Organization* 34(4): 571–604.

Ojo, Olatunde, D. K. Orwa, and C.M.B. Utete (1985). *African International Relations.* London: Longman.

Okolo, Julius E. (1989/99). "Obstacles to Increased Intra-ECOWAS Trade," *International Journal* 44(1): 171–214.

Organization of Economic Cooperation and Development (1998). *Geographical Distribution of Financial Flows to Developing Countries.* Washington, DC: OECD.

O'Toole, Thomas (1997). "The Central African Republic: Political Reform and Social Malaise," in John F. Clark and David E. Gardinier, eds., *Political Reform in Francophone West Africa.* Boulder: Westview Press.

Oyediran, O., ed. (1979). *Nigerian Government and Politics Under Military Rule.* New York: St. Martin's Press.

Parker, Ron (1991). "The Senegal-Mauritania Conflict of 1989: A Fragile Equilibrium," *The Journal of Modern African Studies* 29(1): 155–171.

Pazzanita, Anthony G. (1992). "Mauritania's Foreign Policy: The Search for Protection," *The Journal of Modern African Studies* 30(2): 281–304.

Pfaff , William (1995). "A New Colonialism? Europe Must Go Back into Africa," *Foreign Affairs* 74 (January/February).

Plano, Jack, and Roy Olton (1988). *The International Relations Dictionary.* Oxford: Oxford University Press.

Popovic, Alexandre (1999). *The Revolt of the African Slaves in Iraq in the Third and Ninth Century.* Princeton, NJ: Markus Wiener.

Prendergast, John (1999). "Building for Peace in the Horn of Africa: Diplomacy and Beyond," *United States Institute of Peace.* Washington, DC: U.S. Institute of Peace (Special Report, June 28).

Quilles, Paul (1998). *Mission d'Information sur le Rwanda: Enquête sur la Tragedie Rwandaise (1990–1994).* Tome 1, vols. 1 and 2. Paris: Assemblée Nationale.

Reed, William Cyrus (1992). "Directions in African International Relations," in Mark W. Delancey, ed., *Handbook of Political Science Research in Africa.* Westport, CT: Greenwood Press.

Reisman, W. Michael (1983). "Somali Self-Determination in the Horn: Legal Perspectives and Implications for Social and Political Engineering," in I. M. Lewis, ed., *Nationalism and Self-Determination in the Horn of Africa*. London: Ithaca Press.

Reno, William (1996). "The Business of War in Liberia," *Current History* 95(601).

——— (1998). *Warlord Politics and African States*. Boulder: Lynne Rienner.

Reyntjens, F., and S. Marysse (1996). *Conflits au Kivu: Antecedents et Enjeux*. Antwerp: Center for the Study of the Great Lakes Region of Africa.

——— (1997). *Conflits au Kivu*. Paris: l'Harmattan.

Rose-Ackerman, Susan (1999). *Corruption and Government: Causes, Consequences, and Reform*. New York: Cambridge University Press.

Rosenau, James (1966). "Pre-Theories and Theories of Foreign Policy," in R. Barry Farrell, ed., *Approaches to Comparative and International Politics*. Evanston, Ill.: Northwestern University Press.

Rubenson, Sven (1976). *The Survival of Ethiopian Independence*. New York: Holms & Meir.

Sacharoff, Ariadne (1998). "Multinationals in Host Countries: Can They Be Held Liable Under the Alien Tort Claim Act for Human Rights Violations?" *Brooklyn Journal of International Law* 23: 927–946.

Said, Abdul A. et al. (1995). *Concepts of International Politics in Global Perspective*. Englewood Cliffs, NJ: Prentice-Hall.

Salih, M. A. Mohamed (1998). "Political Narratives and Identity Formation in Post-1989 Sudan," in Mohamed Salih and John Markakis, eds., *Ethnicity and the State in Eastern Africa*. Uppsala: Nordiska Afrika Institutet.

Saro-Wiwa, Ken (1992). *Genocide in Nigeria: The Ogoni Tragedy*. London: Saros International.

——— (1995). *A Month and a Day: A Detention Diary*. New York: Penguin Press.

Saul, John (1997). "'For Fear of Being Condemned as Old Fashioned': Liberal Democracy vs. Popular Democracy in Sub-Saharan Africa," *Review of African Political Economy* 73: 339–353.

——— (1997). "Liberal Democracy vs. Popular Democracy in Southern Africa," *Review of African Political Economy* 72: 219–236.

Schraeder, Peter J. (1994). "Elites as Facilitators or Impediments to Political Development? Lessons from the 'Third Wave' of Democratization in Africa," *The Journal of Developing Areas* 29(1): 69–90.

——— (2000). "Cold War to Cold Peace: Explaining U.S.-French Competition in Francophone Africa," *Political Science Quarterly* 115(3): 1–25.

Schraeder, Peter J., with Nefertiti Gaye (1997). "Senegal's Foreign Policy: Challenges of Democratization and Marginalization," *African Affairs* 96(385): 485–508.

Schraeder, Peter, Steven Hook, and Bruce Taylor (1998). "Clarifying the Foreign Aid Puzzle: A Comparison of American, Japanese, French, and Swedish Aid Flows," *World Politics* 50(2): 294–323.

Shaw, Timothy (1980). "Foreign Policy, Political Economy and the Future: Reflections on Africa and the World System," *African Affairs* 79(315): 260–268.

Shaw, Timothy, and Olajide Aluko (1984). *The Political Economy of African Foreign Policy: A Comparative Analysis.* New York: St. Martin's Press.

Shearer, David (1998). "Outsourcing War," *Foreign Policy* (Fall): 68–81.

Skurnik, W.A.E. (1993). *The Foreign Policy of Senegal.* Evanston, IL: Northwestern University Press.

Smith, Joel, and Lloyd D. Musolf, eds. (1979). *Legislatures in Development: Dynamics of Change in New and Old States.* Durham, NC: Duke University Press.

Smith, Stephen (1995). "France-Rwanda: Lévirat Colonial et Abandon dans la Région des Grands Lacs," in André Guichaoua, ed., *Les Crises Politiques au Burundi et Rwanda (1993–1994): Analyses, Faits et Documents.* Paris: Karthala.

Solomon, Hussein (1996). "Southern Africa: Security in the 1990s," *Strategic Analysis* 19(3): 303–391.

Solomon, Hussein, and Jakkie Cilliers (1998). "The Southern African Development Community and Small Arms Proliferation," in Virginia Gamba, ed., *Society Under Siege: Licit Responses to Illicit Arms.* Institute for Strategic Studies Towards Collaborative Peace Series 2, Johannesburg.

Sorenson, John (1993). *Imagining Ethiopia: Struggles for History and Identity in the Horn of Africa.* New Brunswick, NJ: Rutgers University Press.

Southall, Roger (1995). "A Critical Reflection on the GNU's Foreign Policy Initiatives and Responses," in Chris Landsberg, Garth le Pere, and Anthoni van Nieuwkerk, eds., *Mission Imperfect: Redirecting South Africa's Foreign Policy.* Johannesburg: Foundation for Global Dialogue and Center for Policy Studies.

Staniland, Martin (1987). "Francophone Africa: The Enduring French Connection," *Annals* 489 (January): 40–50.

Stremlau, John (1977). *The International Politics of the Nigerian Civil War, 1967–1970.* Princeton, NJ: Princeton University Press.

Tegenu, Tsegaye (1996). *The Evolution of Ethiopian Absolutism: The Genesis and the Making of the Fiscal Military State, 1696–1913.* Uppsala: Acta Universitatis Upsalensis (no. 180).

Thiam, Cheikh Tidiane (1993). *Droit Public du Sénégal (Vol. 1): L'état et le Citoyen.* Dakar: Les Éditions du CREDILA.

Thompson, V. B. (1969). *Africa and Unity: The Evolution of Pan-Africanism.* London: Longmans, Green and Company.

Thioub, Ibrahima (1994). "Le Sénégal et le Mali," in Momar-Coumba Diop, ed., *Le Sénégal et ses voisins.* Dakar: Societes-Es-paces-Temps.

Thompson, W. (1969). *Ghana's Foreign Policy, 1957–66.* Princeton: Princeton University Press.

Thompson, Lisa, and Anthony Leysens (1997). "The Elusive Quest for the National Interest," *Global Dialogue* 2(1): 43–48.

Toffler, Alvin, and Heidi Toffler (1993). *War and Anti-War: Survival at the Dawn of the Twenty-first Century.* Boston: Little, Brown.

Touval, Saadia (1963). *Somali Nationalism: International Politics and the Drive for Unity in the Horn of Africa.* Cambridge: Harvard University Press.

Tuso, Hamdesa (2000). "Indigenous Processes of Conflict Resolution in Oromo Society," in I. William Zartman, ed., *Traditional Cures for Modern Conflicts: African Conflict "Medicine."* Boulder: Lynne Rienner.

Ungar, Sanford (1986). *Africa: The People and Politics of an Emerging Continent.* Rev. ed. New York: Simon and Schuster.

United Nations Conference on Trade and Development (1999). *World Investment Report 1999.* New York: UN.

United States International Trade Commission (1997). *U.S.-Africa Trade Flows and the Effects of the Uruguay Round Agreement and U.S. Trade and Development Policy.* Washington, DC: USITC.

Vale, Peter, and Ian Taylor (1999). "South Africa's Post-Apartheid Foreign Policy Five Years On—From Pariah to 'Just Another Country,'" *Round Table* 352: 629–634.

Van der Westhuizen, Janis (1998). "South Africa's Emergence as a Middle Power," *Third World Quarterly* 19(3): 435–455.

Venter, Al J. (1998). "Market Forces: How Hired Guns Succeeded Where the United Nations Failed," *Jane's International Defense Review*: 23–26 (March).

——— (1998). "Winds of War Set to Blow Across Angola," *Jane's Intelligence Review* 10(10): 37–39 (October).

Venter, Denis (1996). "Regional Security in Sub-Saharan Africa," *Africa Insight* 26(2): 173.

——— (1996). "South Africa, Brazil and South Atlantic Security: Towards a Zone of Peace and Co-operation in the South Atlantic," in S. Pinheiro Guimarães, ed., *South Africa and Brazil: Risks and Opportunities in the Turmoil of Globalization.* Brasília: National Council for Scientific and Technological Development and the International Relations Research Institute.

——— (1996). "The Indian Ocean Rim Initiative: A Vehicle for South-South Co-operation," *Indian Journal of African Studies* 7(1-2): 15–35.

——— (1997). "South Africa and Africa: Relations in a Time of Change," in Walter Carlsnaes and Marie Muller, eds., *Change and South African External Relations.* Johannesburg: International Thomson.

——— (1998). "South African Foreign Policy in a Time of Change: The African Dimension," *Journal of the Third World Spectrum* 5(2): 14.

Verba, Sidney (1961). "Assumptions of Rationality and Non-Rationality in Models of the International System," *World Politics* 14: 93–117.

Villalón, Leonardo A. (1995). *Islamic Society and State Power in Senegal: Disciples and Citizens in Fatick.* Cambridge: Cambridge University Press.

Wai, Dunstan M. (1981). *The African-Arab Conflict in the Sudan.* New York: Africana.

Watson, James L., ed. (1980). *Asian and African Systems of Slavery.* Berkeley: University of California Press.

Weiss, Thomas G., and Leon Gordenker, eds. (1996). *NGOs, the UN, and Global Governance.* Boulder: Lynne Rienner.

Wesley, Derek A. (1996). *The Kingdom of Kush: The Napatan and Meriotic Empires.* London: British Museum Press.

White, Brian (1989). "Analysing Foreign Policy: Problems and Approaches," in Michael Clark and Brian White, eds., *Understanding Foreign Policy: The Foreign Policy Systems Approach.* London: Edward Elgar.

Widner, Jennifer (1991). "The 1990 Elections in Côte d'Ivoire," *Issue* 20(1): 31–40.

Willame, Jean-Claude (1997). *Banyarwanda et Banyamulenge: Violences Ethniques et Gestion de l'Identitaire au Kivu.* Paris: l'Harmattan.

Willet, Susan (1998). "Demilitarization, Disarmament, and Development in Southern Africa," *Review of African Political Economy* 77: 413–414.

Wiseman, John (1993). "Leadership and Personal Danger in African Politics," *Journal of Modern African Studies* 31(4): 657–660.

Wright, Stephen, ed. (1999). *African Foreign Policies.* Boulder: Westview Press.

Yates, Douglas (1996). *The Rentier State in Africa: Oil Rent Dependency and Neocolonialism in the Republic of Gabon.* Trenton, NJ: Africa World Press.

Young, Crawford (1994). *The African Colonial State in Comparative Perspective.* New Haven: Yale University Press.

——— (1999). "The Third Wave of Democratization in Africa: Ambiguities and Contradictions," in Richard Joseph, ed., *State, Conflict, and Democracy in Africa.* Boulder: Lynne Rienner.

Young, Crawford, and Thomas Turner (1985). *The Rise and Decline of the Zairian State.* Madison: University of Wisconsin Press.

Yousuf, Hilmi S. (1986). *African-Arab Relations.* Brattelboro, VT: Amana Books.

Zack-Williams, Alfred (1995). *Tributors, Supporters and Merchant Capital: Mining and Underdevelopment in Sierra Leone.* Aldershot: Avebury Press.

Zartman, I. William (1966). "Decision-Making Among African Governments in Inter-African Affairs," *Journal of Development Studies* 2(2).

———, ed. (1995). *Collapsed States: The Disintegration and Restoration of Legitimate Authority.* Boulder: Lynne Rienner.

———, ed. (1997). *Governance as Conflict Management.* Washington, DC: Brookings Institution.

The Contributors

Clement E. Adibe is assistant professor of Political Science at De-Paul University, Chicago. His research interests include economic integration and regional security in West Africa and United Nations peace operations. He is the author of *Managing Arms in Peace Processes: Somalia* (1995).

John F. Clark is associate professor of international relations at Florida International University, Miami, where he has worked since 1991. His research focuses on democratization, ethnic conflict, political development, state politics, and great power intervention in francophone Africa. He has conducted field research in Congo-Brazzaville in 1990 and 1997, and in Congo-Kinshasa in 1994. He is coeditor, with David Gardinier, of *Political Reform in Francophone Africa* (1997), and has published in such journals as *Studies in Comparative International Development, Journal of Democracy, Africa Today,* and *SAIS Review.*

Ruth Iyob is assistant professor of political science at the University of Missouri–St. Louis. She is the author of *The Eritrean Struggle for Independence: Domination, Resistance, and Nationalism, 1941–1993,* and has published extensively on nationalism, citizenship, and gender.

Gilbert M. Khadiagala is associate professor of comparative politics and African studies at the Johns Hopkins School of Advanced

International Studies. He is author of *Allies in Adversity: The Front-line States in Southern African Security, 1975–1993.*

René Lemarchand is currently the Carter Visiting Professor at Smith College (Northampton, Mass.). He served for four years as USAID regional consultant on governance and democracy in Abidjan and, more recently, with the USAID mission in Accra. He has written extensively on Rwanda, Burundi, and the Congo. His publications include *Rwanda and Burundi: Ethnic Conflict and Genocide* (1996).

Terrence Lyons is assistant professor at the Institute for Conflict Analysis and Resolution, George Mason University. His publications include *Voting for Peace: Postconflict Elections in Liberia* and *Sovereignty as Responsibility: Conflict Management in Africa.*

William Reno is associate professor of political science at North-western University. He is the author of *Warlord Politics and African States* (1999) and other publications on the political economy of warfare in Africa. His latest project is a comparative study of the role of violent commercial organizations in rebuilding political authorities in Africa and Central Asia.

Peter J. Schraeder is associate professor in the Department of Political Science at Loyola University, Chicago, specializing in international relations theory and comparative foreign policy, particularly in regards to Africa. His most recent field research in Africa was funded by a two-year Fulbright grant to Senegal (1994–1996). He has published in the *Journal of Modern African Studies, Journal of Politics, Politique Africaine,* and is the author of *United States Foreign Policy Toward Africa: Incrementalism, Crisis, and Change* (1994) and *African Politics and Society: A Mosaic in Transformation* (1999).

Denis Venter is managing director of Africa Consultancy and Research in Pretoria, South Africa. He is the former executive director and head of academic programs at the Africa Institute of South Africa, Pretoria. He has published on African politics, foreign policy, and regional security.

Index

Presidential Decision Directive
(PDD), 25, 100, 191
Prester John, 112
People's Republic of China, 116
Piggs Peak Draft, 145
Pointe Noire, 76
Pope John Paul II, 54
Popular Movement for the
Liberation of Angola (MPLA),
68, 133
Pragmatic internationalism, 168
Preferential Trade Area (PTA), 137

Quiet diplomacy, 175

Radio France International, 53
Rational Actor Model, 72
Rawlings, Jerry, 28
Realpolitik, 27–28
RECAMP. *See* French Reinforce-
ment of Capabilities of African
Missions of Peacekeeping
Regional organizations and security,
9
Reno, William, 31
Revolutionary United Front (RUF),
27, 29, 195
Rice, Susan, 100, 190
Rivers State Task Force, 196
Romeo, Dallier, 91
Rose-Ackerman, Susan, 190, 193
Royal Dutch Shell, 31
RPA. *See* Rwandan Patriotic Army
RPF. *See* Rwandan Patriotic Front
RUF. *See* Revolutionary United
Front
Rwanda, 74, 79, 87, 90–91, 101,
121; civil war in, 74; Clinton
visit, 100; genocide, 91; ethnic
exclusion, 91, 94; foreign policy,
95; invasion of Congo, 92, 96,
101–102; refugees, 97; relations
with France, 91; relations with
UN, 93; U.S. policy, 100
Rwandan Patriotic Army (RPA), 89,
92
Rwandan Patriotic Front (RPF), 42,
74, 87, 88

Rwigyema, Major General Fred, 88

SACU. *See* South African Customs
Union
SADC. *See* Southern African
Development Community
SADCC. *See* South African
Development Coordination
Conference
SADC Council of Ministers, 145
SAHRNON. *See* South African
Human Rights Network
Saleh, Major General Salim, 104
Samuyira, Nathan, 141
Sandra, MaClean, 150
Sankoh, Foday, 29–30
Saro-Wiwa, Ken, 31
SARPCCO. *See* South African
Regional Chiefs Cooperation
Organization
SASS. *See* South African Secret
Service
Sassou Nguesso, Dennis, 68, 70,
73, 76, 79, 80, 103
Save the Children Fund, 32
Safe havens, 99
Savimbi, Jonas, 68, 146
"Second liberation," 134
Seiler, John, 143
Selassie, Emperor Haile, 4, 113,
121
Self-determination, 117
Senegal, 41, 47; Committee on
Foreign Affairs, 52; constitution,
50, 52; constitutional crisis, 51;
foreign policy, 50; elections in,
52; media, 52–53 ; National
Assembly, 51; military, 51;
Ministry of Foreign Affairs and
of Senegalese Abroad, 50, 53;
reforms in, 61; structural
adjustment, 52
Senghor, Léopold Sédar, 44
Sese Seko, Mobutu, 68–72, 81–82,
90, 94, 96, 121, 187, 209
SFTU. *See* Swaziland Federation of
Trade Unions
Shell Oil, 197

Sierra Club, 31
Sierra Leone: diamond economy,
29; elections in, 33; and
Executive Outcomes, 33; mining
in, 195; multilateral creditors,
190; political elites in, 18; race
relations, 18; and RUF, 29
Soglo, Nicéphore, 48, 55
Somali Democratic Republic, 119
Somali National Movement (SNM),
120
Somalia: ethnicity, 111, 115–116,
120; colonialism, 114; collapse
of, 117; and irrendism, 116;
nationalism, 116, 122; and the
UN, 191
Somaliland, 201
SNM. *See* Somali National
Movement
South Africa, 6; as "economic
engine," 136; entry into SADC,
139; and EU, 139; foreign
investments, 172; Government of
National Unity, 135; national
identity, 160–162; National Party,
159; political transition in, 135;
and regional leadership, 178
South African Customs Union
(SACU), 137
South African Defense Force, 33
South African Development
Coordination Conference
(SADCC), 131, 133–135
South African foreign policy, 159,
160–164; actors in, 160–161,
167, and Africa, 171; and Angola,
175; and conflict resolution, 175;
coordination of, 169; defining,
160; and Department of Defense,
167; Department of Foreign
Affairs, 161; and Department of
Trade and Industry, 166;
economic interests in, 173; goals
of, 164, 160, 169; human rights
in, 163; idealists in, 178; and
international organizations,
172–173; intervention in Lesotho,
166, 167; and Namibia, 164; and

national interest, 160, 161;
Nelson Mandela, 162; norms in,
162; Parliamentary Portfolio
committee on Foreign Affairs'
(PPFCA) role in, 162, 166; and
peacekeeping, 174–175; and
postapartheid era, 162;
pragmatists in, 178; redefined,
178; "securocrats," in, 167; shift
in, 171, 179
South African Human Rights
Network (SAHRNON), 151
South African Regional Chiefs
Cooperation Organization
(SARPCCO), 142
South African Secret Service
(SASS), 167
Southern Africa: "Congo effect" in,
145; democratization in, 131,
140; and domestic instability,
140; economic interdependence
in, 135; elites in, 132; foreign
policy making, 132; and human
rights, 140; and institution
building, 149; NGOs, 140;
foreign policy norms, 140;
security in, 134, 140–146; and
traditional monarchies, 133
Southern African Development
Community, (SADC), 83, 136;
aims, 136; Article 5, 140; Article
37, 136; collective intervention,
141; common currency, 136;
conflicts in, 137, 142, 176; and
EU, 36; HIV/AIDS, 137; human
right in, 150; intervention in
Lesotho, 150; Interstate Defense
and Security Committee, 142;
institutional overlap in, 137, 173,
174; Ministerial Workshop on
Democracy, Peace, and Security,
140; Organ for Politics, Defense,
and Security, 141, 161, 176; and
peacekeeping, 142; political
values, 176, 177; Program of
Action, 139; Protocol on Illicit
Drug Trafficking, 142; "Smart
Partnership," 137; member states,

246

(WNBLF), 96
Wilson, Woodrow, 19
WNBLF. *See* West Nile Bank
  Liberation Front
Working Group on Indigenous
  People, 31
World Bank, 58
World Health Organization, 32
World Wildlife Federation, 31

Youou, Fulbert, 73
Yamoussoukro peace talks, 47

Zambia, 133, 134

ZANU. *See* Zimbabwe African
  National Union–Patriotic Front
Zartman, 5
Zenawi, Meles, 8, 88, 100
Zimbabwe, 81, 83, 102, 121;
  decolonization, 133; economic
  decline, 152; elections in, 135;
  intervention in DRC, 144; white
  farms, 152
Zimbabwe African National
  Union–Patriotic Front (ZANU-
  PF), 135
Zimbabwe Union of Democrats, 144
Zulu militias, 103

About the Book

In this comprehensive treatment of the interplay between domestic and international politics, the authors analyze efforts by African states to manage their external relations amid seismic shifts in the internal, regional, and global environments. The authors' nuanced analysis of foreign policy issues and themes traverses the continent; they identify patterns of change, examine constraints, and give careful attention to the processes that so powerfully influence policy outcomes.

Gilbert M. Khadiagala is associate professor of comparative politics and African studies at the Johns Hopkins School of Advanced International Studies. He is author of *Allies in Adversity: The Frontline States in Southern African Security, 1975–1993*. **Terrence Lyons** is an assistant professor in the Institute for Conflict Analysis and Resolution, George Mason University. His publications include *Voting for Peace: Postconflict Elections in Liberia* and *Sovereignty as Responsibility: Conflict Management in Africa*.